S E V E N

T R A I L S

W E S T

Arthur King Peters

SEVEN TRAILS WEST

ABBEVILLE PRESS PUBLISHERS
New York London Paris

To my wife, Sarah, with whom I first crossed the Mississippi in 1946

Front cover: NORTH FROM BERTHOLD PASS, 1874. *Photograph by W. H. Jackson.*
See page 52. • Back cover: THE JOSEPH HENRY BYINGTON FAMILY,
"A MORMON FAMILY," NEAR CALLS FORT, UTAH, 1867. *See page 90.*
Pages 2–3: STAMPEDING BUFFALO, LAMAR VALLEY, YELLOWSTONE PARK,
1916. *Photograph by Jack Ellis Haynes. See page 45. • Pages 4–5:* DONNER LAKE AND
RAILROAD SNOW SHEDS, *n.d. Photograph by A. J. Russell. See page 212.*

EDITOR: Nancy Grubb
DESIGNER: Molly Shields
PRODUCTION EDITOR: Owen Dugan
PRODUCTION MANAGER: Richard Thomas
PICTURE EDITOR: Paula Trotto
MAP DESIGNER: Claudia Carlson

First paperback edition, 2000
10 9 8 7 6 5 4 3 2 1
Hardcover
10 9 8 7 6 5 4 3

The Library of Congress has cataloged the hardcover edition as follows:
Seven trails West / Arthur King Peters.
    p.   cm.
Includes bibliographical references and index.
ISBN 1-55859-782-4
  1. Trails—West (U.S.)—History—19th century.
  2. Transportation—West (U.S.)—History—19th century.
  3. Telegraph—West (U.S.)—History—19th century.
  4. West (U.S.)—Description and travel. I. Title.
F591.P425   1996
978'.02—dc20   ·   95-39095
Paperback ISBN 0-7892-0678-1

CONTENTS

INTRODUCTION

IN LESS THAN SIXTY-FIVE YEARS, FROM NOVEMBER 17, 1805, when Lewis and Clark reached the Pacific Ocean, to May 10, 1869, when the Golden Spike was pounded home, America's western frontier leaped two thousand miles from the Mississippi River to the westernmost edge of the continent. Even more impressively, in that short interval the awesome technology of the Industrial Revolution was applied to nearly two-thirds of the American continent, which, at the turn of the nineteenth century, had never heard the creak of a wagon wheel or the crack of a rifle, nor felt the blade of plow or ax. Great and terrible things were suddenly asked of the virgin land whose riches seemed as inexhaustible as its dimensions.

The trails across the table-flat prairie at first paralleled the north and south banks of the Platte and North Platte Rivers. This conglomerate formed the major corridor of western expansion, known as the Great Platte River Road, before leading to high passes in the Rockies or Sierra Nevada where unwary emigrants such as the unlucky Mormon handcart companies, the Donner Party, and even the experienced explorer John C. Frémont were trapped by sudden blizzards that cost many lives. The trails did not forgive mistakes, but for a Jedediah Smith, a Jim Bridger, a Susan Magoffin, a James Clyman, or a Jean Baptiste Charbonneau, even the danger held a certain fascination.

Some half-million Americans turned west on the trails between 1800 and 1870, constituting the greatest voluntary mass migration in history. Motives for emigration differed, but most pioneers, with the exception

ECHO CANYON, UTAH, *1867. Photograph by Charles W. Carter.*

of the get-rich-quick gold rushers, were ordinary folk in search of a better life. A profile of the trail complex and the critical role it played in this migration is vital for an understanding of how America came to be. Such an overview—presented in this book through highlights of people, places, and events along seven major trails—reflects the continuing reexamination of our western roots in America's quest for a national identity.

America's western frontier was born to die. It was, in fact, a succession of frontiers, the first being the Atlantic coast and the final one the Pacific, with many others in between, moving ever farther west. In 1800 the frontier's border was the roughly north-to-south line traced on the landscape by the Mississippi and Missouri Rivers, with the major jumping-off place at Saint Louis—then a village with just three streets. But the frontier was more than a line on the map distinguishing "civilized" from "primitive" America. It was an unknown land of unfathomed opportunities lying between the Mississippi and the Pacific—a vast region twice the size of the eastern United States. By 1870, after the Golden Spike ceremony completed the first Transcontinental Railroad, it can reasonably be said that the western frontier had ceased to exist.

Out of the frontier's seedbed grew the trails that opened the trans-Mississippi West. Their tendrils quickly stretched from Missouri and Nebraska to present-day New Mexico, Utah, California, and Oregon, forming a network that bound the growing nation together and fashioned the armature for later national development.

The four trails blazed by the explorers, fortune seekers, and pioneers of the Lewis and Clark expedition, the Santa Fe, the Oregon-California, and the Mormon Trails proved, at a heavy cost, that the continent could be crossed overland. Three others deserve a special place in the trail pantheon: the Pony Express, the first Transcontinental Telegraph, and the first Transcontinental Railroad, which constituted trails of a new order that enabled speed of communication and transport. After they had been opened—all in the

Right: TOPOGRAPHICAL MAP, UNITED STATES AND TERRITORIES. *Published by Mathew Dripps, 1876.*

By 1876, seven decades after the appearance of Arrowsmith and Lewis's New and Elegant General Atlas of 1804 (see page 14), the trans-Mississippi West was still only on the threshold of the booming development to come, as the vast blank areas on this map confirm.

Opposite: MANDANS, SURVIVORS OF SMALLPOX EPIDEMIC, *1872.*

Diseases introduced by the Europeans killed more Indians than white bullets. The 1837 smallpox epidemic ravaged the Mandan tribe, leaving only thirty-one survivors from a tribe of sixteen hundred. Pictured here are two of the lucky ones.

but also white by whites, and Indian by Indians. A devastating clash of cultures was inevitable when the western European-Americans encountered Paleolithic Native Americans who had not yet invented the wheel, written language, textiles, glass, or metallurgy. Inevitable, too, was the culminating white "victory," but that would come farther down the trail, at Wounded Knee, South Dakota, in 1890.

Fortunately for students of the western trails, many emigrants kept diaries and journals and later wrote reminiscences describing their treks west. Merrill Mattes, patriarch of western-trail history, has identified and classified over three thousand such documents, and many more doubtless still await discovery in dusty attic trunks and scattered archives. The reminiscences, often written long after the fact, must be read with discrimination, but one can only marvel at the steadfastness of the diarists, often young women, who faithfully penned their accounts in a clattering covered wagon or by a campfire at the end of an exhausting day, conscious that they were making history. They have left us an eyewitness heritage beyond price.

The trail experience in itself changed the emigrants. To judge from their individual accounts, it impelled many of them to shuck off their outworn European attitudes and ways, just as they abandoned cherished household possessions crossing the deserts. For some, the trail hardships amounted to a purification. Even today the simple trail testimonies continue to enrich a vision of the West that, sometimes inspiring, sometimes disturbing, remains deeply imbedded in the nation's conscience and in the world's perception of us as Americans.

course of a single decade—people recognized that the country had changed irrevocably: from sea to sea, America was now one nation.

Blood was spilled on every one of the seven trails, and not simply Indian blood by whites and vice versa

THE
LEWIS AND CLARK
EXPEDITION

THE AMERICAN TRAILS WEST BEGAN IN PARIS.

After two frustrating years of negotiation limited primarily to the acquisition of American rights in the New Orleans area, Thomas Jefferson's agents in Paris were astounded by Napoleon's sudden decision to sell all the French landholdings west of the Mississippi River to the United States, a strategic move aimed at thwarting the English. Accordingly, at Paris, on "Deux Prairial an onze de la République Française" (which translates from the postrevolutionary calendar as May 22, 1803), the flourish of Napoleon's unexpected signature on the treaty of sale turned the key in the lock to America's western frontier.

At the stroke of a pen, the size of the United States more than doubled, yielding what is now the central third of the country—some 909,000 square miles—at a cost of about four cents an acre. With the acquisition of this vast territory, whose exact boundaries were not even clear at the time, the American frontier made a giant leap over the Mississippi River and across the Great Plains to the Rockies. From that moment on, a grand sweep of migration to the Pacific became inevitable, bridging the rest of the continent, although it would take three more generations to accomplish.

Jefferson had not yet concluded the Louisiana Purchase Treaty when, in January 1803, he convinced Congress to secretly give Captains Meriwether Lewis and William Clark $2,500 for their historic (and under the circumstances somewhat illegal) military mission

GREAT FALLS OF THE MISSOURI RIVER, MONTANA, *1977. Photograph by David Muench.*

to the Pacific Ocean. Never mind that the purchase from France was still up in the air, that Spain claimed a huge landmass west of the Louisiana Territory, and that British and Russian interests in the Pacific Northwest had yet to be resolved. Jefferson had long dreamed of finding a water route from the Mississippi to the Pacific: the fabled Northwest Passage that would lead to rich trade with the Orient. This geopolitical temptation prompted him to circumvent some of the diplomatic niceties. In a personal order to Lewis, the president directed the captain and his newly formed Corps of Discovery "to explore the Missouri River & such principal stream of it, as, by it's course and communication with the waters of the

Pacific ocean . . . may offer the most direct & practicable water communication across this continent for the purposes of commerce."[1]

When news of the purchase finally reached Washington in June 1803, Lewis had already spent several months making logistical preparations for his expedition.

THE CORPS OF DISCOVERY— WESTBOUND

Meriwether Lewis's family were old friends of Thomas Jefferson, and it was through this connection, backed by his own outstanding military record, that in 1801

Opposite, left: François-Pascal-Simon Gérard (1770–1837). PORTRAIT OF BONAPARTE, IST CONSUL, *1803. Oil on canvas. 24¼ x 21¾ in. (62 x 53 cm). Musée Condé, Chantilly, France.*

Opposite, right: Rembrandt Peale (1778–1860). PORTRAIT OF THOMAS JEFFERSON, *1800. Oil on canvas. 23⅛ x 19¼ in. (58.7 x 48.8 cm). White House Historical Association, Washington, D.C.*

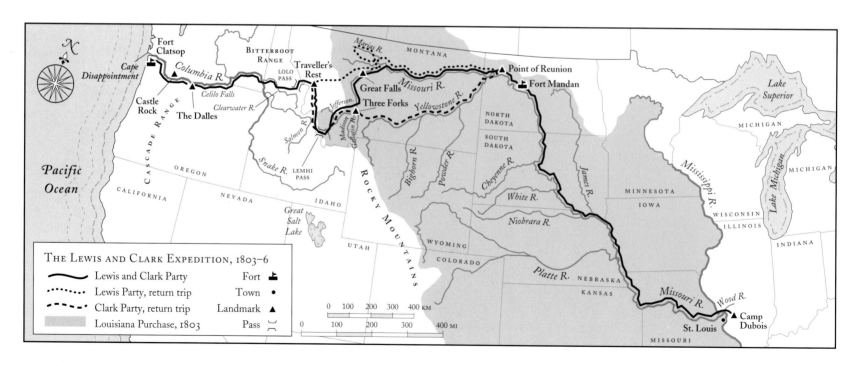

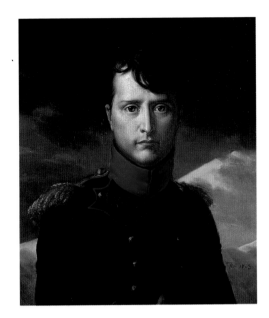

Far right: SIGNATURE PAGE
OF THE FRENCH EXCHANGE
COPY OF THE LOUISIANA
PURCHASE TREATY,
*April 30, 1803. National Archives,
Washington, D.C.*

*The Louisiana Purchase Treaty,
embellished with Napoleon's signature,
conveyed the vast land tract to America
at a cost of about four cents an acre.*

Lewis had been appointed a private secretary to the
president so the young officer could work on Jefferson's
search for the Northwest Passage. With Jefferson's
approval Lewis urged his friend William Clark to join
with him in the still-secret venture.

Meriwether Lewis and William Clark had much
in common. Both had served in the militia and in the
regular army, and Lewis had briefly seen duty as an
ensign in Clark's rifle company. Both were Virginians,
sturdy six-footers well trained in military discipline,
woodsmanship, and Indian matters. Despite their
relative youth—Lewis was twenty-nine and Clark
four years his senior—both clearly were born leaders
whose adventuresome spirits responded wholeheart-
edly to the expedition's challenge. Moreover, the two
men complemented each other well in temperament,
Clark being gregarious and practical, and Lewis more
introspective, moody, and theoretical by nature. They
worked together in a harmony unparalleled in the
annals of American exploration, unfailingly support-
ing each other under the most difficult circumstances.

The exchange of letters that led to their collaboration confirms their deep mutual trust. Lewis's seven-page letter of June 19, 1803, issues an irresistible invitation to Clark: "If therefore there is anything . . . in this enterprise, which would induce you to participate with me in it's dangers and it's honors, believe me there is no man on earth with whom I should feel equal pleasure in sharing them as with yourself."[2] Clark's reply of July 17 was immediate. "My Friend I can assure you that no man lives with whom I would prefer to undertake or shear the Difficulties of such a Trip."[3]

The two young officers left Saint Louis—then a town of only 2,400 souls—in December 1803 and assembled thirty handpicked expedition soldiers for winter training at the mouth of the Wood River on the east bank of the Mississippi. Aboard a little fleet of three vessels—a fifty-five-foot keelboat with twenty-two oars and a square sail, manned by a French Canadian crew, and two smaller pirogues, one red and the other white—they officially began their western odyssey on Monday, May 14, 1804.

An intriguing twist to Lewis and Clark's westward expedition had occurred early in March 1804, when Brigadier General James A. Wilkinson, the ranking general of the U.S. Army, submitted a clandestine report (for which he was allegedly paid) to

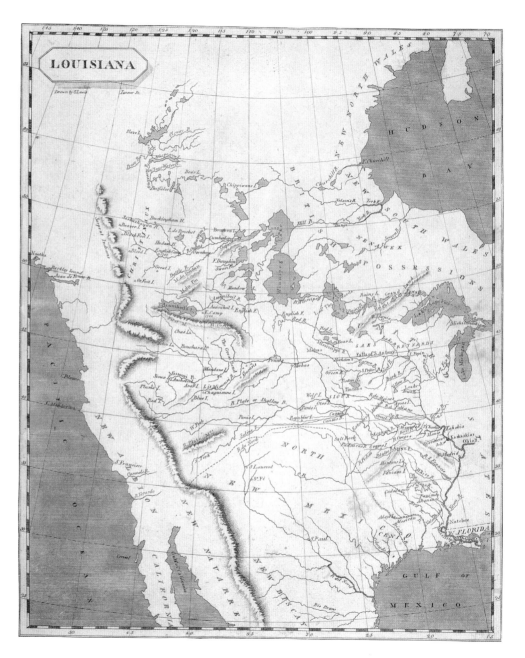

Right: MAP OF LOUISIANA, *from Aaron Arrowsmith and Samuel Lewis,* A New and Elegant General Atlas: All the New Discoveries, to the Present Time *(Philadelphia, 1804).*

This early map reveals both the untouched emptiness of the vast region from the Mississippi River to the Pacific Ocean and the utter lack of knowledge about it at the time of Lewis and Clark's expedition.

the Spanish authorities. Wilkinson's memorandum confirmed Lewis and Clark's objectives and urged their arrest in order to protect Spanish interests. The two leaders apparently never realized that they had become the quarry of Spanish troops, and between 1804 and 1806 three, possibly four, expeditions were dispatched north, charged with arresting "Captain Merry Weather" (as the Spanish called him) and his detachment. (Two were led by Pedro Vial, who in 1793 had opened a trail similar to the later Santa Fe Trail, but in reverse, starting from Santa Fe and ending in Saint Louis.) All these attempts proved unsuccessful, although the first effort missed Lewis and Clark's party by only a matter of days.

From a military viewpoint, the Corps of Discovery had a remarkable record of tight security, good health, and few disciplinary problems. Most of the latter cropped up during the first ninety days after breaking up winter training camp on the Wood River. Seven infractions such as drunkenness, absence without leave, or falling asleep on guard duty brought swift punishment by the lash. Moses B. Reed, who deserted

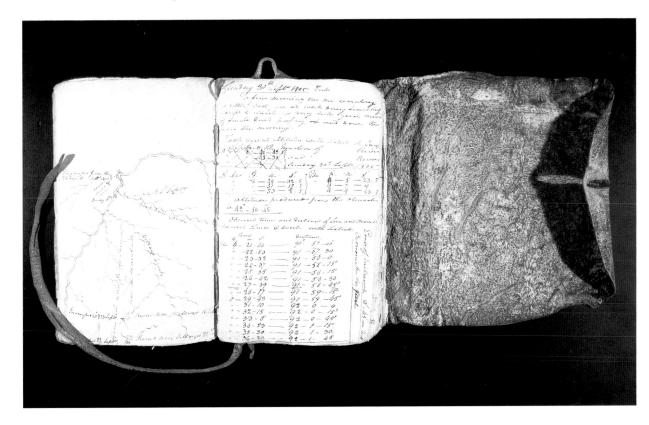

WILLIAM CLARK'S ELKSKIN-BOUND JOURNAL, *open to September 30, 1805. Missouri Historical Society, Saint Louis.*

Clark's field journal includes notes of daily events, distances, and sketches of the trail.

August 4, 1804, was court-martialed, sentenced to run the gauntlet four times through the party, and discharged from the corps. As for health, at various times the enlisted members suffered from boils, dysentery, and venereal disease acquired by fraternizing with Indian women along the route. Lewis and Clark frequently expressed shock in their journals at the custom among certain tribes of prostituting their wives for a twist of tobacco, a strand of beads, a fishhook, or similar trinkets. Lewis had evidently anticipated the venereal disease problem, however, and had stocked a mercury compound with which he successfully treated not only his men but also the Indians.

Every man who set out with Lewis and Clark returned home safe and sound, except one. Sergeant Charles Floyd died August 20, 1804, of what Clark referred to as a "Biliose Chorlick" (now thought to have been a ruptured appendix). After Floyd was buried on a bluff overlooking the Missouri River, Clark wrote in his journal: "Serj.' Floyd Died with a great deel of Composure, before his death he Said to me, 'I am going away' ['] I want you to write me a letter.' . . . He was buried with the Honors of War much lamented. . . . This man at all times gave us proofs of his firmness and Deturmined resolution to doe Service to his County and honor to himself after paying all the honor to our Decesed brother we Camped in the mouth of *floyds* river . . . a butifull evening."[4]

All along the rivers, the expedition would follow a fairly set routine when establishing contact with the native chieftains: first a presentation of gifts such as food, clothing (coats and hats), American flags, presi-

Left: Charles Willson Peale (1741–1827). WILLIAM CLARK, *1810. Oil on canvas, 23 x 19 in. (58.4 x 48.5 cm). Independence National Historical Park, Philadelphia.*

When William Clark was commissioned as only a lowly second lieutenant of artillery by a niggardly War Department, his old friend Meriwether Lewis designated Clark a captain anyway, with equal rank as co-leader of the Corps of Discovery.

Right: Charles Willson Peale (1741–1827). MERIWETHER LEWIS, *1807. Oil on canvas, 23 x 18 in. (58.4 x 46.5 cm). Independence National Historical Park, Philadelphia.*

Captain Meriwether Lewis was four years younger than Clark but the better educated of the two. Prior to the expedition's departure, he had received special training in celestial navigation and botany to prepare him for the journey into the unknown.

dential medals, certificates of good behavior, and the always-coveted twist or "carrot" of tobacco. On occasion Lewis and Clark even proffered a dram of liquor, sometimes to their regret. The offerings were accompanied by long pipe-smoking sessions while Lewis and Clark steered the conversation (held in sign language unless their interpreters happened to speak the local language) to the subjects of peace and trade, extracting pledges from numerous tribes to cease intertribal warfare and to prepare for barter with the American traders who would soon follow the corps. Many peace pledges were made by the Indians, but it appears that few were kept after Lewis and Clark disappeared from view around the next bend in the river.

Pulling up the Teton River (a side branch of the Missouri in present South Dakota) in September 1804, the expedition faced its first major crisis when it was forced to square off with a large band of Teton Sioux led by chiefs Black Buffalo and Partisan. Making a rare tactical error, Lewis and Clark invited the chiefs and some braves aboard the keelboat and plied them with whiskey, which, as Clark noted in his journal, "they appeared to be verry fond of, Sucked the bottle . . . & Soon began to be troublesome." In a second error, Clark then escorted the unruly Indians ashore in a pirogue, which they seized and refused to release. Clark continued: "The 2nd Chief [Partisan] was verry insolent both in words & justures (pretended drunkenness & staggered up against us) declareing I Should not go on, Stateing he had not recved presents Suffient from us." Offended and alarmed, Clark drew his sword and Lewis instantly ordered all personnel in the boat to hold rifles at the ready. With great understate-

ment, Clark added in his journal, "I felt my Self warm & Spoke in verry positive terms."[5]

Tempers then cooled on both sides, and Lewis's party withdrew upstream to camp for the night. Next morning they received Black Buffalo and his braves for an exchange of gifts. A red coat, cocked hat, and medals were bestowed on the Sioux chief, who nonetheless seized the pirogue hawser and refused to let go. Lewis's patience snapped. He barked a command to his crews to load their three swivel guns and aim them at the natives. After a short speech by Lewis, assuring the Sioux that they would all be killed unless the expedition went on unmolested, the crisis ended as abruptly as it had begun. Lewis and Clark's refusal to be bullied by the Sioux, recounted through the Indian grapevine, smoothed their passage all the way to the Pacific.

The corps arrived at the cluster of Mandan villages (near present Bismarck, North Dakota) on October 27, 1804, after rowing, dragging, and sailing their keelboat and two pirogues nearly a thousand miles up the Missouri—against the current. They were well received by the Mandan, who were fascinated by Clark's black servant, York, considering him "great medicine." Given the lateness of the season, the two corps leaders decided to stay the winter before continuing west. Not far from one of the villages the expedition erected a small log barracks, Fort Mandan, to be their home for a winter when temperatures would plummet to seventy-four degrees below zero. The boats were buried under snow and ice thick as concrete, and as Clark noted dolefully in his journal: "My Servents feet also *frosted* & his P---s a little."[6]

As they had done with the Sioux, Lewis and Clark gathered voluminous data on the Mandan culture and urged the tribe to maintain peaceful relations with their neighbors. They signed on Toussaint Charbonneau, a French Canadian, as a Minetaree interpreter. His wife, a seventeen-year-old Shoshone girl named Sacagawea, though pregnant, was also allowed to join the expedition. Several weeks before the corps left the Mandan villages, Clark recorded the birth of her infant in his journal for Monday, February 11, 1805:

About five o clock this evening one of the wives [Sacagawea] of Charbono was delivered of a fine boy. it is worthy of remark that this was the first

child which this woman had boarn and as is common in such cases her labour was tedious and the pain violent; Mr. Jessome informed me that he had freequently administered a small portion of the rattle of the rattle-snake, which he assured me had never failed to produce the desired effect, that of hastening the birth of the child; having the rattle of a snake by me I gave it to him and he administered two rings of it to the woman broken in small pieces with the fingers and added to a small quantity of water. Whether this medicine was truly the cause or not I shall not undertake to determine, but I was informed that she had not taken it more than ten minutes before she brought forth.[7]

The expedition had reached the Mandan villages on October 27, 1804, but not until March 31, 1805—a week before he was to leave Fort Mandan—did Lewis finally write a letter home to his mother, Mrs. Lucy Marks. The extremely long missive, which he may have thought could be his last, might have reassured Mrs. Marks—her son was at least alive—but the harrowing descriptions of his adventures would have made most mothers reach for the smelling salts:

So far, we have experienced more difficulty from the navigation of the Missouri, than danger from the Savages. the difficulties . . . of this immence river, arise from the rapidity of it's current, it's falling banks, sandbars, and timber which remains wholy or partially concealed in it's bed . . . if your vessel happens to touch the sand, or is by any accident turned sidewise to the current it is driven

Opposite, top: George Catlin (1796–1872). TORTURE SCENE IN THE MEDICINE LODGE. *5¼ x 7¼ in. (13.3 x 18.4 cm). From* Catlin, Being a Supplement to O-kee-pa: A Religious Ceremony; and Other Customs of the Mandans *(London: Trubner and Company, 1867).*

Catlin depicted the ceremony in which young Mandan braves hung from rawhide thongs attached to pegs skewered through their back or pectoral muscles.

Opposite, bottom: George Catlin (1796–1872). MISSOURI RIVER, *1866. Color engraving from* Illustrations of the Manners, Customs, and Conditions of the North American Indians, *vol. 1, 1866.*

The half-sunken snags shown in Catlin's sketch were the scourge of river steamboats. By 1897 they had sent over 289 boats to the bottom between Saint Louis and Pierre, South Dakota. One such unlucky vessel, the 181-foot side-wheeler Arabia, *making her way from Saint Louis to Council Bluffs in 1856, sank in ten minutes after a submerged sycamore tree crashed through her oaken hull like a torpedo. Miraculously, the 130 passengers survived, but the steamboat and her two-hundred-ton frontier-bound cargo were lost.* See pages 50–51.

Left: Karl Bodmer (1809–1893). PÉHRISKA-RÚHPA, MOENNITARRI WARRIOR IN THE COSTUME OF THE DOG DANCE, *completed after the return of the 1832–34 North American expedition. Engraving with aquatint, hand-colored with oil, 15 x 21½ in. (38.1 x 54.6 cm). Joslyn Art Museum, Omaha; Gift of the Enron Art Foundation.*

on the bar, and overset in an instant, generally destroyed . . . the banks being unable to support themselves longer, tumble into the river with tremendious force, distroying every thing within their reach. the timber thus precipitated into the water with large masses of earth about their roots, are seen drifting with the stream, their points above the water, while the roots more heavy are draged along the bottom untill they become firmly fixed in the quicksands which form the bed of the river, where they remain for many years, forming an irregular, tho' dangerous chevauxdefrise to oppose the navigator.[8]

Just before leaving Fort Mandan, Lewis and Clark sent the keelboat and its crew back to Saint Louis loaded with boxes and trunks of specimens for Thomas Jefferson, many of them animals and plants never before seen east of the Mississippi: antelope skins and skeletons, mountain-sheep horns, fox pelts, a tin box of mice and insects, and cages of live ground squirrels and magpies. The expedition left Fort Mandan on April 7, 1805, heading up the outer reaches of the largest river system in the United States: thirty-two people in all, traveling in two pirogues and six canoes. On the morning of departure Lewis registered the mixed feelings of doubt and joy that assailed him:

We were now about to penetrate a country at least two thousand miles in width, on which the foot of civillized man had never trodden; the good or evil it had in store for us was for experiment yet to determine, and these little vessels contained every article by which we were to expect to subsist or defend ourselves . . . entertain[in]g . . . as I do, the most confident hope of succeading in a voyage which had formed a . . . da[r]ling project of mine for the last ten years. I could but esteem this moment of my . . . departure as among the most happy of my life.[9]

Once on the river, Clark most often stayed in a boat, since he was the more adept at water navigation, while Lewis spent much time on land hunting and collecting the samples of flora and fauna that Jefferson impatiently waited for; he also scanned the heavens to fix their locations. Together they compiled a study of the Plains and Northwest Indians—documenting their chieftains, territories, languages, and customs. At night the two expedition leaders usually shared their tent of dressed skins with Sacagawea and her little boy, Jean Baptiste, as well as with Charbonneau and the hunter-interpreter George "Drewyer" (probably Drouillard). Sacagawea and her son habitually traveled in Clark's boat, a propinquity that knit strong bonds between the redheaded captain and the child, whom Clark called "Batiest, my little dancing boy."

Going up the Missouri in May 1805, Lewis recorded a ritual that had been performed by Native Americans for over two thousand years:

Today we passed on the Stard. side the remains of a vast many mangled carcases of Buffalow which had been driven over a precipice of 120 feet by the Indians and perished. . . . In this manner the

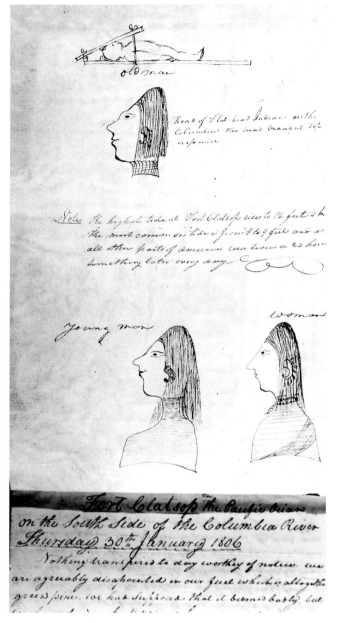

William Clark (1780–1838).
SKETCHES OF FLAT HEAD
INDIANS, *1806. From Clark's
elkskin-bound journal. Missouri
Historical Society, Saint Louis.*

*To fill the dreary winter days at
Fort Clatsop, Lewis and Clark
compiled their notes on the tribes
they had met in the course of their
journey. As Clark's sketches show,
he was intrigued by the Flathead
Indians' tradition of compressing
the skull to achieve a shape they
found beautiful.*

Indians of the Missouri distroy vast herds of
buffaloe at a stroke; for this purpose one of the
most active and fleet young men is scelected and
disguised in a robe of buffaloe skin, having also
the skin of the buffaloe's head with years and
horns fastened on his head in form of a cap, thus
caparisoned he places himself at a convenient
distance between a herd of buffaloe and a precipice proper for the purpose. . . . The other Indians
now surround the herd on the back and flanks and
at a signal agreed on all shew themselves at the
same time moving forward towards the buffaloe;
the disguised indian or decoy has taken care to
place himself sufficiently nigh the buffaloe to be
noticed by them when they take to flight and
runing before them they follow him in full speede
to the precipice, the cattle behind driving those
in front over and seeing them go do not look or
hesitate about following untill the whole are precipitated down the precipice forming one common mass of dead an[d] mangled carcases: the
. . . decoy in the mean time has taken care to
secure himself in some cranney or crivice of the
clift which he had previously prepared for that
purpose. the part of the decoy I am informed is
extreamly dangerous, if they are not very fleet
runers the buffaloe tread them under foot and
crush them to death, and sometimes drive them
over the precipice also, where they perish in
common with the buffaloe.[10]

By far the greatest part (perhaps 90 percent) of
Lewis and Clark's westbound transcontinental journey

was by water, chiefly on the Missouri, Jefferson, Clearwater, Snake, and Columbia Rivers. At many places supplies and equipment were cached underground in anticipation of the return trip, and portages had to be made around the most dangerous falls and rapids. Perhaps the most strenuous portage of all came at the Great Falls of the Missouri, while the party was still east of the Rockies. From June 21 to July 15, 1805, the corps carried out an eighteen-mile portage around the falls, their moccasined feet bloodied by the cactus spines blanketing the trail. With resourcefulness characteristic of the seasoned corpsmen, they mounted rough cart frames on wheellike disks cut from cottonwood trunks to ease hauling the heavy loads of dugouts and supplies. The severity of this portage was a

rude disappointment, for Jefferson and others had conjectured that a portage from the headwaters of the Missouri on the Atlantic slope to the headwaters of the Columbia on the Pacific side of the Continental Divide would take less than a day.

Farther west, on the Pacific slope, another cache was buried, and one more laborious portage successfully executed at the Columbia's Celilo (or Great) Falls. Still farther downriver, at the Dalles, the party boldly decided to shoot the rapids. Crowds of skeptical Nez Percé lined the riverbanks to watch. Even the usually imperturbable Clark, after surveying the situation from a large rock, was impressed by the sight: "I deturmined to pass through this place notwithstanding the horrid appearance of this agitated

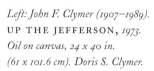

Left: John F. Clymer (1907–1989). UP THE JEFFERSON, *1973. Oil on canvas, 24 x 40 in. (61 x 101.6 cm). Doris S. Clymer.*

The late John F. Clymer, the most authentic of modern western historical artists, visualized the Corps of Discovery hauling their pirogues up the Jefferson River in July 1805, with rifles at the ready. Clark leads the party, with Lewis (wearing hat) second in line. Behind is the guide and interpreter Toussaint Charbonneau, closely followed by his wife, Sacagawea, carrying their infant son, Jean Baptiste.

The Hidatsa, one of the Indian tribes encountered by the Corps of Discovery, had kidnapped Sacagawea, a Shoshone girl, and held her prisoner for several years.

Opposite: SALMON RIVER, IDAHO, *1977. Photograph by David Muench.*

Searching for a way through the mountains, Clark reconnoitered twenty miles down the Salmon River before confirming that his Indian informants were right: the river was impassable.

gut Swelling, boiling & whorling in every direction which from the top of the rock did not appear as bad as when I was in it[,] however we passed Safe to the astonishment of all the Inds."[11]

After their backbreaking carry at the Great Falls of the Missouri, the expedition continued west past Hellgate and entered the Rocky Mountains. Just before reaching the Continental Divide they followed the Missouri's sudden turn southward until they came to "three noble streams," the Three Forks. To their immense satisfaction Lewis and Clark identified them as the headwaters of the Missouri and immediately named them the Jefferson, the Madison, and the Gallatin. Correctly judging the Jefferson to be the chief branch, Lewis led the expedition upstream to the Beaverhead River to reach the uttermost source of the Missouri. Here, on August 12, just before dropping over the Continental Divide at Lemhi Pass (between present Montana and Idaho), Lewis wrote exuberantly:

> The road took us to the most distant fountain of the waters of the mighty Missouri in surch of which we have spent so many toilsome days and wristless nights. thus far I had accomplished one of those great objects on which my mind has been unalterably fixed for many years. . . . McNeal [corps member] had exultingly stood with a foot on each side of this little rivulet and thanked his god that he had lived to bestride the mighty & heretofore deemed endless Missouri.[12]

Heady as this moment of fulfillment was, Lewis sensed that there were hard times still ahead: "We are now several hundred miles within the bosom of this wild and mountanous country where game may rationally be expected shortly to become scarce and subsistence precarious without any information with rispect to the country not knowing how far these mountains continue, or wher to direct our course to pass them."[13] To cross the mountains with all their baggage, the corps desperately needed horses. At this point Sacagawea came to their rescue. Recognizing the area they were passing through as the place where she had been captured by the Hidatsa years before, she assured the leaders that they would soon meet her people, the Shoshone, who were famous for their horses. This shortly proved to be the case; the expedition bartered for some mounts and continued north, crossing the forbidding Bitterroot Range at Lolo Pass and then working west to the Snake River and the Columbia.

Lewis celebrated his thirty-first birthday, on August 18, 1805, by confiding a vow to his journal: "This day I completed my thirty first year, and conceived that I had in all human probability now existed about half the period which I am to remain in this Sublunary world. I reflected that I had as yet done but little, very little indeed, to further the hapiness of the human race or to advance the information of the succeeding generation. . . . I . . . resolved in future . . . to live for *mankind* as I have heretofore lived *for myself.*"[14]

The Corps of Discovery reached the mouth of the Columbia River early in November 1805. That is not to say that they gazed then for the first time on the broad Pacific, which was still a few miles and sev-

eral days off. Clark, in fact, had written in error on November 7: "Ocian in view! O! the joy!" What he actually saw was the estuary of the Columbia. The expedition set up temporary camps around Point Ellice and Chinook Point from which they explored Cape Disappointment, but none proved satisfactory for more permanent lodging because of the rain and high winds that sent giant waves crashing ashore, endangering their canoes and camp. Earlier it had been swarms of seabirds that kept Clark from sleep; now he grumped in his journal that the ocean "roars like a repeated roling thunder." Finally, on December 7, they established a site for Fort Clatsop not too near the shore, set to work erecting a simple square stockade with seven cabins and a tiny parade ground inside, and moved in on New Year's Day, 1806.

The next three months at Clatsop must have seemed the longest of the entire expedition: perpetual

Above: GALLATIN RIVER AT THREE FORKS, MONTANA, UNDER STORMY SKY, *n.d. Photograph by George Wuerthner.*

The Three Forks, in present-day Montana, where the Gallatin, Jefferson, and Madison Rivers join to form the headwaters of the Missouri River. Albert Gallatin was then secretary of the treasury and James Madison, secretary of state.

rain; a deadening diet consisting largely of pounded salmon with "pore elk meat and roots"; no "ardent spirits" to lift the chill; and no human contacts aside from the decadent (as Lewis and Clark described them) coastal Indians. Fortunately, the long winter gave the expedition leaders time to transcribe their voluminous logs and journals, especially those recording their observations of native tribes met along the route. The journals for the Fort Clatsop period are heavy with sober entries to the effect that "nothing of interest happened today." To keep the enlisted men busy, a salt-extraction operation was set up near the ocean. A high spot of the winter was Clark's visit to the seashore to view a beached whale with Sacagawea,

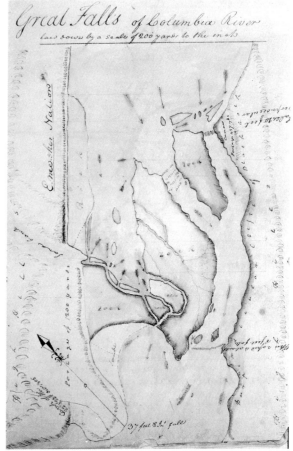

who had never seen the ocean and was eager to examine the great mammal. Unfortunately, by the time the party reached the scene, the Indians had stripped the carcass clean. Even the giant skeleton, however, made a lasting impression.

THE RETURN

All mountaineers learn that the descent is more dangerous than the ascent; a tiring climber often grows careless, opening the way for accidents or disaster.

And so it would be with the Corps of Discovery as they retraced their footsteps, with variations, from miserable Fort Clatsop back to Saint Louis. After the soggy winter of 1805–6, with no sign of the ship that Jefferson had promised to carry them home around Cape Horn, the detachment was eager to start eastward by canoe, horse, and foot—whatever it took. They finally pulled out of Fort Clatsop on March 23, 1806. At the Columbia River they put dugout canoes in the water, hugging the Oregon shore to avoid the heavy waves and strong current. Towing the canoes up the rapids by elk-thong ropes and portaging when necessary, the sodden party made their way upriver through the Cascades to the Dalles, where they portaged again with horses bartered from the natives. Detouring around Celilo Falls, the little expedition continued on land due east, aiming for Traveller's Rest, at the eastern edge of the Bitterroot Range.

Along the way, Lewis grew increasingly annoyed by the Indians' thievery of horses and property; finally he came to blows with one and threatened to kill them all and burn their houses unless the depreda-

tions ceased. Lewis's impatience (which eventually came through in his journal as frank dislike) with the Indians and with what he perceived as their insolence verged on violence several times during the return trip. This antipathy was only slightly softened by sympathy when he encountered bands of Indians reduced to living on boiled pine moss before the salmon runs began.

By early June the corps had grown short of food, fodder, and trade trinkets—a triple dilemma. Over-eager to reach Saint Louis by autumn, Lewis was determined to cross the Bitterroots two weeks earlier

than the Indians counseled. But after his horses floundered a few days through belly-deep snow, the party was forced to retreat, recruit (i.e., feed and rest the horses), and resume the march later, this time aided by an Indian guide. After untold effort they made it through to Traveller's Rest, and once they found themselves on the Atlantic slope everything literally ran downhill to Saint Louis. Events now swept past in a rush; the swift current, no longer their enemy but a friend, carried them down the Jefferson over ninety miles the first day. In July the portage at the Great Falls of the Missouri took days instead of weeks.

At Traveller's Rest, Lewis and Clark had separated so that Lewis could make an exploratory loop north to the Marias River and Clark could reconnoiter south and east on the Yellowstone. They agreed to meet below, at the juncture of the Yellowstone and Missouri. While the two leaders were separated, at the end of July, Lewis's camp was infiltrated by Blackfeet intent on stealing his horses and rifles. In the ensuing fracas two Blackfeet were shot and killed, one by Joseph Fields and the other by Lewis, who described the scene: "The other . . . turned arround and stoped at the distance of 30 steps from me and I shot him through the belly, he fell to his knees and on his wright elbow from which position he partly raised himself up and fired at me. . . . He overshot me, being bearheaded I felt the wind of his bullet very distinctly."[15] These deaths have often been cited as one possible cause of subsequent Blackfoot hostility toward white traders and trappers.

Farther downstream, at the Mandan villages, the detachment began to break up. Corps member John

Colter left to go back upstream with two trappers, Joseph Dixon and Forest Hancock. The Charbonneau family also dropped out, their work done; Toussaint Charbonneau received $500.333 for his services. In August the corps nearly lost one of its leaders when a hunting party took a comic-opera turn. Lewis was accidentally shot in the buttocks—painfully but not dangerously—by Cruzatte, the expedition's one-eyed hunter, fiddler, and helmsman. Lewis passed much of the ensuing descent downstream stretched out in the bottom of a dugout.

Three months after emerging from the Bitterroots, at noon on September 23, 1806, the Corps of Discovery dugout flotilla feathered their oars triumphantly at Saint Louis, firing their rifles to the answering salute of cheers and gunshots from the crowds on land. Once ashore, Lewis and Clark were feted with dinners and balls and endless honors, and properly so—they had not only opened the continent but stamped a new century with their own hallmark: discovery.

Meriwether Lewis was subsequently appointed governor of the Louisiana Territory, but his time of glory proved brief: only three years later, in 1809, the thirty-five-year-old bachelor died mysteriously of a gunshot, probably by his own hand—at a country tavern in Tennessee—having enjoyed far fewer than the sixty-two years he had once vowed "to live for mankind." William Clark was named superintendent of Indian affairs for the Louisiana Territory and later governor of the Missouri Territory. He is judged by many to have accomplished more to help the American Indian than any other man in history up to that time. York, who had a falling-out with Clark after

their return from the expedition, was finally given his freedom by Clark before his master died in Saint Louis in 1838. Sacagawea's final days remain uncertain; according to John Luttig, clerk at Fort Manuel, South Dakota, she died there "of a putrid fever" in 1812, although a large headstone marks her alleged grave at Fort Washakie, Wyoming. Clark brought her son, Jean Baptiste Charbonneau, to Saint Louis and had him educated.

THE VOYAGE OF DISCOVERY— AN APPRAISAL

Any evaluation of Lewis and Clark's Voyage of Discovery must note its major disappointments: it confirmed that there was no Northwest Passage, thus putting an end to Jefferson's long-cherished dream. And despite Lewis and Clark's brilliant personal and logistical triumph, their difficult northerly, watery route would never attract many followers since it did not permit the wagon-train traffic essential for homesteading emigrants.

But such disappointments, grave as they seemed at the time, were outshone by the light of the expedition's many accomplishments. It had recorded a dazzling number of "firsts." The corps was the first party of whites to cross the continental United States to the Pacific. (Alexander Mackenzie's zigzag crossing via the Arctic in 1793 had occurred in present Canada.) Sacagawea, a Native American, became the first woman known to have crossed the continent from the Missouri to the western ocean. Her infant son, Jean Baptiste Charbonneau, was the first child to

do so. Clark's slave, York, was the first black man to cross the continent. In addition, and of greater significance, Lewis and Clark's records constitute the first serious anthropological observations of western Indian tribes, the first comprehensive collection and description of western flora and fauna, and the first maps of the Northwest based on celestial navigation and on-site notations.

Above and beyond all these achievements, the success of the expedition assumed a vital geopolitical dimension by reinforcing United States claims in the Pacific Northwest vis-à-vis the British, Russian, and Spanish interests. By heightening American awareness of the Far West and its commercial potential—especially the fur trade—the expedition stimulated the notion of western expansion that would mature, for better and for worse, as the powerful concept of Manifest Destiny.

2

MOUNTAIN MEN
AND THE
FUR TRADE

THE HISTORY OF THE AMERICAN FAR WEST is enriched by many archetypal figures: the Native American, the Explorer, the Pioneer Woman, the '49er, the Cowboy, and the Cavalryman, to name only a few. Although active for only a relatively short time, each of them captured a permanent place in the American imagination.

Unique among them all stands the Mountain Man, the epitome of the rugged individual who chose to live wild and free. In some respects he resembles that hypothetical Natural Man, innocent and uncorrupted by society, so revered by early nineteenth-century French Romanticists. And yet the analogy is flawed, for the Rocky Mountain environment was certainly not the bucolic Garden of Eden that Jean-Jacques Rousseau and François-Auguste-René de Chateaubriand dreamed of. On the contrary, mountain man country offered harsh weather, wearying distances, the threat of starvation, and an oppressive solitude that would eventually weigh heavily on even the stoutest heart and mind. As if these hazards were not enough, sporadic harassment by the Indian tribes, from horse stealing to scalp lifting, reduced the mountain man's existence to a Darwinian survival of the fittest—and the luckiest. Only a handful of bold men were willing to allow such brutal conditions to season their character.

The mountain man was essentially born with the opening of the beaver trade in the Far West; 1807, when Manuel Lisa dispatched his first trappers up the

GREEN RIVER RENDEZVOUS SITE, WYOMING, *n.d.*
Photograph by Fred Gowans.

Missouri River, will do for a starting date. The European demand for beaver fur to craft gentlemen's top hats had suddenly set brigades of bearded, buckskin-clad trappers to wading in icy streams and ponds on both sides of the Continental Divide in search of the coveted *Castor canadensis*. Fur-trading companies organized by such private entrepreneurs as John Jacob Astor, Colonel William H. Ashley, and Pierre Chouteau, Jr., built a string of trading posts along the rivers: Fort Laramie above the confluence of the Laramie and the Platte, Fort Floyd on the Yellowstone, Fort Bridger on the Green, Fort Henry on the Snake, and Bent's Fort on the Arkansas, among numerous others. These were key trading and supply centers (*fort* is a misnomer since these were not military posts) where Indians and trappers could bring their peltry, traders could stock their beads, blankets, knives, mirrors, and foofaraw (trinkets and other gaudy adornments), and westering emigrants could often buy supplies and wagon parts or swap worn-out animals for fresh. For thirty years the beaver trade flourished, and there were small fortunes to be made; young Jedediah Smith sent five thousand dollars home to Saint Louis his second year out. Less fortunate were those whose entire season's fur harvest sank to the bottom of the river after their dugouts, canoes, or keelboats capsized floating back downstream to Saint Louis.

After London and Paris dandies came to prefer top hats of silk to those of beaver felt, in the 1830s the beaver trade languished, a falling-off that was only briefly offset by a new commerce in buffalo hides for carriage robes. By 1840 the beaver fur trade was to all

COL. CHRISTOPHER "KIT" CARSON, SAINT LOUIS, *December 1864.*

Perhaps the epitome of the frontiersman was Christopher Houston "Kit" Carson, who ran away from home in Missouri at seventeen; went to Taos, New Mexico; and experienced the full range of frontier life as trapper, trader, hunter, horseman, Indian agent, rancher, and army officer. A tough, daring Indian fighter and scout, he won fame as a guide to John C. Frémont on three of the latter's western expeditions.

Jim Baker—a mountain man, trapper, guide, and scout—survived many a hard time in the wilderness with Kit Carson and Jim Bridger in the 1830s. His face illustrates better than words Frederick Jackson Turner's idea that the frontier formed the American character.

intents and purposes dead, and the mountain men drifted into other occupations: as guides for wagon trains heading to Oregon or California and for the increasing numbers of military expeditions exploring and surveying remote mountain reaches. These were regions that men like Jim Clyman, Joe Walker, Old Bill Williams, Kit Carson, and their colleagues often knew more intimately than did the Indians. Even John C. Frémont, the famous Pathfinder himself, felt obliged to enlist such men as guides for his five expeditions across the continent between 1842 and 1853. The trappers and mountain men broke trails into every nook and cranny of the western ranges without U.S. government help and before military forts existed for protection. It was these trailblazers who discovered the passes through the mountains, established trading relationships with many of the Indian tribes, and identified viable travel routes, thus clearing the way for the first great waves of westward emigration in the 1840s.

And so, aided first by the illustrious Bonaparte, then by the humble beaver, and now by the simple mountain man, the juggernaut of Manifest Destiny slowly creaked and rumbled on its way to the Pacific.

| ASHLEY'S CHALLENGE

In 1822 the muddy streets of Saint Louis bustled with all the crowded activity of a grand-opera stage, peopled with a variety of races that defined the melting-pot character of the early frontier town. In summer the scene teemed with prowling Indians from various tribes, some with shaven heads, some roached and feathered, each decked out distinctively with jewelry,

Colonel William H. Ashley's advertisement in the February 13, 1822, Missouri Gazette (Saint Louis) sounded a clarion call to aspiring young mountain men like Jim Bridger, James Clyman, and Jedediah Smith.

bone and quill ornaments, and colored blankets; with sauntering Spanish traders up from Chihuahua, Santa Fe, or Taos, in broad sombreros and adorned with silver accoutrements; with French Canadian *voyageurs,* Mexican mule drivers, and bullwhackers. All mingled in the dust and mud with a flood of local teamsters, boatmen, soldiers, farmers, and traders, to the background strains of creaking wagons, cracking whips, bellowing animals, clanking sabers, and curses in several languages—the music of the frontier.

Among that surging street crowd were restless young men who looked longingly to the West. It is no wonder that on February 13, 1822, when Saint Louis fur trader Colonel William H. Ashley ran his famous advertisement in the *Missouri Gazette* challenging young would-be frontiersmen to apply for a one-to-three-year stint trapping beaver in the Rockies, the response was immediate. A number of the men who signed up to accompany Ashley and his associate Major Andrew Henry became the elite of the frontier for the next two decades; that roster

TO
Enterprising Young Men.

THE subscriber wishes to engage ONE HUNDRED MEN, to ascend the river Missouri to its source, there to be employed for one, two or three years.—For particulars, enquire of Major Andrew Henry, near the Lead Mines, in the County of Washington, (who will ascend with, and command the party) or to the subscriber at St. Louis.

Wm. H. Ashley.

February 13   —98 tf

included such future legends as Jim Bridger, Jedediah Smith, James Clyman, Thomas "Broken Hand" Fitzpatrick, Mike Fink, Jim Beckwourth, David Jackson, Etienne Provost, and Hugh Glass.

Many were farm boys from Pennsylvania, Virginia, and other points east, eager to be their own men and to hone their modest skills as woodsmen and hunters on the thousand-mile-long whetstone of the Rockies. The chance to acquire quick wealth in two or three good seasons on the streams was certainly not to be scorned. But it was more than just the lure of money, for like Lewis and Clark before them, they also heard the call to adventure. If it is true that every voyage is a search for the self, nothing promised to reveal a man to himself like a couple of years in the mountains.

The rugged life of a mountain man was a young man's game. He started early: Kit Carson ran away at

seventeen; Jim Bridger was all of eighteen; Peg-leg Smith (who later amputated his own leg with a knife) was nineteen; and Jedediah Smith and James Clyman were old men of twenty-three and thirty-one, respectively. And he generally finished early, if he walked away at all before starving or freezing to death or "going under" to a tomahawk.

Although many hundreds of men made up the fur brigades and the rough fraternity of western scouts and guides, most have passed anonymously into history. The few dozen whose lives are recorded were so colorful that even the briefest profile of some of those who went up the Missouri with Ashley and Henry conveys a vivid composite image of the mountain man.

JIM BRIDGER

Born in 1804 in Virginia, James Bridger was apprenticed at age fourteen to a blacksmith. Four years later—six feet tall, gray-eyed, and rawboned—he joined Henry's fur brigade. If Bridger was looking for adventure, he soon found it. In the spring of 1823 the party lost four men in a skirmish with the Blackfeet and had to withdraw to the Yellowstone. On the way, there occurred one of the most traumatic episodes in Bridger's entire career. Hugh Glass, a member of the company, was attacked by a female grizzly and her cubs. As they savagely tore chunks of flesh from his head and thigh, Glass could hear their teeth grinding on his bones. When help finally arrived, he seemed on the verge of death and certainly beyond moving. Fearing fresh Indian attacks, Henry's party did not wait

Left: Alfred Jacob Miller (1810–1874).
INTERIOR VIEW OF FORT
LARAMIE, *1837. Watercolor on paper, 11⅝ x 14⅛ in. (29.5 x 35.8 cm). Walters Art Gallery, Baltimore.*

Fort William, Wyoming (better known by its later name of Fort Laramie), was built by William Sublette in 1834 as a trading post—not a military post, as the name implies. Strategically placed on what would become the Oregon-California Trail, for years it was a major stopping place for westbound emigrants. Miller recorded this rare view of the fort's interior in 1837, long before photography reached the frontier.

for Glass to die but pushed on, leaving two men to bury their comrade when his time came. After several days had passed and his time still hadn't come, Glass's companions, believing death was imminent and anxious for their own safety, decided to abandon him. Taking his rifle and knife, they sped down the trail to catch the main party, explaining that Glass had died and they had buried him. The company continued to Henry's Fort on the Big Horn, and there, months later, Glass appeared in camp, bloody and emaciated. It is generally accepted that Jim Bridger was one of those who had abandoned Glass, and that Glass pardoned him only because of his youth.

Bridger would trap for another fifteen years or so in the Rockies and the Southwest with Jedediah Smith, Milton Sublette, Thomas "Broken Hand" Fitzpatrick, Kit Carson, and Joe Meek. He was credited by some with the discovery of Great Salt Lake in 1824 (which he mistook for an arm of the Pacific Ocean) and became a regular celebrant at the mountain men's annual Rendezvous. At one such rampaging bacchanal, in 1835, Bridger saw Kit Carson shoot a bully named Shunar in a duel, receiving as prize a young Arapaho woman, who became Kit's first wife. A few days later Bridger himself, until then a bachelor, took a Flathead woman for his wife, later followed in succession by a Ute and a Snake, by whom he had five children. (The fact that many trappers such as Jim Beckwourth, Jim Bridger, and Beaver Dick Leigh took Indian wives undoubtedly smoothed relationships between trappers and tribes.) At the same Rendezvous, Dr. Marcus Whitman, the noted medical missionary from Waiilatpu, Washington, finally dug from Bridger's back an old Blackfoot arrowhead that he had carried for several years.

A sometime trapper–sometime trader, the illiterate Bridger was a canny businessman. One of the organizers of the Rocky Mountain Fur Company, he later become associated with the American Fur Company, and in 1843, with Louis Vasquez, he built Fort Bridger on the Green River in present-day Wyoming. Strategically placed halfway along the trail to California, the fort became a major trading post, later including a Pony Express station and a military post.

Later in life Bridger acquired some property in West-port, Missouri, and a farm nearby, where he settled down when his health failed. He died on his farm in 1881, having lost his sight but nonetheless rich in years and unparalleled experiences.

JEAN BAPTISTE CHARBONNEAU

In Lewis and Clark's winter quarters at Fort Mandan, Jean Baptiste Charbonneau was born to the seventeen-year-old Sacagawea. In the course of the long journey to the Pacific and back, William Clark became so fond of little Jean Baptiste that after returning home in 1806 he acted as the child's surrogate father, later bringing him to Saint Louis for education at Clark's expense. In a Baptist school under the watchful eye of the Rever-

end J. E. Welch, Jean Baptiste studied French, Latin, and history until he returned to the Mandan villages to live at about sixteen. Two years later, on the Kansas River, he was befriended by Prince Paul of Württem-burg, a scientist, artist, hunter, and explorer who was collecting animal and plant specimens. Prince Paul was intrigued by the gifted young métis and received Clark's permission to take him back to Württemburg for further polishing. No doubt seeming to the prince's circle like Rousseau's Natural Man personified, Jean Baptiste spent the next six years tasting the worldly life at Paul's court, hunting in the Black Forest, accom-panying the prince on his travels through Europe and North Africa, and adding Spanish and German to the French, English, and several Indian tongues that he already spoke. Prince Paul's court painter, Baldwin Möllhausen, must have painted Charbonneau's portrait during those years in Württemburg, but unfortunately Paul's papers were destroyed during World War II, and Charbonneau remains faceless to this day. In 1829, when Prince Paul returned to the United States for further explorations, he brought the twenty-four-year-old Charbonneau back with him. Apparently they then went their separate ways.

Charbonneau was now a man deeply divided by both blood and culture, having spent half his life in Saint Louis and Europe, and half among the Plains Indians. Both blood tides pulled at him, but the Indian side won. Instead of taking a post in the Bureau of Indian Affairs in Saint Louis, which was then headed by his benefactor William Clark, Charbonneau chose the wilderness life of the mountain man.

For the next thirty-five years his moccasin prints

BEAVER DICK LEIGH AND FAMILY, *1890s. Photograph by Dr. Charles Penrose.*

Beaver Dick Leigh (born in Manchester, England, in 1831) and his second wife, a Bannock Indian named Susan, are pictured with three of their children. Leigh, one of the last of the mountain men, stubbornly remained in the north-western Wyoming area, trapping, guid-ing, and scratching out a meager living until death took him in 1899. Years earlier he had watched his first wife and six children die of smallpox in the course of a few days.

boiled buffalo tongue, and coffee with the luxury of sugar, were soon set before us."[1]

In 1847 Charbonneau was appointed *alcalde* (justice of the peace) at San Luis Rey Mission in California. When gold fever swept the West in 1849, he joined his friend Jim Beckwourth (another formidable mountain man of mixed blood) in gold-mining operations at Murderer's Bar on the American River. Charbonneau evidently never struck it rich in mining, and in 1861 he was listed in the city directory of Auburn, California, as clerk of the Orleans Hotel. In 1866 he was spurred into action again by news of recent gold strikes in Montana; in the spring of his sixty-first year Charbonneau eagerly started out on horseback for the new gold fields. On the way there, while fording the icy Owyhee River in southeastern Oregon, his horse lost its footing. Thoroughly drenched, Charbonneau contracted pneumonia and died soon after, at Inskip Station.

So passed a remarkable child of two cultures. As the Lewis and Clark expedition had marked a watershed in America's coming of age, so had the epoch 1800–1870, which saw a wilderness tamed and the country united. Jean Baptiste Charbonneau had played a direct role in both.

JAMES CLYMAN

James Clyman was another of the bold young men who answered Ashley's call, though at thirty-one he was older than most. He had been raised a Virginia farm boy on land owned by George Washington, then moved farther west with his parents. By age twenty he

appeared and disappeared throughout the Far West. He trapped and traded for the American Fur Company and for the firm of Bent and Saint Vrain; took part in the Green River Rendezvous; and with the great Thomas "Broken Hand" Fitzpatrick, in 1845, guided the U.S. Army exploratory expedition south of Bent's Fort along the Canadian River. Lieutenant John C. Frémont once found him stranded with a boatload of hides on a Platte River gravel bar, which Charbonneau had ironically dubbed Saint Helena after Napoleon's island of exile. Wrote Frémont later: "Mr. C[harbonneau] received us hospitably. One of the people was sent to gather mint, with the aid of which he concocted very good julep; and some had already done military service and fought Indians in the War of 1812. After farming a few years Clyman picked up surveying as a profession, one he continued to practice off and on most of his life. He went to the mountains in 1823 with Ashley and Henry's second expedition as a member of Jedediah Smith's fur brigade, and in the next half-dozen years established himself as a first-class mountain man.

Ashley and Clyman had met in Saint Louis, where Ashley engaged him to help recruit his trapping brigade. Clyman accomplished this mission, as he wrote later, by prowling the "grog shops and other sinks of degredation" for a crew of seventy that made "Fallstaff's Battallion . . . genteel in comparison."[2] Since Clyman could cipher, read (especially favoring Shakespeare, Byron, and the Bible), and write (even composing homespun poetry by the campfire), Ashley appointed him a brigade clerk—at one dollar a day.

When the expedition got underway on March 10, 1823, Clyman recorded in his journal that the party "shoved off from the shore fired a swivel [small cannon] which was answered by a Shout from the shore . . . and porceed up stream under sail." Disaster soon struck. At the Arikara villages the party was attacked in a brief but bloody fight—the worst disaster in western fur-trade history. In only fifteen minutes Ashley lost twelve men, with eleven wounded and several more missing. One of the missing was Clyman, who had swum with difficulty to the far side of the river, shedding rifle, pistols, and part of his buckskin hunting shirt to keep from drowning. With three Indians in pursuit, Clyman "concluded to take to the open Pararie and run for life." After an hour's race at full speed, Clyman was able to

hide in some reeds and escape his pursuers. From a ridge a safe distance off he then showed himself to them and mockingly "made a low bow with both my hand" before continuing downriver to safety.[3]

For Clyman, adventure followed rapidly on adventure. Later that first year, when Clyman's captain, Jedediah Smith, was mauled by a grizzly bear, it was Clyman who sewed up Smith's torn scalp and reattached his ear. Clyman was also in Smith's party in February 1824, when they made the first westward crossing of South Pass at some 7,500 feet above sea level in the southwest corner of present-day Wyoming, a discovery that led to the later opening of the Oregon Trail.

The next summer Clyman missed a scheduled rendezvous with Smith's party on the Sweetwater (in present southwestern Wyoming), so he decided to strike out alone for Fort Atkinson at Council Bluffs, six hundred miles to the east. At the outset Indians robbed him of all his equipment and then turned him loose on foot. Weaponless, he could kill no game for food, although he survived for a time by bludgeoning two badgers to death with bones from a nearby horse carcass. Week after starving week Clyman groped his way east. The last few days of his ordeal, literally walking in his sleep, he frequently stumbled off the trail and fell to the ground in a stupor. At last, after eighty days of intense suffering, during which he had covered six hundred

Below: James Clyman, one of the most respected mountain men, sewed Jedediah Smith's ear back on after a grizzly had torn it off.

Opposite: The Winchester 30–30 would be remembered as the gun that won the West, but it was the cap-lock rifle, shown here, favored by the mountain men that opened the West.

miles on foot, the exhausted and skeletal Clyman collapsed when he recognized the American flag fluttering over the fort.

All this took place in Clyman's first year as a mountain man; much was yet to come. In 1825 he took part in the first Rendezvous on the Green River, and the next year circumnavigated the Great Salt Lake in a skin canoe. He subsequently spent seventeen years as a farmer and businessman in Illinois, and in 1832 served a brief military tour in the same company as Abraham Lincoln. (Also in that company was James Frazier Reed, who fourteen years later helped guide the Donner Party to California.)

Clyman's journal—he was one of the very few mountain men to keep one—abounds with geological observations on the landscape through which he traveled and with cogent philosophical speculations inspired by them:

> 1840 Jany 2—. . . Two things Infinite Time and space. Two things more appear to be attached to the above infinity (wiz) Matter and number Matter appears to prevade the infinity of space and number attempts to define quantity of matter as well as to give bounds to space—which continually Expands before matter and number— and all human speculation is here bounden in matter and number leaving space at least almost completely untouched.[4]

Clyman's trail life was not always unadulterated hardship, and his journal is sprinkled with comments like the following, made in 1844 when he was guiding a party of Oregon-bound emigrants past Chimney Rock: "Supped on a most dlecious piece of venison from the loin of a fat Black taild Buck and I must not omit to mention that I took my rifle and (and) walked out in the deep ravin to guard a Beautifull covey of young Ladies & misses while they gathered wild currants & choke chirries which grow in great perfusion in this region."[5]

In June, during his 1846 journey from west to east, Clyman circled the Wind River Range and dropped down to the Sweetwater River. "It gave [me] Quite a cheering satisfactory Idea allthough at so greate a distance to think that I was once more on the waters of the Missisippi and its ripling waters sounded in Idea like sweet home." Over the next few days, east of Independence Rock, Clyman encountered "all most one continual stream of Emigrants wending their long and Tedious march to oregon & california." This was the vanguard of the Great Migration of 1846. On he rode, past the old landmarks of Chimney Rock and Ash Hollow where "familiar noisis such as the whistleing of Quails and the croakings of the Bull frog," sounds not heard in the Far West, fell on his ears like long-forgotten music. Finally reaching Independence, Missouri, on June 22, Clyman sold his mules "and mad[e] my appearance at Mr. Noland's Tavern and a Rough appearance it was."[6] He was a master of understatement.

Clyman went west again in 1848, guiding a party of emigrants to California; this time he settled there and spent the balance of his life dairy ranching and fruit farming. In 1849, at the age of fifty-seven, he married for the first time, and with his wife, Hannah,

had five children, four of whom died early of scarlet fever. Although Clyman lost the sight of one eye in an accident, this did not deter him from spending the last years of his life planting his garden, hunting, or sitting in the sun writing verses on a slate for his one remaining daughter to copy out. He died at eighty-nine in Napa, California, having lived through the era of the mountain man and into the modern age of highways and iron roads. Like every mountain man, Clyman was one of a kind, yet he still strikes us as possessing what we like to think of as typically, though certainly not exclusively, American traits: curiosity, endurance, fair-mindedness, good humor, and common sense.

MIKE FINK

One of the more dubious characters that Clyman rounded up from the Saint Louis fleshpots for Ashley's 1823 expedition was Mike Fink. Notorious as a boatman and a kick-gouge-and-bite brawler—equally expert at both—Fink was a familiar figure in barrooms from Saint Louis to New Orleans. His standard whiskey-soaked entrance was a stamping, shouting declaration that he was "half-man, half-alligator" who could "whup" any man on the river, and who was a wild one with "the wimming." These were impressive qualifications in a man already over fifty. More important was the fact that Fink knew the troubled waters of the Missouri and was a crack shot. Clyman promptly signed him on, with two of his sharpshooting friends, Bill Carpenter and Levi Talbot.

Fink and his friends made their way up the Missouri with a party that later settled for a long winter on the Musselshell River. Fink and Carpenter had a falling out, but patched it up. To confirm there were no hard feelings, Fink proposed to repeat a stunt that he and Carpenter had often performed before: one man would shoot a tin cup of whiskey off the head of the other from a distance of two hundred feet. Carpenter agreed, and they "skied a copper" to see who would shoot first. Fink won the honors and took his usual distance from Carpenter who, not without qualms this time, placed the cup atop his head. Fink smiled and shouted: "Hold your noddle steady, Carpenter and don't spill the whiskey." He then took aim, and squeezed the trigger. Carpenter pitched to the ground. Talbot, who witnessed the scene, rushed to the fallen man and found a bullet hole in the center of his forehead. Fink calmly blew the smoke from his rifle barrel and observed reproachfully, "Carpenter, you have spilled the whiskey!"[7] Furious, Talbot threatened instant revenge but was dissuaded by onlookers. Not long after, however, he caught up with Fink, who affirmed that the killing had been deliberate. Talbot instantly drew his gun and shot Fink through the heart. In a bitter postscript to this double murder, Talbot drowned attempting to swim the Teton River only a few months later.

THE BEAVER AND THE BUFFALO TRADE

Between 1820 and 1840 the fur trade was the biggest business in the trans-Mississippi West. It revolved around a small herbivore with big incisors, a broad tail that could slap the water like the crack of a pistol shot, and—unfortunately for the beaver—a highly coveted fur coat. Caught in an irony more cruel than any steel trap, the fur-bearing logger, dam builder, and marine engineer was nearly obliterated as a species by man— the only other animal on the North American continent whose technologies surpassed the beaver's—in order to satisfy a passing whim of European fashion.

Catching an animal as clever as the beaver was not a simple task. Trappers slogged through the frigid streams and ponds of every valley in beaver country, searching for the telltale dams and lodges built by their quarry. Once the beaver's daily routes from lodge to dam or logging site were determined, traps could be carefully set along the way to intercept the unsuspecting animal on its way to work. More often trappers would submerge a trap underwater, anchoring it with a stake. The trap was then baited with a twig, left protruding above water, which was sprinkled with castoreum, the beaver's own secretion, enhanced with cloves, cinnamon, and other exotic ingredients. Each

trapper concocted his own jealously guarded secret formula. Investigating the seductively scented twig, the beaver would step on the trap spring—its last step on earth and its first on the way to some gentleman's top hat in London or Paris. No one knows for certain how many beaver were killed in this way.

By about 1840 the trade in beaver fur was all but over, yet there remained a coterie of hardened trappers who clung to the old familiar work rather than turn to emigrant guiding or army scouting. Fortunately for them, a popular taste developed for using dressed buffalo hides as lap robes in carriages and this commerce kept the fur trade alive for a few more years. The hunters' good fortune was the buffaloes' curse: their demise was swift and sure. Experts have estimated that in 1800 there were sixty to seventy-five million bison roaming the wilderness west of the Mississippi, clustered in three Great Plains herds: north, central, and south.

Above: Alfred Jacob Miller (1810–1874). TRAPPING BEAVER, *1837. Watercolor on paper, 8⅞ x 13¾ in. (22.6 x 35 cm). Walters Art Gallery, Baltimore.*

Alfred Jacob Miller's romanticized picture of beaver trappers plying their trade hardly conveys the harshness of work that required wading day after day hip deep in icy spring and autumn streams.

Left: John James Audubon (1785–1851). AMERICAN BEAVER, *1844. Plate XLVI of* Vivaparous Quadrupeds of North America.

Castor canadensis, *the semiaquatic rodent whose valuable pelt spurred the opening of the Far West. Trappers and traders were lured west by the profits to be made in this first major business on the far side of the Mississippi.*

Below: BUFFALO BONE PILE OUTSIDE MICHIGAN CARBON WORKS, *1895.*

Mute evidence of the massive extermination of the buffalo herds, this heap of bison skulls tells the final chapter of a sorrowful story. The trade in buffalo robes had long ago died out by the time this picture was taken, but the prairies remained littered with bones polished ivory-clean by carnivores and weather. Toward the close of the nineteenth century these remains were collected and sold for industrial use—some two million tons in all, valued at forty million dollars.

Right: STAMPEDING BUFFALO, LAMAR VALLEY, YELLOWSTONE PARK, *1916.*
Photograph by Jack Ellis Haynes.

The buffalo was at the heart of the Indian way of life, providing food, clothing, and shelter as well as nourishing their mythology.

George Catlin, the American artist who first caught the western Native American culture on canvas, recorded that Indians in 1832 offered two million buffalo hides to trappers, a sign that even before the white hunters' arrival the Indians were steadily diminishing the seemingly limitless bison population. But the more modern rifles and the wanton killing introduced by white hunters greatly accelerated the destruction of the herds. Buffalo Bill Cody alone, hunting to feed the construction crews of the Kansas Pacific Railroad in 1868, was credited that year with a record kill of 4,280 head, which earned him his sobriquet. Passengers on the Union Pacific, steaming west in 1867–69, commonly shot bison for sport through the windows of the moving train, but it was the train itself that most weakened the beleaguered buffalo by breaking up the central herd and dividing the remainder into two groups: north and south. In addition, the barrier of iron tracks between the two herds drastically disturbed ancient

Indian hunting patterns and severely interrupted access to their chief food supply. A quick calculation suggests the scope of that problem: a tribe of ten thousand Indians trying to survive a single winter without their usual two meals of buffalo meat a day would effectively be deprived of some two million meals. That is a giant step toward starvation.

The speed of the systematic slaughter was unbelievable. Colonel R. I. Dodge, standing atop Pawnee Rock in 1867, watched the last great bison herd on the Arkansas River: twenty-six miles wide and fifty miles long, the shaggy mass took five days to pass a given point. Twenty years later, in 1887, only 261 lonely bison were left wandering on the range.

THE RENDEZVOUS

The pelt-hunting mountain men were of two types: traders and trappers. In the early decades of the trade after 1807, a limited number of government-licensed traders circulated among the Great Plains and Rocky Mountain tribes such as the Mandan, Arikara, Crow, Blackfoot, and Shoshone, exchanging trade goods for beaver pelts harvested by the Indians. But as the European desire for beaver hats intensified, brigades of white trappers rapidly replaced the Indians as fur gatherers. Their hunting area covered an immense two million square miles all told, but its heartland lay in the central Rockies, where beaver abounded.

Beaver trapping took place mostly in the early spring, late summer, and fall, when furs were richest. In winter the trappers holed up, if possible, in settlements with a milder climate, like Pueblo, Hardscrabble, or Greenhorn on the Upper Arkansas River. The mountain man trappers led a hard life and were no doubt coarsened by it, routinely clinging to the edge of starvation, and sometimes forced to eat their mules and horses. If they were lucky, they'd feast on slabs of raw buffalo liver or the tasty *boudin*, a prized puddinglike dish made from bison stomach. Their fringed buckskins were usually blackened from the soot and grease of countless campfires and meals, and stained with the dried blood of beaver, buffalo, and other animals. Seldom bearded but often longhaired, usually rank, itchy, thirsty, and randy, and frequently wincing from wounds both old and fresh, the trappers made a colorful caravan as they swarmed into the annual traders' and trappers' Rendezvous from all points of the compass. Eager to unwind for a few weeks of the brief mountain summer, on foot, horse, and muleback they came, greeting each other good-naturedly as "Ol' Hoss!," "niggur," or "child" in their peculiar mountain man jargon liberally punctuated by the emphatic Indian "Wagh!"

At this raucous annual gathering, traders, trappers, and Indians all let off steam built up in the preceding year of dangerous wilderness living. Diversions included brawling, footraces, wrestling, drinking, gambling, sharpshooting contests, wenching with Indian women, and horse racing with Indian men. At the same time, the Rendezvous served as a primitive agora for trading supplies and furs, for exchanging intelligence, and for deal making; trappers switched employers, took on new partners, and planned their operations for the coming season.

The Rendezvous as a fur-trade institution had

Frederic Remington (1861–1909).
I TOOK YE FOR AN INJIN,
November 1890. Frederic Remington Art Museum, Ogdensburg, New York.

After years of living in the wilderness, a mountain man's personal appearance would evolve into an eclectic blend of comfort, camouflage, and practicality, creating a highly eccentric effect.

been Ashley's brilliant idea. A successful and highly respected fur trader himself (and later lieutenant governor, then congressman, of Missouri), Ashley had formed a fur-trading partnership with Andrew Henry in 1822 to develop the beaver trade of the Upper Missouri and in the central Rockies. Their initial ventures were dogged by misfortune: on their first expedition one of the keelboats struck a snag and sank to the bottom with a total loss of ten thousand dollars worth of merchandise, and on their next expedition, in 1823, they suffered the Arikara's fatal attack.

After several years of such harsh experience it occurred to Ashley that instead of incurring the expense and danger of building remote forts as trading posts, it would make better sense to organize a central meeting place each summer where trappers and Indians could bring their peltry for sale to the traders and where the latter could sell them supplies. The new system was put into effect the summer of 1825, when Ashley's inaugural Rendezvous was held near the Junction of Henry's Fork with the Green River, in what is now southwestern Wyoming. Ashley had previously explained to his scattered trapping parties that the exact Rendezvous site would be marked as follows: "The place of deposite as aforesaid, will be the place of randavoze for all our parties on or before the 10th July next & that place may be known—Trees will be pealed standing the most conspicuous near the Junction of the rivers. Sould such a point be without timber I will raise a mound of Earth five feet high or Set up rocks the top of which will be made red with vermillion." The first Rendezvous lasted only a day or two, perhaps because Ashley served no liquor; in later years, when alcohol flowed like water, the Rendezvous would last for weeks. Jim Beckwourth recalled that at the second Rendezvous, in 1826, "the unpacking of the medicine water contributed not a little to the heightening of our festivities."[8] On the Fourth of July of that second

Rendezvous, the men fired their guns wildly and drank spirited patriotic toasts. No doubt some were offered to the president of the United States and author of the Declaration of Independence; the roisterers had no way of knowing that Jefferson had died at Monticello that very day.

Ashley left the first Rendezvous a wealthy man, floating contentedly down the Missouri with some nine thousand pounds of beaver pelts safely stowed aboard three army keelboats dubbed the *Mink, Muskrat,* and *Rackoon.* Following the 1826 Rendezvous he carried out 10,500 pounds of pelts, an unprecedented fur harvest. On average such pelts cost Ashley two to three dollars a pound, for a total cost of close to fifty thousand dollars. He probably sold them, even at depressed prices, at an average four dollars a pound in Saint Louis or New York, for a total value of eighty thousand dollars and a gross profit in the vicinity of thirty thousand dollars. This was, however, a very high-risk business: a loss of horses, damage to the cargo, a sudden drop in market prices—all could easily plunge a year's operations into the red.

Ashley's initial success was a great stimulus to the fur trade, enticing additional trappers, traders, and investors, but after two excursions to the mountains his uncertain health led him to give up personal participation in any more expeditions or Rendezvous. He withdrew to Saint Louis, where he carried on for many years in the fur trade as an agent, merchant, and banker, as a spokesman for western development, and as a model to younger trappers and traders who aspired to his success. Foremost among such followers were Jedediah Smith (whom Ashley had taken on as

partner at the 1825 Rendezvous) and David E. Jackson and William Sublette, who later bought out Ashley's share of the partnership and joined with Smith to form their own trapping and trading company.

The Rendezvous's days were numbered as the fur trade withered and ghost forts multiplied along the rivers. The final Rendezvous, a relatively subdued affair, took place on the Green River in the summer of 1840. Unfortunately, Ashley did not live to see it; he had succumbed to pneumonia on March 26, 1838, and at his own request was buried in an unmarked Indian mound on a bluff overlooking the Missouri. Nevertheless, the memory of Ashley's innovations survived him: the Rendezvous, his decision to buy furs from white trappers rather than from Indians, and his policy of paying generous wages to trappers all mark him as the man who revolutionized fur trapping and trading, transforming them—briefly—into a viable business.

TRADERS

Ashley's experience is not the whole story of the fur trade by any means. Nor is it typical of the experiences of other prominent fur traders, like the Spaniard Manuel Lisa, considered by many to be the wily father of the fur trade, or of John Jacob Astor, the shrewdest operator of them all. Astor, determined to build a rich fur trade with China by wresting control of the Pacific Northwest fur resources from the Russian and British trading companies, boldly sent one trapping brigade overland in 1810 under Wilson Price Hunt and another around Cape Horn by ship to the lower reaches of the Columbia River, where he established in Ore-

gon the trading post known as Astoria. But even the powerful Astor was to know disappointments. One of his ships, the *Tonquin,* was blown up with all hands massacred by the Indians off Vancouver Island; the War of 1812 put another damper on his Astoria project. Wilson Price Hunt's party, making the long trek back east in the fall of 1812, became the first to cross the Continental Divide over South Pass, a feat not to be repeated until 1824—this time westbound—by Jedediah Smith.

During the first four decades of the nineteenth century there were at least twenty prominent fur traders in the Saint Louis area. They conducted probably the most colorful commerce in the country at the time, trading with dozens of Indian tribes from New Mexico to Canada and from Saint Louis to California, supplying provisions to many hundreds of trappers in the field from whom they bought furs, and competing with the formidable British trading firms, the North West Company and Hudson's Bay Company.

Members of the trading organizations combined hands-on trapping and trading experience, contacts with Indian tribes, influence with local political figures, and most important—and problematic—of all, good credit standing. Competition between traders was fierce, and every loophole was exploited in the government's fitful attempts to regulate the fur trade by licensing specific traders to do business with specific tribes and by suppressing the sale of liquor to the Native Americans. Leaders emerged to dominate various regions: Bent and Saint Vrain for the Taos–Santa Fe trade; Astor's American Fur Company and Pacific Fur Company in the Pacific Northwest, Ashley and Henry's Rocky Mountain Fur Company for the central Rockies, and the Chouteau family interests on the Upper Missouri. Many traders had worked up from the ranks as trappers, and some—Lisa, Ashley, and a few others—personally led their brigades into the hunting areas, enduring every risk and hardship, rather than remaining cozily ensconced behind their mahogany desks in Saint Louis.

Equipping a brigade of a hundred or so trappers going out for a year was much like outfitting a small army. Even though trappers generally lived off the

land, outfitting them still entailed borrowing large sums to pay for keelboats, horses and saddles, traps, rifles, powder and lead, blankets, clothing, cutlery, and staples such as flour, bacon, beans, coffee, sugar, and tobacco. For the Indian trade, many of the same goods were in demand as well as needles and thread, beads, feathers, liquor, and decorative gimcracks and gewgaws. A clever trader like Ashley bought his merchandise from many different vendors, so that no single large creditor could use the leverage of the trader's indebtedness to insist on a share of company profits.

Many of the traders' names have a Gallic ring: Cabanné, Chouteau, Pratte, Saint Vrain, Fontenelle, and Robidoux, to name only a few. Of them all, the Chouteau clan stayed in the fur trade the longest, and for a century it was the leading family of Saint Louis (a city founded by Pierre Chouteau, Jr.'s grandfather, Pierre Laclède Ligues). Pierre, Jr. (or Cadet, as he was

Left: JOHN JACOB ASTOR, *1864. Steel engraving after a painting by Alonzo Chappel.*

John Jacob Astor, born the son of a butcher in Heidelberg, Germany, made a fortune in New York real estate, as a fur merchant, and as founder of the American Fur Company in 1808. He became the wealthiest man in America and left an estate of twenty million dollars on his death in 1848.

nicknamed), born in 1789, became the patriarch of a Creole dynasty in the fur trade when fur was virtually the only business in Saint Louis. From 1813 to 1865 he remained a pivotal figure. Starting with Berthold and Chouteau, a small general store in Saint Louis, Pierre soon branched out into the fur trade. Through adroit mergers and acquisitions, and by resorting to cutthroat competitive tactics learned from observing Astor, Chouteau built his firm into a dominant force. In 1826 he became sole western agent for Astor's powerful American Fur Company, and in 1834 he bought out the company's western department, only to sell it under the name of P. Chouteau Jr. and Co. in 1865, after his health and his interest in the fur trade had

65. NORTH FROM BERTHOUD PASS.

both declined. Chouteau died at seventy-six, leaving an estate estimated in the millions and a reputation tarnished by stinginess, sharp dealing, and corruption of Indians, to whom his traders, like many others, routinely sold liquor to overcome competition.

On the whole, fur traders got along surprisingly well with the tribes, probably because each group offered what the other needed. Then, too, the traders seemed less menacing than the trappers, whose activities threatened the old Indian intertribal trade and

hunting patterns. But even the sporadic confronta-
tions like those between Ashley and the Arikara, or
the humiliation visited on individuals like Clyman,
never approached the frequency or viciousness of the
violence between Indians and whites after the Civil
War. Nevertheless, Jedediah Smith did report in an
1829 letter to General William Clark, then superintendent of Indian affairs, that forty-two of his trappers had been killed by Indians over the previous four
years. Except for the murderous Blackfeet, during the
early fur trade years there seems to have been more
stealing of trapper horses by the Indians (often for
prompt resale to the erstwhile owners) than lifting of
trapper scalps.

Rough as their ways may seem to us now, the
mountain men traders and trappers were America's
first western businessmen.
Operating in a vast and un-
familiar territory surrounded
by a strange and sometimes
hostile culture, they could easily have been worse ambassa-
dors of commerce, and they
were ultimately less destructive
than some of those who succeeded them. The best-known
frontiersmen—Kit Carson,
Jed Smith, Jim Bridger—rose
to occupy heroes' niches in
the pantheon of American
archetypes; they will properly
be remembered not for deci-
mating the beaver and buf-
falo populations but for being the first white men to
wrest a livelihood from the prairies and mountains
of the trans-Mississippi West. Beyond that extraordinary feat of survival, they will also be remembered
as trailblazers who opened the way for the Oregon-
California, Mormon, and Santa Fe Trails, and eventually for the Pony Express, the Transcontinental
Telegraph, and the Transcontinental Railroad routes.
Ahead of most military survey and exploration expeditions, the mountain men prowled the West's previously unknown terrain and traced its first crude
maps based on direct field experience.

Alternately sweating, freezing, starving, or bleeding—but at least living free—their simple glory was
to have unlocked the secret paths of the American
wilderness for others to follow.

THE
SANTA FE
TRAIL

3

THE SANTA FE TRAIL SPANNED NEARLY A thousand hot, dry, dusty miles from Franklin, Missouri, to Santa Fe (in present-day New Mexico). Flat and featureless for long stretches, the trail crossed the hunting grounds of fierce Osage, Pawnee, Kiowa, Comanche, and other tribes that harassed the mule pack trains and wagon caravans of the traders and trappers bound for Santa Fe. After the town of Franklin was swept away by the rampaging Missouri River in 1828, the eastern jumping-off place for the trail kept shifting westward to such towns as Independence and Westport Landing (present-day Kansas City).

The Santa Fe Trail began as the first major trans-Mississippi trail whose objective was neither land nor gold nor religious freedom, but commerce. As far back as 1792–93 the Spanish explorer Pedro Vial, under his government's orders, had traveled a very similar route eastbound from Santa Fe to Saint Louis. Nevertheless, the trail is usually considered to have been opened in 1821–22 by trader William Becknell's first caravans from Franklin, thus earning for Becknell, a thirty-three-year-old redheaded Virginian, the title "Father of the Santa Fe Trail." As trade increased after 1822, wagon caravans seeking the quickest way from Missouri to Santa Fe developed two branches for the trail, with a fork in southwestern Kansas where the trail crossed the Arkansas River. At that point the northern trail, or Mountain Branch, continued west to the Purgatoire ("Picketwire" as the trappers called it) River in what is now

SANTA FE TRAIL, RUTS WEST OF DODGE CITY, KANSAS, *February 1993. Photograph by Bruce Hucko.*

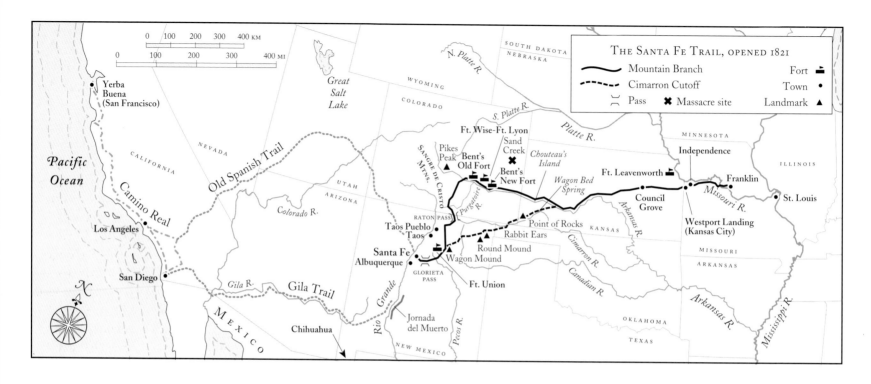

The Santa Fe Trail, opened 1821

— Mountain Branch | Fort
--- Cimarron Cutoff | Town ·
⌣ Pass | ✖ Massacre site | Landmark ▲

Colorado, then ran southwest and climbed over Raton Pass to reach Santa Fe.

The southern branch of the trail, dubbed the Cimarron Cutoff, left the Arkansas River crossing to angle more sharply southwest, passing Wagon Bed Spring, Rabbit Ears, and Round Mound—all familiar landmarks to trail travelers. The Cimarron Cutoff seduced the hurried trader because it was one hundred miles shorter than the Mountain Branch and avoided Raton Pass, which was almost impassable for wagons. But the southern route was also more dangerous since it traversed a fifty-mile dry plain. The two branches of the trail rejoined toward the

southern edge of the Sangre de Cristo Mountains and ribboned into Santa Fe as one.

The trip from Franklin to Santa Fe by wagon train took from fifty to sixty days, with departure from Missouri invariably scheduled for spring in the hope of traveling in good weather. The trains would assemble at Council Grove, west of Franklin, where the participants would organize themselves into a unified large caravan, elect a captain, assign duties, and cut supplies of ash and hickory for spare axles and wagon parts in anticipation of breakdowns on the treeless trail. The conventional wagon used on the Santa Fe Trail came to be the Conestoga, popularly called the Prairie

INSCRIPTION ROCK, OKLAHOMA, *1982. Photograph by Joan Myers.*

Hundreds of travelers down the Santa Fe Trail wrote their names on Inscription Rock, Oklahoma, as signs to following trains that they were alive and well.

Schooner—a large wagon with distinctive outward-leaning sideboards and tailgates designed to help settle shifting cargo toward the center. The wagon body was often painted red and blue with black ironwork, and the bed was covered with white canvas sheets drawn over an arched frame that tilted fore and aft. A large caravan underway with four wagons abreast looked like a flotilla of ships sailing across the sea green prairie.

Upon arrival in Santa Fe, a town of fewer than five thousand inhabitants in 1821, the traders would set up their stores under the arcades around the great central plaza, which was their base for buying and selling throughout the summer. Returning trains usually left Santa Fe in autumn, often carrying their cargo of specie on muleback since the wagons could be sold at a profit in Santa Fe or Chihuahua. On the trail the mule was often favored over the horse or ox as a draft or pack animal. He was more surefooted, and on the rocky trail surface his hooves held up better than those of oxen, who needed leather covers to protect their feet. Most important, a mule was sturdy enough to carry 350 pounds or more for fifteen miles each day and could fare better than an ox on the thin prairie grass. These were all highly desirable

qualities, especially when a mule train (or *atajo*) of perhaps two hundred jacks and jennies was required.

But the mule was not an unmixed blessing. Notoriously stubborn, he demanded special treatment before deigning to accept his burden. He had to be enticed to the loading area by the coquettish *mulera*, or bell mare, and then blindfolded so as not to get spooked while being harnessed. The mule had such a delicate temperament that the sight of his own shadow would sometimes startle him into a panicky gallop, strewing his load and gear across the prairie and provoking a burst of profanity from his handlers, who in calmer moments on the trail might resignedly sing the old lament:

> Git along, Mule!
> Don't you roll them eyes!
> You can teach a fool
> But a doggone mule
> Is a mule until he dies!

Traveling the Santa Fe Trail in Becknell's time offered an important strategic advantage: a trader from Saint Louis could connect at Santa Fe with three other trails. The Gila Trail (running almost due west) and the northwesterly Old Spanish Trail both led to California, effectively linking the Mississippi River with the Pacific Ocean. More important, perhaps, at Santa Fe the Santa Fe Trail also tapped into the Mexican Camino Real, a centuries-old road that ran sixteen hundred miles south through Chihuahua all the way down to Mexico City, the capital of New Spain.

Before 1821, while Mexico was still a Spanish colony, trade was tightly controlled. American traders, trappers, and others were unwelcome in Mexico and were often arrested, had their merchandise and furs confiscated, and could spend years languishing in Mexican jails. Mexican independence from Spain in 1821 and the full-blown opening of the Santa Fe Trail in 1822 changed all that. American merchants could now even compete in New Mexico with the interior trade from Chihuahua, and as the Spanish monopoly on Mexican trade crumbled, annual trade caravans rolled across the Arkansas River border between the United States and Mexico.

In September 1821 Mexico officially threw open its border to American traders. One of the first to cross that frontier was Becknell, ambling along in a mule pack train with four companions and a skimpy assortment of trade goods. Once on the Mexican side, his party was welcomed with a riotous parade featuring villagers dressed as angels with swords, swaying effigies of the Virgin Mary, a tall "liberty" pole (celebrating Mexico's newly won freedom from Spain),

clamorous music, and behavior that even some of the rough traders sanctimoniously condemned as a display of licentiousness beyond description.

The welcoming fiesta augured well for Becknell's dreams of a trade bonanza. Mexican merchandise was relatively cheap: one hundred pounds of flour sold for only two dollars; a load of salt for five; sheep went for one dollar each, horses for eleven dollars a head, and mules for thirty. Such bargains translated into juicy profits in the Missouri resale market, where Spanish mules from Mexico—ancestors of the famous Missouri mule—were in great demand. Mule herds by the hundreds soon became a common sight on the

WAGONS, COVERED, DRAWN BY MULES, *from* Harper's Weekly, *May 1, 1875.*

Raton Pass, on the Mountain Branch of the Santa Fe Trail, was perhaps the most strenuous stretch on the way to New Mexico. Susan Shelby Magoffin's journal records: "It takes a dozen men to steady a wagon with all its wheels locked." And Matt C. Field's wagon train advanced over the pass only a mile and a half in one day.

Santa Fe Trail. Becknell profited hugely in Santa Fe, despite his paltry stock; on his return to Franklin, people stared at the shiny Mexican silver dollars that cascaded out of his saddlebags onto the street.

Despite the comforting clink of Mexican silver coin in American saddlebags, life on the trail proved far from easy. The scarcity of water and the abundance of turbulent weather caused chronic problems, as Becknell soon discovered. His second venture to Santa Fe, in 1822, consisted of a small three-wagon caravan—the first wagons to cross the trail—which Becknell judged unable to climb over Raton Pass. He therefore took the arid shortcut of the Cimarron Cutoff, where his party (like so many others to follow) nearly perished of thirst. Only after desperate expedients, like killing their dogs and cutting off the ears of the mules to drink their blood, were Becknell and company lucky enough to slaughter a buffalo that had recently watered. They survived by imbibing its stomach fluids.

By 1824 Becknell had prospered enough to mount a full-scale caravan of twenty-four vehicles carrying a heavy and diversified cargo worth about $30,000, and armed with a small cannon to impress the Indians. Becknell's associates in this eighty-one-man venture ran the gamut from respected traders like Augustus Storrs (who became American consul in Santa Fe) and Meredith M. Marmaduke (a future governor of Missouri) to Thomas L. "Peg-leg" Smith—a red-necked rowdy later famed as founder of a Taos distillery that concocted a rotgut called Taos Lightning and notorious as the worst horse and mule rustler in California. The first caravan of its size to cross the Missouri River, the Becknell train pulled out for Santa Fe on

May 16, 1824. In September part of the caravan returned to Franklin, bringing with them $180,000 in gold and silver and $10,000 worth of furs—a gross profit of 600 percent on their wagonloads of basic hardware, cutlery, and dry goods.

In the ensuing decades, trade with Santa Fe and Chihuahua had its ups and downs. Back in his home state of Missouri and in Washington, Senator Thomas Hart Benton beat the drums for westward expansion. Disturbed by increasing Indian harassment of trade caravans, he presented several bills in Congress to

BURRO ALLEY, SANTA FE, *c. 1875. One-half of a stereograph by W. Henry Brown.*

Burro Alley, a few blocks from the great plaza in Santa Fe, served as a parking lot for the pack-train mules of incoming traders.

correct matters. One authorized a payment of twenty thousand dollars to the Osage Nation for a guarantee of safe caravan passage through their lands. Another designated U.S. consuls for Santa Fe and Chihuahua, and a third provided for the survey of a road between Missouri and New Mexico. Unfortunately, the road ended up in Taos, not Santa Fe, and the earthen mounds set up to mark the route were often as not disregarded by traders in favor of their own chosen paths to Santa Fe, which facilitated smuggling to avoid the steep duties collected by the Mexican customs agents.

Texas's 1836 revolution seeking independence from Mexico was followed by years of hostility between America and Mexico. The ill-conceived Santa Fe expedition of 1841, purportedly a mission to promote trade, was interpreted (probably rightly) by the suspicious Mexicans as a military invasion. Mexican governor Manuel Armijo had little trouble defeating the 270 exhausted and dispirited Texas volunteers who straggled into his grasp. The Texans were promised freedom if they lay down their arms, but after doing so they were instead shackled together for a "death march" to Mexico City.

In 1843 Colonel Jacob Snively's force of Texas volunteers, intent on disrupting trade traffic along the trail, killed twenty-three New Mexican militiamen in a border incident on the Cimarron Cutoff. Captain Philip Saint George Cooke arrested and disarmed Snively's troops before they could harass the oncoming spring caravan of Mexican and American merchants. A long series of such incidents by Texas marauders finally led Mexico's president, Antonio Lopez de

Santa Anna, to close the New Mexican customs houses in September 1843, thus effectively sealing the border to American traders. But the measure was so unpopular in both New Mexico and Chihuahua that it was repealed the following spring—just in time for trading to resume with the May caravans.

Weather continued to be the main adversary on the trail. In the winter of 1844 the Albert Speyer–Edwin Norris caravan of twenty-five wagons drawn by two hundred mules was caught in a blizzard near Willow Bar, in the Oklahoma Territory, nearly 270 miles short of Santa Fe. By the time the storm cleared, the famished mules had desperately eaten tree bark and chewed off each other's tails in their struggle to stay alive. Unfortunately, most of them perished from cold and hunger, and in later years passing teamsters played a macabre game of rearranging the bleached mule bones into configurations that would amuse the next group traveling through.

Exact statistics for the Santa Fe trade are not available, but the most accurate are probably trader Josiah Gregg's, which reveal that over the years an increasing share of that trade was going not to Santa Fe but farther south to Chihuahua, the city that would one day displace Santa Fe as the chief market for the Missouri merchants. This shift is dramatically evident in a comparison between the years 1837 and 1838. In 1837, the year of a Mexican rebellion, $150,000 was invested in the Santa Fe trade, and of this sum $60,000 went to Chihuahua; in 1838, out of $90,000 in Santa Fe trade, $80,000 went to Chihuahua. The most informed estimates for the total trade in 1846 report that sales with Santa Fe and Chihuahua had reached the impressive level of $1 million from a traffic flow of 363 wagons and 750 men.

By that time Becknell had long ago ended his association with the Santa Fe Trail, having moved in 1826 to Missouri, where he was twice elected to the state legislature, before settling in Sulphur Fork Prairie, near Clarksville, Texas. There Becknell died on April 30, 1856. His passing was nostalgically noted by the *Clarksville Standard* of that date: "The old pioneer is gone, peace to his ashes!"

JAMES OHIO PATTIE

Trapper James Ohio Pattie's action-packed account of his years along the Santa Fe Trail and in the South-west, from 1825 to 1830, reads like a picaresque novel. *The Personal Narrative of James O. Pattie*, published in 1831, has kept perplexed historians trying to untangle his garbled dates and confused trail routes as well as to fill in the blanks left by his exasperating failure to name his associates and to sift out his exaggerations. To add to the confusion, Pattie's editor, Timothy Flint of Cincinnati—a Harvard man, a former clergyman, editor of the *Western Monthly Review*, and a successful author—evidently expanded his own editorial role to that of ghostwriter. But whether pure Pattie or bogus Flint, the narrative captures an authentic flavor of the old Southwest on the brink of radical change.

On his first trip to New Mexico, in 1825, Pattie and his father, traveling with Sylvestre Pratte's trapping party, passed through Taos and Albuquerque, reaching Santa Fe on November 5. "This town contains between four and five thousand inhabitants," noted Pattie, who was charmed by the flat-roofed adobe houses, the snow-clad mountains in the distance, and the many church bells, which "when disturbed, make a noise . . . sufficient to waken the dead."[1] Having received a license from the governor to trap beaver, the Pattie party separated from Pratte and headed southwest for the fur-rich "Helay" (Gila) and San Francisco Rivers. By January 14, 1826, they had taken 250 beaver pelts, which they buried on the banks of the Helay, and by March 3 they had harvested and cached two hundred more on what they named the Beaver River.

Pattie's days seemed never to lack excitement. One night, alone by his campfire, he awoke to find a "panther" (mountain lion) staring at him from six feet away. Slowly, slowly, Pattie drew his rifle up and coolly shot it in the head. On another occasion, charged by an enraged grizzly bear, the young trapper fell over a cliff, broke his jaw, and then nearly bled to death from the knife incisions inflicted by a well-meaning companion. Later that spring, when the party's food ran out, they were grateful to shoot and share a single raven between seven men, drink antelope's blood to slake their thirst, and finally eat some of Pattie's dogs. When Pattie returned in June to dig up the fur pelts he had buried in March, he discovered that the Indians had stolen them all.

According to his *Personal Narrative*, Pattie usually came off the victor in his Indian encounters, but not always. He was surprisingly blunt in admitting that he and his fellow trappers, thirsting for Old Testament revenge, sometimes beheaded, scalped, or hung their enemies, leaving them dangling from trees as a warning to others. Pattie claimed to have rescued Jacova, the beautiful daughter of a Spanish former governor, from Comanche who had abducted her, stripped her naked, and forced her to drive a large herd of horses and sheep ahead of them down the trail. After a flurry of shots, Pattie modestly reported, the blushing young woman rushed into his arms, was quickly draped in his fringed buckskin shirt, and returned unscathed to her aged father. It sounds like a Beadle's dime novel, but it just might have happened.

Pattie had started out from Missouri on his trapping expeditions when he was only twenty-one. He then wandered on and off the Santa Fe Trail for five years, through Kansas, Nebraska, Colorado, New Mexico, Arizona, California—these last three were at the time still part of a foreign country—and northern

Mexico. His assertion that he penetrated as far north as the Yellowstone and Columbia Rivers is discounted by modern historians, but he may have been the first American to look on the Grand Canyon of the Colorado. In 1830, at twenty-six and destitute, his face apparently deeply marked by the years of hardship and disappointment, Pattie left the Southwest to go home to Augusta, Kentucky. On the way back he stopped in Cincinnati, where he met Timothy Flint and arranged to publish his *Personal Narrative.*

Pattie dropped from view so suddenly and so completely after 1831, when his *Personal Narrative* appeared, that it is not known when or where he came to the end of his trail. Clearly, however, the years from 1825 to 1830 had left him disillusioned and embittered. The closing thoughts of his *Narrative*—that all life is vanity, and that he should never have left Kentucky—seem strangely dark for one who had just written his own exciting life story. The ensuing silence and oblivion are ominous enough to suggest that Pattie was, after all, a tragic figure of the trail.

THE DEATH OF JEDEDIAH SMITH

Probably no other fur trader/trapper/mountain man ever knew the West the way Jedediah Smith did in his day, from 1822 to 1831. In only nine years the Bible-toting Jed Smith, eldest of twelve siblings, achieved a remarkable record: he became the first white man to cross South Pass westbound; first to crisscross the Great Basin; first to cross the Sierra Nevada; and first to reach Oregon by traveling

the length of California. He survived the three worst trapper-Indian clashes of the American fur trade: Ashley's defeat by the Arikara in 1823, the Mojave massacre of 1827, and the Umpqua massacre of 1828.

In 1831 Smith took it into his head to visit Chihuahua, the southern terminus of the Santa Fe Trail. He joined up that spring with his former trapping partners William Sublette and David Jackson (for whom Jackson Hole, Wyoming, is named) to make the journey south. On the trail leaving Saint Louis, Smith (perhaps out of simple prudence, perhaps because of some premonition) drew up his will, dated April 31 (*sic*), and named Ashley executor. Once underway, the combined party of seventy-four men was joined by Thomas "Broken Hand" Fitzpatrick, Smith's old comrade from the days when they had both answered Ashley's famous 1822 newspaper ad for would-be trappers. Neither Smith nor his companions had traveled the Santa Fe Trail before, but its difficulties held no terrors for such experienced plainsmen. Apparently, however, they underestimated the merciless Jornada del Muerto of the Cimarron Cutoff during the drought season. After three days without water the party finally split up to conduct a life-and-death search. Smith and Fitzpatrick headed south together but soon separated—Fitzpatrick staying behind to dig desperately in a dry hole, while Smith went ahead to explore further.

The final scene of Smith's life had no known witness and therefore has been painstakingly reconstructed by historians from hearsay, with variations in the details. Not long after his disappearance, Mexican traders who had recently traded with some Comanche acquired Smith's pistols and rifle from them. The Mexicans learned that just over the rise he had dropped into a hollow where there was a water hole. There, according to legend, he was surprised and slain by a small band of Comanche buffalo hunters. What is certain: America's foremost western explorer rode over a rise, never to be seen again.

BENT'S FORTS

Mountain men came from many backgrounds, but Ceran Saint Vrain stands out as unique among them all. Stocky, gray-eyed, and energetic, he exuded a gentlemanly authority. His grandfather had been councillor to the king of France, and his uncle had been lieutenant governor of Louisiana before that territory was turned over to Napoleon by Spain. Ceran's father owned a brewery near Saint Louis, but after the business burned down, the family fell on hard times, and young Ceran—one of ten children—was placed in the foster care of Bernard Pratte, Sr., a well-known Saint Louis fur trader. Saint Vrain began work in his teens for Pratte, Cabanné and Company, earning a responsible position there by age twenty-two. Apparently he met Charles Bent, his future partner, in 1827 on the Green River in Wyoming while both were encamped there for the winter with different trading outfits.

Saint Vrain, then twenty-five years old, and Bent, twenty-eight, in a few short years would revolutionize commerce between Mexico and Missouri. Over the years the partners would build a chain of three forts along the Arkansas and Canadian Rivers: Bent's

Fort (later called Bent's Old Fort) in 1833, Fort Saint Vrain in 1837, and Fort Adobe in 1845. Bent's younger brother, William, would build two more: in 1849 a small log compound at Big Timbers (thirty-eight miles east of Bent's Old Fort) and in 1853, also at Big Timbers near the mouth of the Purgatoire River, a large adobe structure called Bent's (New) Fort. This last outpost was impressive for having ready-made doors and glass windows.

Charles Bent, like Saint Vrain, had cut his eyeteeth in the fur trade, having spent some years operating on the Upper Missouri River with Joshua Pilcher and his Missouri Fur Company. Charles was one of five sons of Judge Silas Bent of Saint Louis, three of whom would later join him in his Santa Fe trade out of Bent's Fort. Small in stature but not in spirit, Bent would later prove himself to be a leader of men as well as a creative and practical businessman.

In the late 1820s John Jacob Astor's American Fur Company was coming to dominate a fur trade in which the buffalo robe was displacing the beaver top hat in popularity. Both Bent and Saint Vrain, not yet partners, astutely shifted their attention to the Santa Fe trade. (In time they both would marry Mexican women, and Saint Vrain even became a Mexican citizen.) In 1830 the two formed the Bent–Saint Vrain trading partnership, with Saint Vrain the partner resident in Santa Fe and Bent the itinerant one, who traveled to and from Missouri with their caravans. The next year was a fat one for the new firm as Bent profitably crossed and recrossed the Santa Fe

Southwestern fur trader William Bent became a respected friend of the Cheyenne tribe, married a Cheyenne, and had three sons with her.

A faithful adobe replica of Bent's Old Fort, seat of the Bent brothers' trading empire, has been reconstructed on the banks of the Arkansas River near La Junta, Colorado.

Trail five times. Eighteen thirty-two proved even better: the wagons of four of the Bent brothers (Charles, William, Robert, and George) carried to Independence a cargo of bullion, furs, and mules valued at $190,000.

Such results justified the firm's expansion into what came to be called "The Adobe Empire"—a vast area controlled by the Bents that comprised parts of New Mexico, Texas, and Oklahoma in the south, and parts of Utah, Wyoming, Colorado, Nebraska, and Kansas to the north and east. Charles Bent and Saint Vrain reasoned correctly that commercial control of this region could be maintained only by creating a central trading station on a grand scale. This bold concept, chiefly Bent's, took form as Bent's Fort. Saint Vrain and William Bent (who had been trading in Taos for several years) located the new fort along the Santa Fe Trail, on the north bank of the Arkansas

River, where it commanded a splendid view of the Spanish Peaks, Pikes Peak, and the flowing valley of the Arkansas. Unlike most frontier trading posts, this enterprise was not planned as a simple stockade with cottonwood picket walls. The partners had in mind something more imposing, more impregnable, and more useful: a huge adobe fortress that could house two hundred men and twice as many animals.

When the fort was completed in 1833, there was nothing like it for a thousand miles in any direction. Solid adobe walls, thirty inches thick and fourteen or more feet tall, enclosed a courtyard (or *placita*) fringed by a veranda. Around this quadrangle ranged twenty-five dwelling rooms of some three hundred square feet each, their roofs made of grass, clay, and gravel. Two towers eighteen feet tall stood like sentinels at the northeast and southwest corners of the trapezoidal fort, while a massive iron-clad entrance faced north, and a corral, nearly as large as the fort itself, adjoined it on the south. The walls sheltered a complex of warehouses, a kitchen, a dining hall, and blacksmith and carpentry shops. A little French tailor had a cubbyhole where he stitched heaps of buckskin shirts and leggings with a three-sided needle. Along the west wall a second tier of apartments rose above the veranda; one of these, used for entertainment and later graced by a billiard table, housed the private rooms of the fort's owners. The whole structure served as a self-sufficient walled oasis in the middle of nowhere.

Over the years Bent's Fort eclipsed even Fort Laramie and Fort Bridger as one of the major trading forts of the West and as the site of pivotal events. In

1834–35 and again in 1840 representatives of six Indian tribes attended important peace conferences at the fort, and in 1845 John C. Frémont and his small party stopped by to sign up Kit Carson as a guide before venturing on to California. Famous frontiersmen like Old Bill Williams, Jim Beckwourth, Jedediah Smith, Joe Walker, Ewing Young, and Peg-leg Smith—as well as Susan Magoffin's party, General Stephen Watts Kearny and his Army of the West, merchant Josiah Gregg, and wayfarers Lewis Garrard and George F. Ruxton—all passed through or bedded down at the fort. Carson, a frequent visitor who named two of his sons after Charles Bent and Ceran Saint Vrain, declared of the partners, "Their equals were never in the mountains."[2]

These events took place in the glory days of

*Opposite, right: John C. Frémont,
illegitimate son of a French refugee,
rose from lieutenant in the army's
Topographical Corps to candidate for
president of the United States in 1856.
In between, from 1842 to 1853, he led
five major exploratory expeditions to
the Rockies and the Sierra Nevada and
mapped overland routes to the Far
West, which whetted public interest
in emigration. An admiring public
dubbed him "the Pathfinder."*

*Opposite, left: Thomas Buchanan Read
(1822–1872).* PORTRAIT OF JESSIE
BENTON FRÉMONT, *1856. Oil on
canvas, 30 x 24½ in. (76.2 x 62.2 cm).
Southwest Museum, Los Angeles.*

*The beautiful and talented Jessie
Frémont, daughter of Missouri Senator
Thomas Hart Benton (of Manifest
Destiny fame) and wife of John C.
Frémont, played a large part in
composing the highly popular reports of
the Pathfinder's expeditions.*

Bent's Fort, and like all such days, they passed. There followed a succession of events hard for William to bear. Charles's brutal death in January 1847 was followed that October by the death of his brother George, presumably of consumption. The youngest Bent brother, Robert, had been killed and scalped by Comanche back in 1841. With his three brothers gone and trade slumping badly in the wake of the Mexican-American War of 1846–48, William dissolved the partnership with Saint Vrain, leaving William as sole owner of Bent's Fort. The U.S. Army, expanding its chain of western forts to protect travelers, had bought Fort Laramie from the American Fur Company for four thousand dollars, but when they offered William Bent a sum variously reported to be between twelve thousand and fifty thousand dollars for his fort, William, contemptuous of the offer, refused to sell. Then, in 1849, a surge of gold seekers passed through, leaving behind them the cramps, convulsions, and deaths of a cholera epidemic that killed almost half of the southern Cheyenne, the tribe that had given William two wives and a number of children. At the same time Ute, Apache, Comanche, and even Arapaho were becoming defiant, circling Bent's adobe fort regularly with taunts and threats.

Suddenly, it all seemed not worth the candle. On August 21 William ordered the fort evacuated and all property removed to a camp five miles downriver. Then he rode back alone, rolled powder kegs into position, and moved deliberately from room to room, setting fire to the wooden roofs. A booming explosion and a mushrooming cloud of black smoke rose above him as he rode grimly back down the trail.

THE MORMON BATTALION

If a handful of Pawnee had been camping on the Santa Fe Trail along the Cimarron River in September 1846, they would have been astonished to hear in the distance a male chorus in full voice. As the song came closer—perhaps "Come, Come Ye Saints" or some other popular Mormon tune—it would have risen above the tramp of four hundred pairs of feet and the wheezing of oxen and mules drawing heavy supply and ammunition wagons. A uniformed officer was no doubt riding at the head of a tatterdemalion column of men dressed in worn farmer's clothes. Women and children must have peered out anxiously from the rear wagons at the Indians, who in turn would have marveled at the file of musket-bearing farmers that materialized over the northern rim and disappeared slowly over the southern, leaving a scrap of song floating behind them like a pennant in the summer air.

These civilian soldiers constituted the volunteer Mormon Battalion, delivered by Brigham Young to support the United States in its four-month-old war against Mexico. While marching southwest out of Fort Leavenworth, Private James S. Brown, from North Carolina, probably expressed the mixed feelings of many volunteers when he noted in his journal that the battalion members were leaving their families in the wilderness to fight their country's battles in a foreign country (Mexico). The Mormon Church was being asked by the U.S. government to raise the battalion while that same government was failing to protect the Latter-day Saints from mob violence at home—an irony that did not pass unnoticed by Brown.

By the time the Mormon Battalion reached Santa Fe, the Mexican governor, Manuel Armijo, had wisely withdrawn, leaving his Mexican garrison to capitulate peacefully to General Kearny. Periodic expresses from Brigham Young were delivered to the battalion as it marched west; these usually contained fatherly and practical admonitions to obey their officers, to attend to prayers, not to steal or plunder, and though in enemy country, not to "disturb fruit orchards or chicken coops or beehives." There were also inspirational words from Young: "I promise you in the name of the Lord God of Israel that not one soul of you shall fall by the hands of the enemy . . . battles will be fought in your front and in your rear, on your right hand and on your left, and your enemies shall flee before you."[3]

The Mormon boys were in Santa Fe a week—barely time to break in a new commanding officer, West Point graduate Lieutenant Colonel Philip Saint George Cooke, and perhaps sneak in a fandango—before starting out October 18 on an important new mission assigned by Kearny: to build a military-supply-wagon road all the way to San Diego. In the end, picks and shovels proved more effective than muskets in leaving the battalion's mark on western history. The new route, through largely uncharted country, proved dangerous in the extreme. Animals and wagons rapidly broke down under the strain, and barefoot soldiers wrapped their feet in rawhide to keep going. When the trail-hardened Saints at last came marching into San Diego on January 29, 1847, John C. Frémont had already (prematurely) raised the American flag over California. The war being effectively

over, the battalion was soon mustered out of service. Some 260 of the men then walked back to Salt Lake City, adding another six hundred miles to their epic march, carrying with them supplies and tools badly needed in Salt Lake Valley. Most important, the battalion's pay fattened the Mormon coffers by some seventy thousand dollars.

In less than four months the battalion had broken open a new wagon trail—the first of its kind—between Santa Fe and California, in effect extending the Santa Fe Trail as a commercial and emigrant wagon route to the Pacific. The day after their arrival in San

Charles Christian Nahl (1818–1878). THE FANDANGO, *1873. Oil on canvas, 72 x 108 in. (182.9 x 274.3 cm). Crocker Art Museum; E. B. Crocker Collection, Sacramento, California.*

Nahl's Fandango *presents a rather demure picture of a fandango dance; far more boisterous were the larger fandango parties, enlivened by the presence of high-spirited, hard-fisted mountain men, overheated by alcohol, who would as soon fight as dance.*

Diego, Lieutenant Colonel Cooke issued a well-earned commendation to his Mormon troops, summing up their remarkable achievement:

Headquarters
Mormon Battalion
Mission of San Diego,
January 30, 1847

Orders No. 1
The Lieutenant-Colonel commanding congratulate the Battalion on their safe arrival on the shore of the Pacific Ocean, and the conclusion of their march of over two thousand miles.

History may be searched in vain for an equal march of infantry. Half of it has been through a wilderness where nothing but savages and wild beasts are found, or deserts where, for want of water, there is no living creature. There, with almost hopeless labor we have dug deep wells, which the future traveler will enjoy. Without a guide who had traversed them, we have ventured into trackless table-lands where water was not found for several marches. With crowbar and pick and axe in hand, we have worked our way over mountains, which seemed to defy aught save the wild goat, and hewed a passage through a chasm of living rock more narrow than our wagons . . . marching half naked and half fed, and living upon wild animals, we have discovered and made a road of great value to our country.[4]

Cooke's forecast proved correct; within two years thousands of emigrants and gold seekers would pour over the route that he and the Mormon Battalion had opened for wagons, and not far behind them would come the Santa Fe and Southern Pacific railroads.

THE TAOS UPRISING

In July 1846, after a stiff march south from Fort Leavenworth, Kansas Territory, Colonel Stephen Watts Kearny halted his seventeen-hundred-man Army of the West at Bent's Fort, in order to replenish supplies and repair equipment before advancing to Santa Fe. There the Mexican army, in all probability, waited to engage him in combat. Feverish activity and confusion filled the air, generated by swarms of Indians and traders that buzzed restlessly around the courtyard, while the fort's population of chickens, geese, sheep, goats, turkeys—and even George Bent's peacocks—excited by the crowds, scurried around frantically, adding their voices to the racket and their droppings to the manure heap.

Army tents lined the Arkansas River bank for miles, and Kearny's soldiers stormed through the gates of Bent's Fort in droves, bawling angrily for food and drink that had long ago vanished from the fort's shelves. Outside the adobe walls similar pandemonium prevailed as twenty thousand horses, mules, and oxen, voicing their discontent at the lack of pasturage, neighed, brayed, bellowed, bucked, snorted, plunged, reared, kicked, wheeled, pitched, nipped, whinnied, pissed, crow-hopped, cavorted, rolled, wallowed, shit, hee-hawed, squealed, coughed, farted, nickered, nuzzled, heaved, spun, ran, dodged, and

Below: FATHER ANTONIO JOSÉ MARTINEZ, *c. 1848. Daguerreotype.*

Padre Martinez, parish priest of Taos in the 1840s, officiated at the wedding of Kit Carson and Josefa Jaramillo. Martinez, a Mexican patriot who had mixed feelings about Anglo intervention in Mexico's affairs, was implicated in the Taos Uprising of 1847.

stampeded in bursts, to the oath-streaked frustration of their herders.

At last Kearny and his army moved on toward Santa Fe. Only a few days out, breathless messengers from the fort brought him news of his promotion to brigadier general, and with a star now gleaming on each shoulder the new general forged eagerly ahead. On reaching Santa Fe, he found that Governor Armijo had already ceded the city without a fight. Once Kearny had taken control of Santa Fe, he announced a humane policy toward the conquered Mexicans, declared New Mexico annexed by the United States, and sought an experienced and respected American to serve as the first territorial governor of New Mexico. That man, not surprisingly, was Charles Bent. But Kearny's appointment turned out to be a death warrant. By the end of 1846, plots of rebellion by the Pueblo Indians and Mexicans flamed into violence: the Taos Uprising. In January 1847 Governor Bent traveled from Santa Fe to his home in Taos to investigate the reports of local unrest. No doubt it felt good, too, to be home again with his wife, Ignacia; their five-year-old daughter, Teresina; and as house guests Kit Carson's wife, Josefa (Ignacia's sister), and Tom Bogg's wife, Rumalda, as well as two boys, Pablo Jaramillo (Ignacia's brother) and his friend Narciso Beaubien.

Just after daybreak on January 19 Charles and his household were startled from sleep by a howling mob brandishing torches and weapons outside the house. What followed has been pieced together over the years by participants, witnesses, and official reports. Bent quickly directed his wife and the others to chop a hole through the back wall and escape to the safety of a neighbor's house. Wielding a large spoon and poker, they finally gouged an opening large enough to squeeze through, while in the front room Charles tried to reason with attackers long past the point of reason. Indians broke through a hole in the roof. The din grew enormous. The front door was suddenly splintered by musket fire, a ball striking Charles in the stomach. Arrows zinged through the doorway, burying themselves in his face and chest. After yanking some of them out, he staggered back to the hole where his wife waited for him, but he could no longer speak. He groped in his pocket for a scrap of paper, but before he could scribble on it ululating attackers closed in, scalped him alive with a bowstring, and began mutilating his body. The two boys, Narciso and Pablo, betrayed by a servant, were caught hiding in a barn and butchered beyond recognition. Ignacia, Josefa, and Rumalda, although spared by the mob—probably because they were women—were forced to stay for two days in the dark, freezing house with Charles's bloody remains until neighbors rescued them.

According to Jim Beckwourth and other outraged mountain men riding to revenge days later, several other Taos officials were not even that fortunate. Sheriff Steve Lee and Prefect Cornelio Vigil were diced and shredded and left in the streets to be scavenged by roving hogs; Circuit Attorney James Leal died a slow death of unspeakable cruelty. Simeon Turley's Taos distillery was sacked and several men killed. The violence and bloodshed surged beyond Taos through the outlying settlements; at Ponil and Vermejo, Bent and Saint Vrain ranches were raided and six hundred horses, mules, and oxen driven off. News of Charles Bent's murder reverberated throughout the Adobe Empire. Even the Cheyenne, friends of William and Charles, were ready to march against Mexico until William dissuaded them, saying this was the duty of white soldiers.

From Pueblo, Bent's Fort, Santa Fe, Albuquerque,

and points in between, mountain men streamed in to join the army troops in an attack on the Taos rebels. Within this little army of 480 men, Ceran Saint Vrain was appointed captain of a small but rugged company of trappers and traders that included Dick Wootton, Lucien Maxwell, and Jim Beckwourth—all good men in a fight. By mid-February, after marching hundreds of miles through deep snow, the Americans launched a savage assault on the Mexican insurgents and Pueblo Indians barricaded in San Geronimo church in Taos Pueblo. At the end of the three-day battle, during which the Americans wheeled a cannon up to a breach in the church wall and fired repeatedly into the nave, the villagers counted 150 dead, decided they had had enough, and sent women and children crawling out to wave white flags and crosses, weeping for mercy. The rebellion was essentially over.

SUSAN SHELBY MAGOFFIN

When she started down the Santa Fe Trail in June 1846, eighteen-year-old Susan Shelby Magoffin was a southern belle from a distinguished Kentucky family. Her husband, forty-five-year-old Samuel Magoffin, a veteran Santa Fe trader, was taking her on a honeymoon from Independence, Missouri, to Santa Fe and Chihuahua, Mexico, with his large trade caravan. The Magoffin caravan impressed the young bride as

> quite a force. Fourteen big waggons with six yoke each, one baggage waggon with two yoke, one dearborn with two mules, (this concern carries my maid) our own carriage with two more mules

Left: Ruins of San Geronimo Church in Taos Pueblo (photographed in 1912), where a bloody and decisive battle was fought during the Taos Uprising in 1847.

and two men on mules driving the loose stock, consisting of nine and a half yoke of oxen, our riding horses two, and three mules, with Mr. Hall the superintendent of the waggons, together with his mule, we number twenty men, three are our tent servants (Mexicans). Jane, my attendant, two horses, nine mules, some two hundred oxen, and last though not least our dog Ring. A gray hound he is of noble descent; he is white with light brown spots, a nice watch for our tent door.[5]

All in all, a substantial equipage to move fifteen hundred miles on a wedding trip across forbidding country.

Susan's journal, as revealing as it is atypical, records the observations and feelings of a privileged, knowledgeable, and sensitive young woman under dramatic circumstances: she was about to enter a foreign country on whom her own nation had declared war only a few weeks before. And she was expecting a child. The early journal entries, usually written in a rain-soaked tent while Susan sat on her bed cross-legged like a tailor, often tell of collecting pebbles, gathering wildflowers and berries, or catching the whistle of a partridge or the chirp of a lark. Interspersed are the words of a girl happily in love: "After dinner I layed down with mi alma [her husband] on a buffalo skin with the carriage seats for pillows and took what few ladies have done a siesta in the sun." Glimpses of sterner stuff also show through even before Independence had quite disappeared over the horizon. "Oh, this is a life I would not exchange for a great deal! There is such independence, so much free uncontaminated air, which impregnates the mind, the feelings, nay every thought with purity."[6] Before her journey through Mexico was over, a more worldly Susan would exclaim in her journal with some exasperation: "After all this thing of marrying is not what it is cracked up to be."[7]

Before long a more sober tone tempered her comments as the shortage of water and fuel, the suffering of the animals, and the bad weather began to erode euphoria. At Camp Twenty-three, for example, Susan reported on the burial of a Mexican who had died of consumption the day before: "The manner of interring on the plains is necessarily very simple. The grave is dug very deep to prevent the body from being found by the wolves. The corpse is rolled in a blanket—lowered and stones put on it. The earth is then thrown in, the sod replaced and it is well beat down. Often the corral is made over it, to make the earth still more firm, by the tromping of the stock. The Mexicans always place a cross at the grave."[8]

While crossing Ash Creek, her carriage overturned and was smashed to pieces, injuring both Magoffins. Alarmed, the caravan hurried on to Bent's Fort for medical help. En route, Susan noted signs of Indians having preceded them. "We passed their sign . . . a post set in the ground, with a fork at the other end, in which a sword and bundle of fagots, *many in number* representing, as I was told a sign to some other tribe passing after them, the army of whites they were numerous: The sword was painted red, for the use they made with it, and it also had several notches cut in it to represent the number of days since they passed."[9]

At Bent's Fort, in an upstairs room with a dirt floor that she sprinkled daily with water, Susan lost her baby, a loss she grievingly accepted as coming from the hands of Providence. Her resignation to the death did not keep her from noting the considerably different experience of an Indian woman in the room below. "She gave birth to a fine healthy baby, about

the same time, and in half an hour after she went to the river and bathed herself and it, and this she has continued each day since. . . . No doubt many ladies are ruined by too careful treatments during childbirth, for this custom of the hethen is not known to be disadvantageous, but it is a 'hethenish custom.'"[10]

As the Mexican War heated up, the Magoffin caravan continued south toward Chihuahua on the theory that the safest course was to follow the American forces. Susan now had to confront the possibility that she and her husband might be captured by the

WAGON MOUND, NEW MEXICO, *1982. Photograph by Joan Myers.*

Wagon Mound, so called because of its fancied resemblance to a prairie wagon, looms above the old Santa Fe Trail. Crosses in the foreground mark the final resting place of early travelers.

Mexicans. Her journal again expresses the working faith that sustained many trail travelers. "I shall be torn from the dearest object to me on earth, perhaps both of us murdered, or at best he will be put into one prison, while I am sent to an other one without even my bible, or my poor journal to comfort me. But though they may deprive me of *these things*, there are others that they cannot move. I have a *soul*, I have a Savior, the means of prayer are always within my reach. It has comforted me more than once."[11]

In her journal for August 31, 1846, Susan Magoffin wrote with justifiable pride of her arrival in Santa Fe two weeks after General Kearny had taken the town. "I have entered the city in a year that will always be remembered by my countrymen; and under the 'Star-spangled banner' too, the first American Lady who has come under such auspices, and some of our company seem disposed to make me the first under any circumstances that ever crossed the plains."[12] One hundred fifty years later, the first part of this observation no doubt remains valid, since it is unlikely that another Anglo woman followed more closely on Kearny's heels than she. Recent research, however, has established that other American women—most notably Mary Donoho, a hotelkeeper from Missouri who reached Santa Fe in 1833—were in the City of Holy Faith before her. Veteran Santa Fe trader (and inveterate bachelor) Josiah Gregg, whose 1844 *Commerce of the Prairies* was a bible of the Santa Fe Trail to his fellow travelers and to later historians, attested: "Other females, however, have crossed the prairies to Santa Fe at different times, among whom I have known two respectable French ladies."[13]

MARY DONOHO, *c. 1859. Tintype.*
It was long thought that Susan Magoffin was the first white woman down the Santa Fe Trail. More recent research, however, has assigned that distinction to Mary Donoho, a hardy hotelkeeper who traveled to Santa Fe in 1833.

In January 1847, after the Taos Uprising and the murder of Charles Bent (whom they had earlier met on the trail), the Magoffins feared they might be caught between Mexican soldiers advancing toward them from the south and Mexican guerrillas mobilizing behind them to the north. (Susan and Samuel Magoffin had good reason to fear for their safety if captured by the Mexicans. Samuel's brother James, also a successful and widely respected Santa Fe trader, had helped negotiate the bloodless American takeover of Santa Fe and eventually of all New Mexico.) Susan energetically pitched in to prepare the caravan's defenses against attack. "All the wagoners are well armed . . . and within our little tent we have twelve sure rounds, a double-barreled shot gun, a pair of holster and one pair of belt pistols with one of Colts six barreled revolvers—a formidable core for only two people to muster."[14] Quite a change from the girl who only six months before had been blithely picking roses and raspberries and taking siestas in the sun.

A month after Colonel Alexander Doniphan's troops planted the American flag in the plaza at Chihuahua, Susan Magoffin and party finally reached that city, on April 4, 1847, having left Santa Fe nearly six months earlier. The march down the trail had been rugged, both physically and psychologically. Susan recorded that she often slept only two hours a night; they covered twenty to thirty-five miles a day for several straight weeks in choking dust and crossed the Jornada del Muerto by moonlight to avoid the heat. On the way south they were wracked by false rumors announcing the death of James Magoffin and

Opposite: On the trail, buffalo chips were commonly used as cooking fuel when wood was scarce. It is said that children learned to sail them through the air.

Below: Yavapai Indians killed six members of the Oatman Family crossing the Arizona desert in 1851. A daughter, Olive, was kidnapped, tattooed by the tribe, and enslaved until 1856, when she was sold to a white man. Slavery had been practiced by a number of tribes since long before the advent of the whites.

disastrous defeats of Zachary Taylor's, Doniphan's, and John Ellis Wool's troops, until the Battle of Sacramento River brought the American forces a strategic victory. General Taylor then ordered U.S. troops and traders out of Chihuahua for security reasons, and the Magoffins proceeded southeast to the towns of Saltillo, Matamoros, and finally Camargo for the boat home.

Susan Magoffin's journal of her fifteen-month ride down the Santa Fe Trail reflects her personal metamorphosis. Her entry for February 16, 1847, confirms: "I am learning a lesson that not one could have taught me but experience, the ways of the world . . . who could by telling me, make me sensible of what I have seen and felt since I left home to travel."[15] Unfortunately, Susan's ordeals, including a bout of yellow fever, undermined her health. A second child died soon after birth, and at the age of twenty-seven Susan Magoffin herself died near Kirkwood, Missouri, in 1855, leaving two daughters.

It might be dangerous to generalize about the impact of the frontier experience based on the journal of only one woman if the pages of western history from 1800 to 1870 were not filled with the accounts of countless other women who buried children or husbands (or both) on the way west, walked thousands of miles in all weather, and stoically suffered every kind of privation. Like Susan Magoffin, every one of them inevitably arrived at her destination a different woman from the one who had left home months before. This is no doubt part of what Frederick Jackson Turner had in mind in 1893 when he advanced his thesis that the frontier experience helped shape the American character.

THE SAND CREEK MASSACRE

In November 1864 one of the most devastating and treacherous attacks on Indians in modern times took place near the Mountain Branch of the Santa Fe Trail, at Sand Creek, Colorado Territory, about forty miles north of Bent's New Fort. On this spot American troops attacked without warning a Cheyenne village whose inhabitants—largely women and children—believed they were safely under the protection of the U.S. government. The massacre remains one of the most shameful American military actions in the West.

All through the spring and summer of 1864 the Plains Indians, growing restive under the restrictions and pressures of increased white encroachment, responded by committing more frequent raids on outlying ranches: stealing horses, driving off stock, attacking wagon trains, killing men, and carrying off women and children as captives. Between April and August, within a two-hundred-mile radius of Bent's New Fort, Cheyenne, Arapaho, and Kiowa carried out some twenty attacks, leaving over fifty dead and reducing ranches and stations to charred ruins. Across an area bounded by the Platte River on the north and the Arkansas River on the south, the violence escalated into what became known as the Cheyenne War of 1864.

Prodded by such bloody provocations, and perhaps resenting the caustic public maxim that it cost a million dollars to kill one Indian, Governor John Evans of the Colorado Territory looked around for a cheap, popular answer to the Indian problem. His solution took the form of a proclamation authorizing citizens to "kill and destroy, as enemies of the country" all hostile Indians on the plains and to confiscate their property. Encouraged by this license to kill and loot, young Coloradans eager for action mustered into the Third Regiment of the Colorado Volunteer Cavalry. Volunteers thirsting for revenge were further emboldened by martial law proclaimed August 23 by Colonel John M. Chivington, a former Methodist Episcopal preacher now the commanding officer of the First Colorado Cavalry. Two years earlier Chivington, then a major, had distinguished himself at the Battle of La Glorieta Pass, near Santa Fe—a victory that turned the tide of the Civil War in the Southwest. This was the largest Civil War battle in the region, and Chivington emerged from it a hero, a full colonel, and commanding officer of the Colorado First. But at Glorieta, his troops had not only routed the Confederates, they also savagely—and pointlessly—burned eighty-five wagons of valuable supplies and bayoneted over five hundred horses and mules. Only two years later Chivington's inexplicably barbarous conduct at Sand Creek again broke the rules of warfare, making his name synonymous with infamy.

Before Governor Evans announced his lethal "kill and loot" proclamation in August 1864, he had issued a benign one in June intended to separate "friendly" from "hostile" Indians. William Bent, who knew the Cheyenne better than any other white man, had been asked to persuade the Cheyenne chief, Black Kettle, to lead his people to Fort Lyon, where they were promised government protection and provisions. Trusting Bent, whose first and second wives, Owl Woman and Yellow Woman, were Cheyenne, Black

Kettle acquiesced. Further assurances of safety, from Major E. W. Wynkoop, post commander of Fort Lyon, had been received in council with other Cheyenne and Arapaho subchiefs.

In the higher echelons of U.S. power, however, a dangerously vindictive attitude prevailed. Governor Evans maintained that the Cheyenne had declared war on the United States and should be punished before peace was made. General S. R. Curtis, commanding the Military District of Kansas, declared, "I want no peace till the Indians suffer more." To make matters worse, Major Wynkoop was replaced in early November by Major Scott J. Anthony, who, like Chivington, was openly seeking an opportunity to punish the Indians. Their chance came about noon on November 28, when Chivington rode unannounced into Fort Lyon at the head of the Colorado Third. He immediately took the extraordinary step of sealing the fort and forbidding anyone to leave, in order to keep the element of surprise in his forthcoming attack on the unsuspecting Cheyenne camped at Sand Creek. Chivington's troops—some seven hundred strong, including Anthony's reinforcements and two howitzers—covered forty miles in an overnight forced march, traveling in the cavalry style of walk-trot-gallop-dismount-and-lead. They arrived on the banks of Sand Creek at first light on the twenty-ninth.

Below them, on the north bank, Black Kettle's village was just coming to life, with sunlight washing the hundred or more lodges, dogs stretching, women emerging from the teepees. A sudden charge by Lieutenant Luther Wilson's three companies severed the village from its horse herd as the mounted soldiers,

Colonel John M. Chivington fell into disgrace after leading a treacherous assault on the Cheyenne village at Sand Creek, Colorado.

firing at will, crashed across the dry creek bed. Chivington shouted "Remember the murdered women and children on the Platte!" A raking cross fire into the defenseless village was quickly set up, while howitzers lobbed grapeshot and canister down on the villagers.

Black Kettle, stunned by the slaughter and understandably thinking that it all had to be a mistake, hoisted a large American flag from a lodge pole with a white flag below to signal peaceful intentions, but the firing continued. Jim Beckwourth, one of Chivington's guides and a friend of the Cheyenne, later testified that Chief White Antelope, long known as friendly to the whites, ran out with hands high, calling "Stop! Stop!" He then stood statue-still, with arms folded across his breast framing the presidential medal he had received in Washington, D.C., in 1851. He was shot down where he stood, then his nose, ears, and genitals were hacked off. Women, children, and a few men ran up the dry creek channel, desperately clawing holes in the loose sand to hide from the frenzied soldiers. The pursuit was evidently merciless, as soldiers and officers scalped and butchered their victims.

Robert Bent, a Chivington guide and half-Cheyenne son of William Bent, later testified to a Senate investigating committee:

> I saw five squaws under a bank for shelter. When the troops came up to them they ran out and showed their persons to let the soldiers know they were squaws and begged for mercy, but the soldiers shot them all. I saw one squaw lying on the bank whose leg had been broken by a shell; a soldier came up to her with a drawn sabre; she raised her arm to protect herself, when he struck, breaking her arm; she rolled over and raised her other arm, when he struck, breaking it, and then left her without killing her. There seemed to be an indiscriminate slaughter of men, women, and children. There were some thirty or forty squaws collected in a hole for protection; they sent out a little girl about six years old with a white flag on a stick; she had not proceeded but a few steps when she was shot and killed. All the squaws in that hole were afterwards killed.[16]

By three o'clock that afternoon the bloodbath was over; then the village was torched. The exact number of dead will never be known. In Chivington's official report to General Curtis, and in his testimony at subsequent hearings, he estimated that four hundred to six hundred Indians and only nine soldiers were killed (no doubt an exaggeration calculated to enhance his "victory"). Other participants in the massacre, perhaps less vainglorious than their commanding officer or seeking to downplay the heinousness of the killing in the face of public indignation, offered more realistic figures, ranging from sixty-nine to two hundred Indian dead.

Despite the several official investigating commissions, congressional hearings, and military inquiries that followed Sand Creek, Chivington was never punished or even court-martialed for his part in the massacre, on the grounds that he was not legally on duty when the massacre took place. His commission, it seems, had expired on September 23, 1864, although he continued in command until resigning from the service on January 6, 1865. Curiously enough, all the inquiries took place after Chivington resigned. Following his resignation, the apparently unrepentant Chivington worked in the freight business for a while in Nebraska, then went off to California, returning to Denver in 1883. There he worked for newspapers before dying of cancer at age seventy-three. It remains a deeply disturbing enigma how Chivington, who as a young man was vehemently opposed to slavery and who spent years as a Methodist Episcopal preacher, could turn into the "inhuman monster" (Wynkoop's words) of Sand Creek.

Although Chivington's official report stated that Black Kettle had died at Sand Creek, the Cheyenne chief escaped with many of his people, only to be killed on November 27, 1868 (almost exactly four years after Sand Creek), by General George Custer's Seventh Cavalry at the Washita. One of the cruelest ironies of the Sand Creek massacre was the role of William Bent and his family. William, with all good intentions, had urged Black Kettle to go into Fort Lyon for protection, a move that had led to the chief's bloody defeat. William's son Robert served as a guide for Chivington, leading the troops to Sand Creek and their rendezvous not with glory but with dishonor. Two other Bent sons, George and seventeen-year-old Charley, were in Black Kettle's camp at the time, and both sided with the Cheyenne. After Sand Creek, George fought for a time with the Cheyenne Dog Soldiers, then later settled on their Oklahoma agency. Charley, who became a Cheyenne guerrilla with a price on his head, was disowned by his father and died miserably of Pawnee wounds and malaria in a Cheyenne camp.

Sand Creek took its place in a decades-long series of Indian massacres by whites: Bear River in Idaho, 1863, with ninety dead; the Washita, in Oklahoma, 1868, with 103 dead; Marias River, in Montana, 1870, with 173 dead; and Wounded Knee in South Dakota, with about 200 dead. In between, Indians inflicted their own share of deaths on whites and on other tribes: in 1866, partly driven by revenge for Sand Creek, a large band of Lakota, Cheyenne, and Arapaho ambushed federal troops along the Bozeman Trail and killed forty-eight soldiers. In 1871, at Camp Grant, Arizona, one hundred Apache were massacred by their traditional foe the Papago. And, of course, on June 25, 1876, at the Little Big Horn in Montana, 209 American soldiers were slain in battle by Cheyenne and Lakota warriors. Given the whites' greater numbers and firepower, it is not surprising that they killed more Indians than the other way around, yet in the Great Plains and the Southwest the estimated total killed on both sides during the nineteenth century represents a very small fraction of either population. Very small, but still too large.

When Jedediah Smith died near the Cimarron in 1831, the Santa Fe Trail was still in its infancy, having been opened by William Becknell only a decade earlier, yet trail commerce had already significantly raised the standard of living in Santa Fe and Chihuahua. That commerce would grow into the economic lever that ultimately pried New Mexico loose from its mother country to become, in 1912, the forty-seventh state of the Union. After 1831 the trail would live on for another half-century before it too died, like most of the trails, under the steel wheels of the railroad.

INTERIOR OF MECHANICS' CORRAL, FORT UNION, NEW MEXICO, *September 1866.*

With the Civil War at an end, obsolete supply wagons and surplus wheels gathered dust in the workshop corral.

THE
OREGON-CALIFORNIA
T R A I L

4

After the Lewis and Clark breakthrough to the Pacific Northwest in 1804–6, forty more years passed before the big overland push west really got underway, in 1843—the year of the first Great Migration. At that time California was still part of a foreign country and Oregon under dispute with the British. To sell one's property, load all earthly belongings into a wagon, and strike out on a two-thousand-mile journey into the wilderness was not a decision lightly taken. Many authorities publicly warned against such folly. Editor Horace Greeley called it "palpable suicide" in 1843, although a decade later he blithely switched signals, proclaiming "Go west, young man." Two years later Daniel Webster blustered that the Far West was a useless "region of savages and wild beasts." Despite such caveats, the tide of westering emigrants reached flood stage with the migrations of 1843, 1846, and 1849–50, driven by several factors: economic need caused by the panic of 1837–42, the prospect of a congressional bill donating land to Oregon settlers, Britain's ceding of present-day Oregon and Washington to the United States in 1846, the settlement of the Mexican War in 1848, and the gold rush of 1849–50.

At first Oregon attracted more settlers than California: in 1843 some 875 pioneers traveled overland to Oregon and only 38 to California. These were not imposing numbers for a Great Migration, but they far exceeded the handful of missionaries and others in previous years. By 1846 the trend had reversed, with fifteen hundred to California and only twelve hundred to Oregon, and by 1860 the Golden State had attracted

CHIMNEY ROCK, NEBRASKA, *n.d. Photograph by Ron Cronin.*

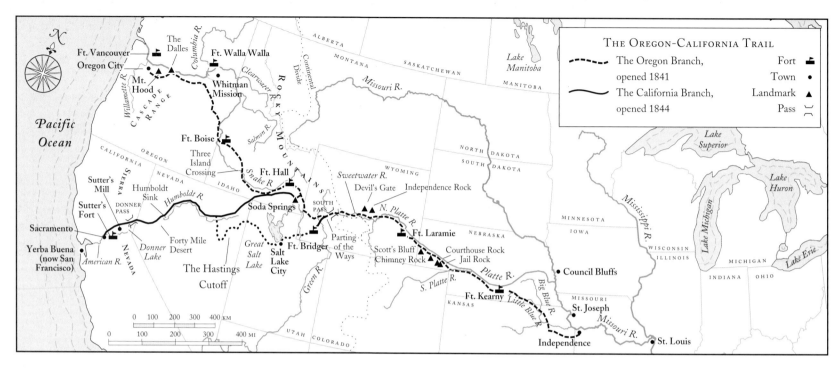

The Oregon-California Trail map showing:

THE OREGON-CALIFORNIA TRAIL
- - - The Oregon Branch, opened 1841 — Fort
— The California Branch, opened 1844 — Town •
Landmark ▲
Pass ⊃⊂

Pacific Ocean

Ft. Vancouver, Oregon City, The Dalles, Ft. Walla Walla, Mt. Hood, Whitman Mission, Columbia R., Clearwater R., Salmon R., Ft. Boise, Three Island Crossing, Ft. Hall, Snake R., Soda Springs, Sweetwater R., Devil's Gate, Independence Rock, South Pass, N. Platte R., Parting of the Ways, Ft. Bridger, Green R., Great Salt Lake, Salt Lake City, The Hastings Cutoff, Humboldt R., Humboldt Sink, Forty Mile Desert, Donner Pass, Donner Lake, American R., Sutter's Mill, Sutter's Fort, Sacramento, Yerba Buena (now San Francisco), Scott's Bluff, Chimney Rock, Courthouse Rock, Jail Rock, Ft. Laramie, S. Platte R., Platte R., Big Blue R., Little Blue R., Ft. Kearny, Council Bluffs, St. Joseph, Independence, St. Louis, Missouri R., Mississippi R.

Continental Divide, Rocky Mountains, Cascade Range, Sierra Nevada, Willamette R.

States/regions: ALBERTA, MONTANA, SASKATCHEWAN, MANITOBA, Lake Manitoba, WYOMING, NORTH DAKOTA, SOUTH DAKOTA, MINNESOTA, IOWA, WISCONSIN, ILLINOIS, MICHIGAN, INDIANA, OHIO, Lake Superior, Lake Huron, Lake Michigan, Lake Erie, OREGON, CALIFORNIA, NEVADA, IDAHO, UTAH, COLORADO, KANSAS, NEBRASKA, MISSOURI

Scale: 0 100 200 300 400 KM; 0 100 200 300 400 MI

more than four times the number that ended up in Oregon. (At that point it would have made sense to change the name of the route west to the California Trail.) Expert advice, bitter experience—nothing seemed to check the slow-motion stampede west that continued on the trail well past the Civil War until the completion of the Transcontinental Railroad.

TRAIL HAZARDS

April and May were the traditional months for wagon trains to head west when prairie grass was greening, water was plentiful much of the way, and weather mild. Such a departure time would put the train in Oregon or California by September or October, before the early mountain winter blocked the passes over the western slope. That was the general plan, and it worked for most emigrants, but for some the ride was far from smooth.

Outfitting wagon trains was big business. Saint Joseph, Independence, Council Bluffs, and other frontier towns brashly touted themselves as the most desirable jumping-off spots, selling the best and cheapest guns, wagons, tools, harness, livestock, and general supplies. Local emigration societies were organized throughout the East and potential emigrants pledged to report in the springtime to an assembly area, usually a few miles outside Independence or Westport,

NOVEMBER SNOW AND COURTHOUSE AND JAIL ROCKS, *1991. Photograph by Greg Ryan–Sally Beyer.*

In the southwest corner of present-day Nebraska, Courthouse Rock (named after the courthouse in Saint Louis) and Jail Rock were among the first landmarks that emigrants saw on their way west. Such curious formations served as milestones to help gauge the distance covered.

where they voted on trail rules, pledged obedience to an elected captain, engaged a pilot, set up companies within the train, and assigned rosters for guard and mess duty.

Stretching between the Missouri River and the Pacific Ocean, the Oregon-California Trail had evolved from ancient buffalo and Indian trails along the banks of the Platte River, to foot and pack trails, then to wagon and handcart "roads," and in 1869 to iron rails. Across the prairie the trail climbed imperceptibly to the Continental Divide at South Pass, a halfway stop for weary travelers. A few miles west of the pass the trail divided, at the Parting of the Ways, into two main branches: one northwest to Oregon Country via the Sublette Cutoff, then Fort Hall (in present Idaho), and down the Snake and Columbia Rivers to Oregon City and the Willamette Valley. The second branch ran southwest past Fort Bridger on the Hastings Cutoff, to follow the Humboldt and Truckee Rivers, up over the Sierra Nevada and down the western slope to Sacramento and Yerba Buena (now San Francisco). So much braiding of diverse routes along the western section of the trail occurred over time that there came to be several "Partings of the Way" west of South Pass, giving a wagon company three or four chances to change its mind before committing to its final destination.

If westbound emigrants anticipated frequent Indian attacks, basing their fears on lurid reports in the eastern press, their apprehensions proved relatively groundless. Indians frequently stole horses along the trail, but they caused surprisingly few deaths; between 1840 and 1860 perhaps four hundred emigrants were killed by Indians, mostly west of South Pass. Accidents accounted for many deaths, but disease fostered by poor sanitation and polluted water was far deadlier, especially the waves of dysentery, "mountain fever," smallpox, and malaria that periodically engulfed white travelers and Indians alike. Cholera alone, carried from New Orleans by riverboat to Saint Louis and then out on the trail, is estimated to have felled five thousand emigrants among the gold rushers. Other travelers toiling west over the years recorded seeing fresh graves every hundred yards along some sections of the trail, and the estimated total of Oregon-California Trail deaths exceeds twenty thousand.

Animals suffered more than the humans. In the Nevada Forty Mile Desert, exhausted oxen often had to be cut loose from the wagons to fend for themselves—how successful they were can be judged by one count there in 1850 that tallied ninety-seven hundred dead animals and three thousand abandoned wagons. Personal belongings succumbed too. Heavy nonessentials were jettisoned, and the trailside litter ranged from pots and pans to family antiques and furniture of all kinds. The bitter feelings born during such forced abandonment of cherished property sometimes showed up in unexpected ways, as when flour or sugar were spitefully doused with kerosene to make them unfit for following travelers.

EARLY TRAVELERS

Until the first wagons made it all the way to California or Oregon, prospective caravans of settlers (often families with women and children) were not yet convinced

Opposite: INTERIOR OF AN EMIGRANT WAGON, *c. 1936. Old-fashioned schooner wagon brought across the plains by John Bemmerly in 1849 from Cincinnati to Yolo County, California. Photograph by the Work Projects Administration.*

Treasured household belongings were often the first things to be jettisoned on the trail in order to lighten the load. Farther on, oxen would be cut loose as they gave out, and finally the wagons themselves would be left behind.

Below: Ezra Meeker, who crossed the plains to Oregon as a boy in 1852, studies a trail rut hollowed out by emigrant wagon wheels that once rolled toward Oregon. Photographed in 1923.

Opposite: THE JOSEPH
HENRY BYINGTON FAMILY,
"A MORMON FAMILY," NEAR
CALLS FORT, UTAH, *1867.*

*Crossing the plains by wagon was a
rugged journey, as the stress written on
these faces testifies. Women found trail
life hard enough itself, but if a husband
perished along the way, as many did,
the trip was even grimmer.*

———————————

Right: THE PARTING OF
THE WAYS, *n.d. Photograph by
William Hill.*

*Near South Pass, after crossing the
Continental Divide, emigrants came to
a fork in the trail: the Parting of the
Ways. To the right waited Oregon, to
the left, California. Many a route was
doubtless determined here by the toss
of a coin or a hat.*

———————————

that overland migration by householders would even be possible.

It is easier to tell who got to Oregon first by wagon than it is to document the first to California. Peter H. Burnett organized an emigrating company to Oregon in 1843 that included Daniel Waldo, James Nesmith, and Jesse Applegate and his brothers. A few of the company's wagons made it through to the Willamette Valley after a relatively uneventful trip, arriving at Oregon City by boat down the Columbia on November 6, 1843.

As for California, contemporary western historians still disagree over which emigrants arrived first. The Bidwell-Bartleson company of 1841—the first planned wagon train to California from the East—is a case in point. Apparently a party of real greenhorns— John Bidwell himself asserted they knew California

was west, but that was all— the group was lucky enough to fall in with mountain man Thomas "Broken Hand" Fitz- patrick's company, en route to Oregon as escort to the peripatetic Jesuit priest Pierre Jean De Smet. Fitzpatrick shepherded the Bidwell-Bartleson wagons as far west as Soda Springs, in present Idaho, where the company turned shakily southward, aiming for California. Bidwell's group was finally forced to abandon their wagons before reaching the Humboldt River, and they continued on horseback to John Marsh's ranch at the base of Mount Diablo in California.

In 1843 another mountain man, Joseph Reddingford Walker, also piloted wagons from the east into California (but barely over the border). Since he had to abandon them east of the Sierra Nevada, Walker retains the rather technical distinction of having been first to bring wagons into California but not over the Sierras. More important, however, is that Walker had opened part of what shortly became the Oregon-California Trail.

The summer of 1843 also found a somewhat exotic group on the trail, though it was not bound for either California or Oregon. William Sublette was guiding the party on a nostalgic journey to the former Green River site of the old fur trappers' and traders' Rendezvous,

which had been discontinued in 1840. The caravan had been organized by Sir William Drummond Stewart— Scotsman, big-game hunter, world traveler, and professional soldier, who had fought under the Duke of Wellington at Waterloo. Sir William was no greenhorn, although he provoked smiles when he wore his tartans on the trail. He had taken part in many fur trappers' Rendezvous, starting in 1833, and he had taken the artist Alfred Jacob Miller to the one in 1837 to paint the mountain men in their chosen environment. Stewart was friend to many of the celebrated frontiersmen of the time, including Sublette, Fitzpatrick, and Jim Bridger, to whom Stewart once gave a full suit of English armor (immortalized in Miller's portrait of Bridger in full regalia, now in the Joslyn

Art Museum in Omaha). Bridger, in turn, gave his Scottish friend the iron arrowhead that Dr. Marcus Whitman had dug out of Bridger's back at the 1835 Rendezvous. Young journalist Matt C. Field of the *New Orleans Picayune*, also in the party, called this the "first pleasure excursion" to the Rocky Mountains.

Stewart's party left Independence in June 1843, working their leisurely way west to South Pass and then southwest to the Green River and the old Rendezvous site. Now it was peopled only by ghosts of bygone days, even though the party tried to recapture the old spirit by hunting, betting on horse races run among themselves, and conscientiously observing the "Weinstein hour" held daily in Stewart's well-stocked tent. It was a sentimental journey by men who saw the wilderness world dissolving and wanted to savor its primitive delights together one more time.

The Elisha Stephens (or Stevens) party of 1844 finally became the first to get at least some of their wagons across the Sierra Nevada and all the way to John Sutter's New Helvetia settlement at present-day Sacramento. Stephens, with a hawk-nosed, strikingly homely face, was a blacksmith by trade who sought that will-o'-the-wisp, Opportunity, in California. Despite his offputting features, the forty-year-old Stephens inspired confidence and won election as captain, the general opinion being that he was born to command. Stephens plus twenty-six other men, eight women, and seventeen boys and girls (two were born on the journey), left Council Bluffs, Iowa, in eleven ox-drawn wagons about May 18, 1844, bound for California. Their route followed the established Platte River road to Fort Laramie, then took them across present-day Wyoming, where they rested, watered, and fed their stock for the week of July Fourth at Independence Rock. Then they went to South Pass, where they

Harold Von Schmidt (1893–?).
ROUGH GOING OVER THE
SIERRAS, *n.d. Oil on canvas.*

Wagons crossing the Sierra Nevada sometimes had to be emptied of loads and disassembled. Using chains and rope pulleys, snubbed around trees, they could then be hoisted in pieces up and over the granite ledges.

established the wagon route later known as Sublette's Cutoff, up to Fort Hall, and then southwest along the Raft River to the Humboldt River and the Sink (where the Humboldt disappeared into the ground). From that point west to the Sacramento Valley, Stephens's party blazed their own trail, opening a major wagon way eventually called the Truckee Route (named after Chief Truckee, the Paiute Indian who showed them the way). On or about November 15, the wagons reached what later became famous as Donner Lake. In effect, Stephens had discovered Donner Pass.

Stephens split his party twice, sending a detachment on horseback across the summit to Sutter's Fort, where help could be had if necessary, and then sending five of the more determined wagons over the pass. In snow two feet deep, the wagoners unloaded all the wagons and carried the contents to the summit. The oxen, unhitched from the wagons, were squeezed one at a time up a wide cleft in a ten-foot vertical granite wall and then chained to the wagons. Pulled by the oxen above, and pushed by the men below, the wagons were inched over the wall. From then on, the way down the western slope seemed relatively easy, and Stephens's party ultimately made it through to Sutter's Fort. They can properly be considered, as historian Hubert H. Bancroft put it, "the first wagons that ever made tracks in California soil, brought across the mountains."[1]

Perhaps the most dramatic event of the entire Stephens journey from Council Bluffs to Sutter's Fort was the decision of seventeen-year-old Moses Schallenberger to stay at the Donner Lake camp all winter, alone, guarding abandoned wagons filled with property he expected to sell in California. The rest of the Stephens party, after helping him build a shelter, went on to California. For nearly three months of deep winter, Moses lived alone in a log cabin with no windows and a doorway without a door—a log cave. If young Schallenberger wanted to test himself by going it alone, this was a worthy sanctuary, with no habitation within nearly a hundred miles and the only signs of life the delicate tracks etched in the snow by the foxes he trapped and devoured to stay alive. At the end of his self-imposed isolation, when a rescue party returned for him in late February, Moses Schallenberger no doubt knew himself far better than before. Leaving the snowy forest, the boy turned his back on the cabin— the same one in which the Breen family of the Donner Party would survive the dread winter of 1846.

VOICES FROM THE TRAIL

Between 1840 and 1870 the American continent seemed to tilt toward the Pacific coast when 250,000 to 400,000 emigrants (depending on which historian is consulted) took to the Oregon-California Trail. Behind such a statistical image of western migration lies a second, more vivid image: the record of individual pioneers reacting to sights and events along the trail. Well over two thousand emigrants kept journals or diaries or wrote letters home describing the pleasures, hardships, and perils of the trail experience, which they called "seeing the elephant." What follows are extracts from some of these personal accounts.

Pouring out the cornucopia of California's natural assets before their readers to promote westward

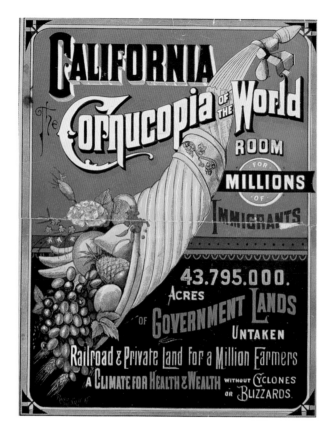

CALIFORNIA, CORNUCOPIA OF THE WORLD, *c. 1870. Lithograph poster by Rand McNally and Co. The New-York Historical Society.*

Luscious posters such as this enticed eastern emigrants by touting California as a paradise overflowing with nature's bounty and assuring easy prosperity.

expansion, the *Saint Louis Weekly Reveille* wrote on March 9, 1846:

> There is no country holding forth such great inducements to emigrants as California. Its natural advantages are of the most important character—a most salubrious climate, a perpetual spring, as it were, without the sultriness of summer or the chilling winds of winter—a soil unsurpassed for richness and productiveness, some

of the principal articles of agriculture growing in a wild, uncultivated state, and in excessive abundance—immense herds of wild cattle, whose hides, tallow, meat &c., would be most profitable articles of traffic—the wealth of the woodland and rare water privileges—a prize for industry and enterprise—the gold, silver and precious gems that the earth is holding in its flinty bosom, and which, in some cases, nature has so exposed as to render them available without the cost of labor and expense.

Peter H. Burnett—the Weston, Missouri, storekeeper who organized the first wagon train to Oregon in 1843—drummed up public support for it by street-corner speeches. Edward Lenox, whose family was caught up in the Oregon fever, later recalled: "Mr. Burnett hauled a box out into the sidewalk, took his stand upon it, and began to tell us about the land flowing with milk and honey on the shores of the Pacific. . . . And then, with a twinkle in his eye, he said 'They do say that out in Oregon the pigs are running about under the great acorn trees, round and fat, and already cooked, with knives and forks sticking in them so that you can cut off a slice whenever you are hungry.'"[2]

Jesse Applegate, a thirty-two-year-old farmer from Saint Clair County, Missouri, joined the Great Migration of 1843 to Oregon in command of the Cow Column, a special company responsible for the wagon train's extensive livestock. He later described his daily routine:

> It is four o'clock A.M.; the sentinels on duty have discharged their rifles—the signal that the hours of sleep are over; and every wagon and tent is pouring forth its night tenants. . . . Sixty men start from the corral, spreading as they make through the vast herd of cattle and horses that form a semicircle around the encampment, the most distant perhaps two miles away.

OREGON TRAIL RUTS, *n.d. Photograph by Randall A. Wagner.*

It took many thousands of emigrant wagons to carve these ruts on the Oregon-California Trail, still visible today near Guernsey, Wyoming.

The corral is a circle one hundred yards deep, formed with wagons connected strongly with each other, the wagon in the rear being connected with the wagon in front by its tongue and ox chains. It is a strong barrier that the most vicious ox cannot break, and in case of an attack of the Sioux would be no contemptible entrenchment.

From 6 to 7 o'clock is a busy time; breakfast is to be eaten, the tents struck, the wagons loaded and the teams yoked and brought up in readiness to be attached to their respective wagons. All know when, at 7 o'clock, the signal to march sounds, that those not ready to take their proper places in the line of march must fall into the dusty rear for the day.

There are sixty wagons. They have been divided into fifteen divisions or platoons of four wagons each, and each platoon is entitled to lead in its turn. The leading platoon of today will be the rear one tomorrow. . . .

The pilot, by measuring the ground and timing the speed of the wagons and the walk of his horses, . . . [has selected] the nooning place, as nearly as the requisite grass and water can be had at the end of five hours' travel of the wagons. . . . The wagons are drawn up in columns, four abreast, the leading wagon of each platoon on the left. This brings friends together [for the noon rest] . . . as well as at night.[3]

Matt C. Field—the reporter for the *New Orleans Picayune* who went west with Sir William Drummond Stewart's party of 1843—recorded his impressions of camp sounds on the trail:

The drivers' "gee," "wo-ho" and "haw" were caught up by echo and went bounding away and back again from rock to rock—an echo so lively and clear that it seemed to mock even the mosquitos buzz—the driving of pickets, the tinkling of the lead-mare's bell, the horses' neigh, the mules' bray, the chopping of wood, and the merry *chansons* of the Frenchboys.

[Of camping in the dark:] Remember . . . the white tents rising—the pitchy darkness gathering—the fires lighting up around—the confusion of finding animals in the dark—men calling to each other—the circle of fires like magic—then the busy cooking time and the stillness after supper—capped by the dismal howling of wolves all around us![4]

D.G.W. Leavitt of Arkansas, organizing a California-bound wagon train in 1843, recommended the following trail equipment to participants: "The

Left: APPLEGATE TRAIL, *1992. Photograph by Dick Ackerman.*

An old wagon trace of 1846, remnant of the Applegate Trail leading to southern Oregon. Normally covered by the waters of Clear Lake Reservoir, these tracks were recently exposed after a severe drought.

Opposite: DR. MACBETH IN COSTUME HE WORE CROSSING THE PLAINS TO FLEE CHOLERA, *c. 1848. Daguerreotype.*

Dr. MacBeth's arsenal proved useless, for en route to the gold fields he died from cholera, not an Indian's tomahawk.

expense of outfit will be about \$125 to \$150, including everything. Every man should have two horses or mules to ride and carry his baggage, or for baggage every five men can unite and obtain a wagon and eight cattle or four horses or mules. Every five men must have a tent and camp equipage sufficient for comfort, but not burdensome. Also every man must have a good rifle or heavy double barrelled shot gun, 16 lb. lead, 4 lbs. powder, caps &c. &c."[5]

The Fourth of July anywhere on the trail, as Field noted, provoked noisy and colorful celebrations: "A banner of stripes & stars, constructed out of 2 red silk handkerchiefs, a lot of Dr. Tilghman's white bandaging stuff, some blue calico, several hat bands and tassels, and the usual quantum of *fixed* stars, was raised as the sun peeped, and a volley of some 25 guns, besides 56 others that went off at random, saluted the national flag in the heart of the wilderness!"[6]

A '49er doctor, Samuel M. Ayres, of Missouri, wrote a graphic letter to his wife telling her more about a cholera epidemic than she probably wished to know:

I am sorry to inform you that since I last wrote you there has been very much distress on the road. Hundred[s] have been summoned to their long homes and others are still lingering on the shores of time, ready to launch out into the abyss of eternity. The disease is called cholera by the most of the emigrants. . . . They are taken with diarrhoea and vomiting, both of which are uncontrollable except by the strongest means. The discharges are very thin,—coffee grounds color. After these symptoms have lasted from 12 to 24 hours cramps commence and the patient soon falls into a stage of collapse and dies. Perhaps the average amount of deaths among those who die of this disease is one half, which, you know, is very bad.[7]

Overton Johnson, part of the Great Migration of 1843, described the resourcefulness of trail-wise emigrants crossing the South Fork of the Platte River: "We procured . . . a sufficient number of green [fresh] Buffalo hides, and having sewed two of them together for each boat, we stretched them over the wagon beds as tight as we could, with the flesh side out, and then turned them up in the sun to dry; and when they became thoroughly dry, we covered them with tallow and ashes, in order to render them more impervious to water."[8]

In 1849 Elijah Bryan Farnham was impressed by the appearance and behavior of Sioux warriors met along the Platte River. "There was a great many Sioux

Indians here at the ford. . . . They are a proud noble looking race of good proportion tall strong athletic and good horsemen They dressed with little clothing The only clothes that most of them had was a breechcloth over their hips. . . . One of these nakedly dressed Indians took quite a fancy to one of the women that was travelling in company with us and offered her husband before her face 3 horses for her She must of felt herself highly flattered"[9]

Rebecca Ketcham's awed reaction to Scott's Bluff, in 1853, was like that of other wayfarers confronting that spectacle as well as the nearby cliffs on the Platte: "On each side the bluffs assume every imaginable form. They are said to be 400 feet high and look in the distance like castles and churches with towers and domes and chimneys."[10] South Pass, on the Continental Divide, was perhaps the most famous milepost on the trail and also the most disappointing visually, since there was no dramatic mountain pass from the Atlantic to the Pacific slope. William T. Newby was utterly unimpressed: "The mane mountain is a graduel desente up & allso the same down. If you dident now it was the mountain you woldent now it from aney outher plane."[11]

Women's duties on the trail included a lot of laundering in the river, under a merciless sun, as Rebecca Ketcham found out:

We washed close to the bank of the river in cold river water, dipping it up ourselves. All around us on each side the river were sheep, cattle, horses, wagons, men, women, and children—more cattle and sheep than I ever saw before in my life: drove

Left: SUNSET ON THE NORTH PLATTE RIVER WITH SCOTT'S BLUFF IN THE BACKGROUND, *n.d.*

The towering stone faces of Scott's Bluff near the border between today's Nebraska and Wyoming looked to some emigrants like a vast city built by giants. The bluff is seen here across the Platte, a river so wide and shallow that many travelers said it was not a river at all but simply moving sand.

Opposite: THE TYPICAL HIGH PLAINS OF WESTERN KANSAS, WESTERN OKLAHOMA, AND NORTHWEST TEXAS. ABANDONED HOUSE ON HORIZON. HASKELL COUNTY, KANSAS, *1897. Photograph by W. D. Johnson.*

In a bleak house, without a shade tree or a neighbor for miles around, a frontier wife had to create her own world or suffer from the extreme isolation.

after drove, thousands, yes, tens of thousands. . . .
It is astonishing to see what a multitude is moving
on, and now when it is so late in the season, and
the great rush is supposed to be over.

Camilla and I both burnt our arms very badly
while washing. They were red and swollen and
painful as though scalded with boiling water. Our
hands are blacker than any farmer's. . . . Our faces
are pretty well tanned, but nothing like our hands.
I am getting so I like a sunburn very much.[12]

Even at the end of a trying day, according to
Jesse Applegate's somewhat syrupy account, younger
members of his wagon train still found enough energy
for music and relaxation: "Before a tent near the river
a violin makes lively music, and some youths and
maidens have improvised a dance upon the green; in
another quarter a flute gives its mellow and melan-
choly notes to the still air. . . . It has been a pros-
perous day; more than twenty miles have been
accomplished of the great journey."[13]

Perhaps the worst conditions existed along the
Humboldt River bottoms, in present-day Nevada.
Henry Wellenkamp observed in his laconic way:
"Complete quagmire Our animals give out fast The
River is lined with dead horses Mules & Oxen, shattered wagons in every direction."[14] The lack of safe
water in the Humboldt Desert became acute for
Wellenkamp and his fellow emigrants: "The odor
of carions, water tepid & highly alkaline, the countless
dead Oxen Horses Mules and Men in it, make it a
fine flavored Soup."[15]

John M. Shively reported in 1843 that along the

Columbia River robberies staged by the Indians
"were an everyday occurrence until we reached the
Dall[e]s. If the party robbed made no resistance,
the Indians would let him retain what he had on his
back, and also his pony, nor did they whip any that
made no resistance."[16]

For Oregon emigrants, the trail saved some of its
harshest trials until the end, when both men and beasts
were exhausted and least able to cope with them, as
Rebecca Ketcham indicated: (September 1) "Phill had
a great deal of trouble with his pack animals. Their
packs came loose, got tangled in the bushes, got wet in
crossing the river. . . . Crossed Burnt River 9 or 10
times during the day." (September 11) "I will try to be
cheerful and patient."[17]

FREIGHT WAGON STUCK IN
MUDDY RAVINE, *n.d.*
*Steep riverbanks and badlands gulches
presented special problems as men and
teams strained to free wheels buried in
mud and to keep heavily loaded wagons
from tipping over.*

The final water challenge for Oregon emigrants—descending the Columbia River on rafts at the Cascades—was described in 1843 by N. M. Bogart:

When trying to pass some of the Cascades, their frail craft would get caught in one of the many whirlpools, the water dashing over them, and drenching them through and through. Then the men would plunge in the cold stream and carry the half drowned women and children ashore, build

THE PASSAGE OF THE DALLES, COLUMBIA RIVER, OREGON, *1867. Photograph by Carleton E. Watkins.*

The Passage of the Dalles on the Columbia River was one of the final and most daunting water hazards that Oregon-California Trail emigrants had to overcome on their long trek to Oregon City.

huge bon-fires so they could partially dry themselves and goods, then proceed again on foot, the mothers clambering over rocks and fallen timber carrying the smallest child in their arms, with one or two clinging to their skirts, whilst the men would help tow the boats to smoother water.[18]

Countering the still exuberant press accounts of California gold, Dr. Samuel M. Ayres, shortly before his death in California in 1850, wrote a gloomy letter to his wife expressing his disillusion with El Dorado:

Well now, about California. Everybody is disappointed in this place. Hundreds are returning home immediately after their arrival here, a great many of whom beg money of their friends to take them home. The emigrants of this year are all very much discouraged. The mines are failing, property depreciating, the country full of poverty stricken people. Many are committing suicide, and others are wishing themselves dead, while others still are working with brilliant expectations, but very few are prospering.[19]

Individual emigrants carried away reactions that were as different as the emigrants themselves. Henry Wellenkamp's were blunt and honest, tinged with justifiable pride:

Passed Sutter's Fort & entered Sacramento City C. 9 o'clock a.m. on Wednesday Aug. 21, 1850 . . . after an Absence from home of 17 weeks or 119 Days from Washington [Missouri]. So ended our

hard dangerous and toilsome Journey across the Rocky Mountains, Great Basin & Sierre Nevada Mountains. It Stands relieved by a great many pleasant Scenes, natural curiosities fine and Romantic Passages, yet the iminent emigration 50–70,000 Persons constantly crowding, making clouds of Dust, grazing away the grass—obstructing many passes by their dead animals & imparting the air with stench—made it on the whole—unpleasant and toilsome.[20]

THE DONNER NIGHTMARE

On a spring morning in 1846, Sarah Keyes, seventy-five years old and ailing, was carried out of her house in Springfield, Illinois, and propped up on a large featherbed aboard the strangest covered wagon that ever crossed the plains. It had been specially built for her by James Frazier Reed, her son-in-law and organizer of the Springfield emigrant party for California. Mrs. Keyes's granddaughter, Virginia, described the contraption in a letter years later as the "Pioneer Palace Car." The extraordinary vehicle boasted a side entrance that opened into a small central room complete with high-backed spring seats, a sheet-iron stove, and a good library of standard works. Planks running the full length of the wagon supported a roomy second-story bedroom, a unique feature for a prairie wagon. Keyes's daughter, Margaret Reed, also traveling in the wagon, had been given a large mirror by friends who hung it opposite the entry door as a constant reminder "to keep her good looks" on the long journey to California.

California, published in 1845 by Lansford W. Hastings, and been seduced by Hastings's colorful description of the region as a paradise-by-the-Pacific, easily reached by a new shortcut, "bearing west southwest, to the Salt Lake," as Hastings put it, "and then continuing down to the bay of St. Francisco." A seemingly simple hop, skip, and a jump across some eight hundred miles of desert and mountains. Reed would have frequent occasion to recall those siren words with bitterness in the months ahead.

James Frazier Reed, shown here with his wife, Margaret, was the leader of the Donner Party until he was banished from the train for having stabbed a teamster to death in self-defense.

Patty Reed was only eight years old when her family was stranded in the Sierra Nevada with the Donner Party.

As the four yoke of oxen slowly pulled out of the yard that April 16, another granddaughter, eight-year-old Patty Reed, lifted the wagon cover to give her grandmother a last look at her old home. In her innocent way Patty thus raised the curtain on the most spectacular catastrophe of all western migration. Within weeks Sarah Keyes would lie buried by the side of the trail in Kansas, and in September, on Utah's Great Salt Desert, the Pioneer Palace Car would be an abandoned derelict, its mirror gleaming dully in the darkened interior.

James Frazier Reed, a forty-six-year-old railroad man and furniture manufacturer, was smarting from financial reverses and dreamed of greener fields in California as well as a milder climate for his invalid wife. He had read *The Emigrants' Guide to Oregon and*

The Reed party of three wagons out of Springfield (including Reed's wife, Margaret, and their four children) was joined by two brothers: Jacob Donner, age sixty-five, and his family of eight, and George Donner with a family of six. This was the core of what has come to be known as the Donner Party, although the title is misleading since these three families accounted for only twenty-two (their teamsters and servants added another nine) of the eighty-one men, women, and children who ultimately suffered together in California's Sierra Nevada through the baneful winter of 1846–47.

*A wagon train fords a river in Kansas—
perhaps the Big Blue. Although wagon
beds were often sealed with pitch to help
them float like boats, capsizing—with
loss of contents and even life—was a
constant threat.*

The Donner Party's progress west was like a chess game in which the early moves greatly determined the final outcome. At the Big Blue River in Kansas, rain-induced floods kept them on the bank for five days waiting to cross, a delay whose consequences would be felt only later, in the high Sierras. Farther west the company struck the North Platte River in Wyoming before reaching South Pass and the Little Sandy River. At Little Sandy, still almost a thousand miles from California, a basic decision had to be made: travel southwest to Fort Bridger and the Hastings Cutoff, which reportedly saved three hundred miles (three weeks of travel time) but also required crossing mountains eight thousand feet high and the vast Great Salt Desert. The second choice was to take the old route northwest to Fort Hall, thence southwest to the

Humboldt River in Nevada, up the canyon of the Truckee River, and over the pass into the Sacramento Valley. A number of emigrants with the Donners opted to play it safe by taking the Fort Hall route, but James Reed spoke out for the Hastings Cutoff. The Donner brothers and several other families threw in their lot with him—a fatal error. At Fort Bridger, Reed was shocked to learn that Lansford Hastings, who had promised to guide the Reed-Donner party over the cutoff, was now leading a train of some sixty-six wagons and had gone ahead without them, leaving word for Reed to follow his tracks west.

On the last day of July 1846 the Donner train, now made up of eighty-seven people and about twenty-three wagons, started out on the Hastings Cutoff. Reed's journal for the second and third weeks of August describes in surprisingly understated terms the nasty surprises that befell them crossing the Wasatch Range, where the party spent backbreaking days hacking out a new route through willow trees and undergrowth. Forward progress slowed to two miles a day or less. On August 24 Reed recorded: "It took 18 days to get 30 miles."[21] On the thirtieth, still gasping for breath from their Wasatch exertions, the company embarked on "the long drive through the Salt desert." Reed's entry for Monday, August 31, reports ominously: "In dessert drive of Sixty 60 miles." Tuesday, September 1, records only: "In dessert."

While crossing the desert, their trials multiplied: oxen gave out and wagons had to be abandoned; Indians made off with much of the stock; thirst, hunger, and cold exacted their toll. At one point Reed and his wife and children walked all night in the white and

freezing desert of sterile salt to catch up with the main group ahead. At the far side of the desert, near Pilot Peak, the company camped from September 3 to 8 to recruit—another delay that would cost them dear. By early October they were crossing the Humboldt Desert in a second "long drive" that frayed tempers and brought simmering animosities to the surface. On October 5, in an altercation with teamster John Snyder, Reed stabbed him to death in self-defense. As punishment, Reed was banished from the company and sent on alone (he was shortly joined by Walter

A rotten wheel is all that remains of the wagon believed to have been abandoned by the Reed family in Utah's Great Salt Desert.

Herron), in the hope that he would get through four hundred miles of snow-covered Sierras to Sutter's Fort on the Sacramento River. On October 8 an elderly traveler, one Hardkoop (first name unknown), was left behind on the trail to die when he could not keep up, and on October 20 William M. Pike was shot to death by his brother-in-law, William M. Foster, in a gun accident. (By the time the party reached camp at Truckee [later named Donner] Lake, some in wagons and others on foot, they had lost six people one way or another.) There followed a five-day rest at Truckee Meadows, a third crucial delay that in effect made them almost three weeks late in reaching the vicinity of Truckee (later Donner) Pass.

Between October 25 and 30 the party, now numbering eighty-one, struggled upward toward the pass, only to collapse three miles below the summit, lacking the strength to cross over to safety. Blanketed during the night with deep snow, on November 4 the desperate company retreated to Donner Lake and Alder Creek, located in the bottom of a great granite bowl below the pass, to set up what turned out to be their camps for the next four months.

Judging from the testimony of the victims' few journals and later reminiscences, the company rather oddly dispersed at that point, living in curious isolation from each other. The camps were strung out over eight some miles, and instead of group cohesiveness— common enough in a disaster—an every-man-for-himself-spirit seemed to take over. The elderly Donner brothers and their families were left to spend the winter in tents. Lewis Keseberg had injured his foot and could manage only to prop a brush lean-to against

Patrick Breen's cabin (Moses Schallenberger's former log cave) for his wife and two children, one of whom was only a year old. No one seemed to be in charge of camp life, and during the terrible winter ahead, this leadership vacuum became critical.

The camp's animals were soon slaughtered for food, but many of their carcasses were buried in snow ten to fifteen feet deep and never found again. Inside the rude cabins, totally submerged beneath the white drifts, darkness prevailed day and night except for the flickering light from little pine sticks burning on the mantels. Animal hides covered the cabin roofs to keep the snow at bay; men, women, and children were soon reduced to boiling and eating strips of those hides and to splitting off pieces of log from inside the walls for firewood.

In early November it snowed continuously for two weeks, frustrating two attempts to escape over the pass on foot. Finally, on December 16, a party of fifteen left Donner Lake on improvised snowshoes. The survivors of the Snowshoe Party (five women and two men) arrived on January 18 at Johnson's Ranch in the Bear River valley, forty miles from Sutter's Fort. Eight members had perished on the way to safety, and the first ghoulish communions of flesh eating by some survivors had begun a few days after Christmas.

The surviving seven snowshoers brought out word of the Donner situation, and plans for rescue efforts got underway at once. The so-called First Donner Relief, captained by A. Glover and R. P. Tucker, left Johnson's Ranch on February 4, arriving at Donner Lake two weeks later. Moving with urgency, Tucker and his men quickly handed out the few provisions they carried (having left caches of food hung in trees along the trail for the return trip) and started back to Bear River valley with twenty-one refugees.

On the way out they met several members of the incoming Second Relief, including James Reed, who had survived his earlier banishment from the party. Shortly afterward he was overcome with relief to see his wife and two of their children (Patty and Tommy Reed were still back at Donner Lake), gaunt and tattered, staggering toward him through the heavy snow with a scattering of other survivors. Reed and his men had already unpacked their horses days before, since the animals floundered helplessly in snow too deep and soft to bear their weight. The Second Relief continued on foot up over the pass to Donner Lake, carrying the horses' loads on their own backs, sometimes through snow thirty feet deep. On arrival at the lake, Reed also quickly distributed food, collected a few refugees, and started back out.

It was a time for hard decisions: who was to go out, and who stay behind? George Donner's wife, Tamsen, a former schoolteacher, elected to remain in the tent with her sick husband rather than leave him. They died together at Donner Lake. Patrick Breen and seven of his family preferred to wait for the soon expected Third Relief, which later left them at "Starved Camp" on the trail to California. When discovered there in mid-March by William H. Eddy and others, the Breens were stretched out, apathetic but breathing, in a snowhole twenty-four feet deep and twelve feet wide that had been melted out by their campfire. Scattered among the Breens, according to Eddy, were two dead Donner children, the partly devoured corpse of

Mrs. Graves, and her thirteen-month-old infant, who was still alive and crying inconsolably.

That gruesome sight was a mild precursor to the scene that greeted mountain man William Fallon and the Fourth (and final) Relief when they broke trail into the Donner Lake camp on April 17, 1847. Extracts from Fallon's journal (whose accuracy is sometimes questioned) appeared in the *California Star* for June 5, 1847. When he reached the cabins, Fallon found Lewis Keseberg, the only person left alive. Scraggle-bearded and emaciated, Keseberg sat before a pot of stew made from human brains, lights, and liver—surrounded, as Fallon reported, by "bodies terribly mutilated, legs, arms, and sculls scattered in every direction." Outside, dead bodies, torn by animals, littered the melting snow. The bodies remained there until June, when General Stephen Watts Kearny's troops, returning east after their California campaign, marched through the Donner Lake area and paused long enough to bury some of the victims. Of the original eighty-seven members of the Donner Party who rolled out of Fort Bridger on the Hastings Cutoff nearly nine months earlier, thirty-nine had died on the trail west, at Donner Lake, or on the way to the California settlements.

A survivor of the Donner disaster, Georgia Ann Donner Babcock was only four years old when the group starved in the Sierra Nevada. Years later Mrs. Babcock wrote that she and other children in the camp had been fed human flesh, which kept them alive until they were rescued.

No single member of the Donner Party has been so excoriated by other members of the party—and the public—as Keseberg. An educated German, thirty-two years old, with a twenty-three-year-old wife and two children, Keseberg was suspected of having murdered Mrs. Murphy—who expired in his cabin at Donner Lake—and three other members of the party. He later admitted to having cannibalized corpses in order to survive, a confession that only one or two others were honest enough to make. Such charges seem to make Keseberg the villain in the tragedy, yet interviews with him in later years—by such authorities as historians Hubert H. Bancroft and C. H. McGlashan as well as Donner Party survivor Eliza Donner Houghton—seem to tip the scale back toward balance with respect to his character. In any event, Keseberg clearly bore no responsibility for bringing on the Donner disaster; the true villains were forces of nature—distance, time, and weather. And lurking underneath it all, the human animal's will to live.

The Reeds and the Breens, the only two families to survive their ordeal intact, both prospered in California. James Frazier Reed carried away enough gold from the 1849 gold rush to develop a successful fruit-farming business near San Jose. Before he died in 1874, Reed and his wife adopted little Mary Donner, whose parents had died in the Sierra Nevada. Patrick Breen and several of his sons became respected businessmen in the area of San Juan Bautista. Breen's daughter, Isabella, who was less

Below: After his rescue Lewis Keseberg eventually became proprietor of a California hotel, although he never fully overcame the public's horror at his earlier gruesome experience.

Right: The dream of finding California's gold nuggets drove more than a hundred thousand argonauts west in 1849 alone.

than a year old at Donner Lake, lived until 1935—the last survivor of the Donner Party.

THE GOLD RUSH

After the Mormon Battalion was discharged in San Diego in 1846, some of the soldiers stayed on in California. Six Mormon veterans were at work in Sutter's Mill that January of 1848 when one of them, James Marshall, noticed grains of gold in the mill-race. The story of the strike and its consequences has already been so thoroughly told and retold elsewhere that it does not bear repeating here in detail. Suffice it to say, however, that the cry "Gold!" seems to have made carpenters drop their tools, bakers drop their loaves, and sailors abandon their ships in a headlong rush to the gold fields. Newspaper readers were inflamed with gold fever by letters like the one from Philadelphian John Thibault, written from San Francisco and printed in the *Missouri Republican* on June 4, 1849: "Here I am in the golden country, and really a golden country it is; for I never, in my life saw as much gold as I have seen in the five days since my arrival.

. . . The poorest man in this place can show from $500 to $1500 in gold dust, that has been gathered by his own hand in a month or so. . . . No one,

with the least labor, finds less than $15 to $20 per day." The public read, openmouthed, and packed their bags for California. They apparently did not heed Mark Twain's witticism: "A mine is a hole in the ground owned by a liar."

The discovery of gold touched off an unprecedented emigration, both overland and by sea, that had a dramatic impact on the trail. "Pawnee," a correspondent for the *Missouri Republican* who was stationed astride the Oregon-California Trail at Fort Kearny, Nebraska Territory, noted that by June 19, 1849, 5,092 wagons had already passed the fort that spring. The influx of aspiring millionaires to California in 1849 alone pushed the state's population from 14,000 to 115,000, changing California forever and paving a golden road to statehood in 1850.

Fortunes were made and lost, and made again and lost again, and Sutter himself was ultimately driven from his own property by the unruly horde. Sharpers made more money fast-shuffling cards and buying and selling claims in the wide-open mining towns than by getting their feet soaked in the placer streams or their hands callused by a pick in the mines. The stereotypical solitary prospector, doggedly tilting his pan all day in the broiling sun, soon gave way to sophisticated, capital-intensive drilling and flotation processes that could profitably handle many tons of ore a day to separate a few ounces of gold from the rock. Miners went underground, in work more grueling than golden, and for every California mother lode that took millions of dollars' worth of gold from the earth, there were thousands of miners who never made ends meet. Even worse, an 1867 government-sponsored survey found that in California during the last half of 1849, one-fifth of the ninety thousand immigrants perished within six months after arriving in El Dorado.

THE WHITMAN MASSACRE

By strange coincidence, two of the grimmest disasters in western frontier history occurred within a few months of each other on separate branches of the Oregon-California Trail: the Donner tragedy in California's Sierras and the Whitman massacre at Waiilatpu Mission, Oregon, in November 1847.

For over a decade missionaries of various persuasions, including the Catholic church and several Protestant denominations, had cast covetous eyes toward the souls of the Flathead and Nez Percé Indians of Oregon. Some of the religious fervor of these church men and women shines through the 1836 journal entries of Eliza Hart Spalding, a missionary's wife headed for Oregon: "The love of Christ has . . . made me not only willing but anxious to spend and be spent in laboring to promote my Master's cause among the benighted Indians." The theme was repeated again and again: "The hope of spending the remnant of my

days among the heathen, for the express purpose of pointing them to the Lamb of God who taketh away the sins of the world, affords me much happiness."[22] For the next eleven years, Eliza and her husband, Henry, would live out that conviction in a life filled with toil and peril, culminating in 1847 with the death of her dearest friend, Narcissa Whitman.

Other missionaries matched the Spaldings' zeal. Mary Walker and Myra F. Eells, two of four brides in the 1838 church company for Oregon, rode sidesaddle for a record-breaking nineteen hundred miles. Unlike most women emigrants, Eells could be blunt, and her journal entry for July 23 refers to "the most filthy Indians we have seen . . . many of them are as naked as when born." The next day she wrote peevishly: "Scenery awful. . . . We often say that this journey is like going to sea on dry land." Fort Boise, in mid-August, was no better: "A restless night; the dogs bark, the wolves prowl, the horses take fright and break loose, some of the men about the Fort have a spree, the wind blew our tent over, the Indians about are watching for an opportunity to take whatever they could get."[23] In spite of the hardships, Eells rode on.

Eliza and Henry Spalding were newlyweds when they struck out from New York with Dr. Marcus Whitman and his wife, Narcissa (also newlyweds), in February 1836. Adding a little spice to the situation was the fact that some years earlier Henry had proposed to Narcissa but had been rejected. Marcus had been sent west the year before by the Congregational and Presbyterian churches, and he had attended the 1835 Rendezvous.

After traveling up the Missouri by steamboat, the

Whitman-Spalding party reached the Loup Fork of the Platte River, where they fell under the protection of the American Fur Company's spring caravan, headed by mountain man Thomas "Broken Hand" Fitzpatrick, then en route to the summer Rendezvous. On July 4 the party crossed South Pass, where Eliza noted simply, "Crossed a ridge of land they called the divide." Not a word was recorded of the fact that she and Narcissa were the first two white women to cross the pass to the Pacific. On July 6 Eliza wrote, "Arrived at the Rendezvoux this evening. Were met by a large party of the Nez Percés, men, women, and children. The women were not satisfied short of saluting Mrs. Whitman and myself with a kiss." What Eliza doesn't describe is the wildness of the welcome: thundering horses, rifle shots in the air, bloodcurdling war whoops, daredevil riding, and general pandemonium as the Indians showed their enthusiasm for the new missionaries who were coming to serve them.

Arriving at last, on September 3, at Fort Walla Walla on the Columbia River—after a seven-month journey—the couples were assigned to different missions, the Whitmans going to Waiilatpu some twenty-five miles from Fort Walla Walla to minister to the Cayuse tribe, and the Spaldings to the Nez Percé. On November 28, 1836, Eliza recorded their arrival "at this desirable spot, where we expect to dwell the remainder of our earthly pilgrimage," but some curious restraint kept her from confiding until December 3, even to her journal, that on November 15 she had delivered a baby girl, also named Eliza.[24]

Over the next decade at Waiilatpu, the Whitmans built a sanctuary for emigrants in difficulty, with a school for Indian and other children, a flour mill, blacksmith shop, corral, farm plots, storage, and other facilities. Meanwhile, Narcissa Whitman had also delivered a child, and the two women, living at separate missions many miles apart, set a daily fixed hour when they could simultaneously "observe a season of special prayer" for their infants.

The doctor and his wife developed their little Waiilatpu Mission as an outpost of Christian civilization, serving the Cayuse with a devotion that seemed to be appreciated. Converts were made, and the needs of both Indians and missionaries were accommodated. But in the fall of 1847 a hitherto benevolent Providence seemed to turn against Waiilatpu when a virulent measles epidemic swept the settlement, killing perhaps half the Cayuse in a matter of months. Dr. Whitman's treatments of sick Indian children were often counteracted by the native cures of sweat huts followed by cold plunges, with the result that many Indians died but few white children succumbed. Because of this, Whitman was considered to be a dangerous medicine man, or *te-wat,* and as such could rightfully be killed by a relative of any deceased person he had treated. The Cayuse also grew suspicious that the Whitmans were poisoning them in order to take over their property, and these groundless fears were fanned by a half-breed named Joe Lewis and other hostile members of the mission community.

In late November 1847, seventy-five people lived at Waiilatpu: twenty men, ten women, and forty-five children under the age of eighteen. This included the two Whitmans; seven Sagers (the Whitmans' foster children, whose parents had died on the trail west);

Jim Bridger's daughter, Mary Ann, age eleven; mountain man Joe Meek's daughter, Helen Mar Meek, age ten; and Eliza Spalding, age ten. On November 29 the residents were at work, scattered among various mission buildings: the main Mission House, the Emigrant House, the blacksmith shop, the Sawmill Cabin, and an Indian lodge. Also on the mission grounds were Chief Tiloukaikt, Tamsucky, Tomahas, Clokamus, Isaklome (or Wet Wolf), and Joe Lewis. It was on that day that Cayuse suspicion and anger erupted in a bloodbath that engulfed the mission.

Catherine Sager, thirteen at the time, lived through the entire horror and supplied probably the fullest account in a reminiscence written many years later. She described the main Mission House on that Monday as a hospital bulging at the seams with sick children and adults, upstairs and down. In the living room Catherine and her sister Elizabeth were in a tub being bathed by Narcissa Whitman. Catherine described the scene: "Mother started for the pantry for milk for the youngest child. The kitchen was full of Indians. One demanded milk. She told him to wait until she could give her baby some. He followed her to the door of the sitting room and tried to force his way in, but she shut the door in his face and bolted it. The Indian called loudly for the Doctor and she said, 'Doctor, You are wanted.' Father went out, telling her to bolt the door after him."[25]

In the kitchen Dr. Whitman found John Sager (age seventeen) and Mary Ann Bridger, who was washing dishes, as well as a noisy crowd of Indians including Tiloukaikt, Tamsucky, and Tomahas. When the doctor sat down to talk with Tiloukaikt, apparently Tomahas came up behind and struck Whitman on the head with a club:

> As he started forward he was shot in the neck. . . . It is true that old Teiloukite chopped the Doctor's face so badly that his features could not be recognized. . . . My brother John Sager was making brooms when Dr. Whitman was attacked and in an effort to prevent what was happening made an attempt to defend him with a pistol. There was such a crowd when he was attempting to take aim an Indian caught him and held him by the arm while another shot him, and he fell at the same time as the Doctor.

Mary Ann Bridger ran screaming from the kitchen into the living room, where she calmed down long enough to tell Mrs. Whitman that her husband was dead. Mrs. Whitman dragged the bleeding doctor, barely alive, into the living room. "She asked him if he knew her. 'Yes.' 'Are you badly hurt?' 'Yes.' 'Can I do anything to stop this blood?' 'No.' 'Can you speak with me?' 'N-no.' 'Is your mind at peace?' 'Yes.'"

Everyone had rushed upstairs and fastened the door. Outside there were shouts, people running, shots fired. Narcissa went to the window. "A rifle shot echoed through the clearing and Mother fell back, her hand clutching her shoulder, gasping. Blood spotted the wall and floor." A short time later Tamsucky came upstairs and persuaded Narcissa, Andrew Rodgers, and some of the children to come down, saying they must leave the house at once as the Indians were going to burn it down. As they left the kitchen and walked into the yard, carrying the injured Narcissa on a settee, Rodgers realized Tamsucky's treachery, threw up his hands, cried "Oh, my God!" and was instantly shot down. "Mrs. Whitman," Catherine continued, "was shot through the face by a blood-crazed savage as she lay helpless on the settee. Every groan made by the sufferers was answered by blows from clubs. One Indian snatched at Mrs. Whitman's hair, holding her while another calmly took aim and shot at her. . . . When they were satisfied that she was dead, they threw her into the mud and left."

In the first twenty-four hours of the melee nine people suffered agonizing deaths; four more would die in the following week. There were a few fortunate escapes. Henry Spalding had gone on a trip to the Umatilla River with Marcus Whitman and was to have returned with him to Waiilatpu on November 28. But Spalding had been injured when his horse rolled on him and thus was obliged to put off his return—a delay that saved his life. John Mix Stanley, the noted western artist, had been at Waiilatpu a few weeks earlier and was returning to the mission when word of the massacre reached his camp not far from Waiilatpu. Peter Hall escaped under cover of dark, made his way to Fort Walla Walla to report the massacre, and then disappeared forever, presumed to have drowned while crossing the Deschutes River. W. D. Canfield also eluded death at Waiilatpu. He was butchering a beef outdoors when the killing began, and he was shot in the side. Nevertheless, he gathered up his family, secured them indoors, and that night set out alone and afoot on a 120-mile trip to warn Eliza Spalding at the Lapwai Mission. The Osborn family saved themselves by hiding under the floorboards of the Mission House, where they spent the night listening to the groans of the dying Andrew Rodgers above them. Rodgers's last words were "Come Lord Jesus, come quickly!" and faintly, soon after, "Sweet Jesus." Then silence.

After the massacre the surviving men, women, and children were held captive for a month. Lorinda Bewley was demanded as wife by Chief Five Crows, and when she rejected him with some rather blunt talk, she was dragged off to his lodge by force. Eventually Peter Skene Ogden, factor at the Hudson's Bay Company at Fort Vancouver, ransomed the survivors and arranged for their passage down the Columbia River to Fort Vancouver and then to Portland. Troops were sent into Cayuse country by Governor Joseph Lane of the Oregon Territory to bring the guilty to justice. Although Joe Lewis, the agent provocateur in the affair, escaped arrest, five Indians—Tiloukaikt, Tomahas, Clokamus, Left Hand, and Wet Wolf—were brought in, identified by Catherine Sager at their trial, and condemned to die. Although they requested to be shot—alleging they had shot their victims at Waiilatpu—they met death on the scaffold on June 3, 1850.

5 THE MORMON TRAIL

OF ALL THE TRAILS THAT OPENED THE WEST, the Mormon Trail alone had a specifically religious purpose: to lead to a land governed by the spiritual doctrine of the Church of Jesus Christ of Latter-day Saints, or Mormons. Church tradition holds that this doctrine was engraved in ancient tongues on tablets of gold buried in the earth long ago. The tablets were revealed by an angel on the evening of September 21, 1823, in Palmyra, New York, to eighteen-year-old Joseph Smith. Miraculous powers bestowed upon Joseph later enabled him to translate the tablets' inscriptions, and in 1830 they were published as the *Book of Mormon.* This text, subtitled *Another Testament of Jesus Christ,* is what would sustain Mormon hearts on their grueling trek to Utah.

Attempting to flee persecution for their beliefs, the Mormons moved westward in three main stages: first from Kirtland, Ohio, to Nauvoo, Illinois (with much backing and forthing across Missouri in between), and then from Nauvoo to Winter Quarters (site of modern Florence, Nebraska). The third stage took them from Winter Quarters to the valley of the Great Salt Lake. This part, generally considered the crux passage of the Mormon Trail, was opened in 1847 by Mormon Prophet Brigham Young and his Pioneer Company of 148 Latter-day Saints, searching for a place to establish their holy kingdom, the New Zion. Earlier, Young and his Council of Twelve Elders had weighed several options as to where New Zion might be established: "somewhere in the Rockies"; farther west in California; or even on Vancouver Island.

DEVIL'S GATE, WYOMING, *1992. Photograph by Randall A. Wagner.*

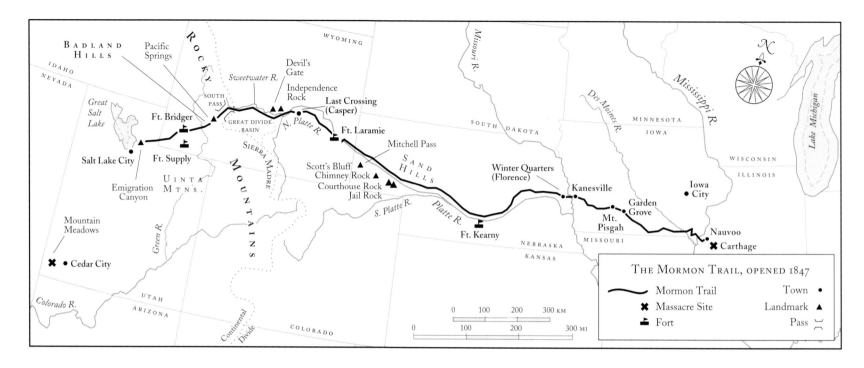

The Mormon Trail, opened 1847

~~~ Mormon Trail   Town •
✖ Massacre Site   Landmark ▲
⚓ Fort   Pass ⊃⊂

Ultimately they came down in favor of the Rockies, and the final trail began when the company pulled out of Winter Quarters on April 17; it terminated in the valley of the Great Salt Lake on July 24, 1847. On that historic day Brigham Young, weak from mountain fever, was carried to the mouth of the last of the many canyons they had penetrated (later named Emigration Canyon) and, tradition has it, gratefully announced, "This is the right place!"

It was a prophetic utterance in more ways than one. The Great Salt Lake Valley was not only a favorable environment for the Latter-day Saints but Salt Lake City would one day sit astride the routes of the Pony Express, the Transcontinental Telegraph, and the Transcontinental Railroad, becoming a nexus of the western trail system.

THE PROPHETS

No firmly authenticated photograph of Joseph Smith is known to exist, but verbal descriptions offer an imposing and charismatic portrait. A strapping six feet two inches tall and weighing well over two hundred pounds, Smith took pride in both his physical strength and his powers of moral suasion. His rather triangular face was dominated by a broad brow and compelling, wide-set eyes that seemed to glow with sparks from some supernatural forge. The same year the *Book of*

Joseph Smith, founder of Mormonism, was murdered in jail at Carthage, Illinois, in 1844. This is said to be a rare "photograph of the Prophet," though its authenticity has never been verified.

Mormon was published, 1830, Smith gathered around him five like-minded associates in Fayette, New York, and together they formed the Church of Jesus Christ (later renamed the Church of Jesus Christ of Latter-day Saints). In a spiritual sense, Fayette might be said to represent the point of origin of the Mormon Trail. From these first six members, the Mormon church—eventually guided by a complex hierarchy of Apostles, Elders, and Bishops, with Smith as the first Prophet—has grown to its present global membership of over nine million people.

Although Smith's congregation grew rapidly, his career following the founding of his church was marred by controversy and violence as he sought to lead his Saints to the promised New Zion. Paradoxically, the very traits he demanded of members—cleanliness, virtue, industry, and uncompromising obedience to a church that dominated both spiritual and temporal life—made the Mormon community at once envied by and suspect to its Gentile neighbors. The Saints' stiff-necked assertion that their religious precepts were the only ones that assured salvation, coupled with the rumor that some Saints practiced polygamy, added fuel to the fires of resentment.

Smith and his people became virtual pariahs for years, driven back and forth by mobs across Illinois, Missouri (Smith was jailed in both states), and Ohio, where he was tarred and feathered. On October 27, 1838, Governor Lilburn Boggs of Missouri issued an order to his militia directing them to either drive the Mormons out of Missouri or exterminate them. Three days later the militia, really an armed mob two hundred strong, massacred seventeen Mormon men, women, and children at Haun's Mill. Subsequent riots and armed conflict between Mormons and Gentiles caused many deaths and deepened bitter feelings on both sides. Finally, in 1844, the state of Illinois granted the Mormons a charter to establish a city at Nauvoo; it seemed that the Promised Land was at hand and the site of New Zion delivered. Within two years Nauvoo, once a swamp, became the most flourishing city in Illinois. Too flourishing, at least to suit its envious neighbors.

The year 1844 proved to be a fateful one for the Prophet and his Saints. It started off with great promise: in March, Smith was ordained and crowned King of the Kingdom of God by his secret Council of Fifty, and in May he was nominated in convention as a candidate for the presidency of the United States. Hardly a month later, on June 27, Smith and his brother Hyrum were murdered by militiamen at the Carthage, Illinois, jail. The Latter-day Saints hierarchy quickly designated a replacement: Brigham Young.

Young was born in 1801 in Whitingham, Vermont—a Green Mountain boy, as his friend and mentor Joseph Smith had been. Young came from humble beginnings—with only eleven days of formal schooling—yet he became a shrewd and highly successful businessman, as well as president of the Mormon church for thirty years, governor of Utah Territory for six, superintendent of Indian affairs for six, and founder of more than 250 Mormon settlements.

During the 1850s and 1860s many prominent visitors—Horace Greeley, Richard Burton (the English explorer and soldier), and the humorist Artemus Ward, among others—flocked to Salt Lake City, all curious to see for themselves whether this fabled Mormon leader was a charlatan or a saint. Their composite portrait probably yields a reasonable likeness of Young in his prime: a man "of moderate height"; "portly"; "calm"; "composed"; possessed of "the plain simple manners of honesty"; "clear, sharp eyes and . . . hard, firmly set lips"; with auburn hair, a bass voice, and the appearance of "a gentleman farmer in New England" who seemed to "enjoy life and be in no particular hurry to get to heaven." Ward, who apparently observed Young attending a dance and a play, considered "the Prophet more industrious than graceful as a dancer" and reported that in the theater "Brigham Young usually sits in the middle of the parquette in a rocking chair and with his hat on."

Although a Methodist in his youth, Young had been deeply impressed by the various Mormon spokesmen who spread Joseph Smith's gospel in upstate New York, and he was baptized into the Church of Jesus Christ of Latter-day Saints in 1832, just two years after its formation. First with his family and then on his own, the young future Prophet moved from place to place, working when he could as a painter, glazier, furniture maker, farmer, mason, day laborer, and even boat builder. His proficiency in all these practical crafts, his lack of formal education, and his zeal for Zion matched experiences common to most of his followers, creating a bond of solidarity between Young and his Saints based on the perception that he was one of them. This sense of unity proved invaluable when he led them west to build a civilization in the Utah wilderness.

After the death of his first wife, Miriam, Brigham remarried in 1834, and by the time of his death at seventy-six is said to have accumulated at least nineteen wives and probably as many as fifty-five. A number of them, he once remarked, were old ladies he regarded as mothers rather than wives, whom he had wed because they needed financial and familial support. Be that as it may, the certainty is that he sired one of the largest families ever recorded in America.

Probably fewer than 80 percent of Mormon men adhered to the orthodoxy of plural marriages (or polygamy, as it is broadly referred to), which had been initiated by Smith. (His first wife, Emma, argued with him over this issue.) Polygyny (one husband, several simultaneous wives) was far more common among the Saints than polyandry (one wife, several husbands). Despite the sensationalist jibes of the non-Mormon press and politicians, polygyny as practiced by the Mormon community from 1840 to 1890 did not create harems for satyrs and philanderers. Rather, it was a workaday response to plain necessity: building and sustaining the Kingdom required many hands, and there was a need to create fresh generations of Mormons in a hurry.

Plural marriages (sealed for time and eternity in a church ritual) were solemnized by Mormon covenants that imposed stringent responsibilities on the husband to provide food, clothing, and shelter for the new wife and her children. Many a widow, having lost her husband on the trail west, landed in New Zion exhausted, ill, and utterly destitute. Under such circumstances, polygyny—which even Brigham Young objected to at first—offered a workable solution. However, after the practice was openly acknowledged from the pulpit in 1852, the public's antagonism toward polygamy, as they saw it, sullied both the Mormon image and Young's reputation, weighing heavily in his failure to win reappointment as governor of Utah in 1854 and in delaying statehood to Utah. Not until 1890 was the practice officially prohibited, by Wilford Woodruff, then president of the church. Even so, it took six more years before Utah was admitted to the Union as the forty-fifth state.

EXODUS: NAUVOO TO WINTER QUARTERS

In January 1845, barely six months after Young succeeded Joseph Smith as head of the Mormon church, the state of Illinois responded to Gentile pressures by revoking the Mormon charter for the city of Nauvoo. The state's reversal came as a blow to Young and his Council of Twelve Elders, but to avoid further bloodshed they made an agreement that autumn to leave Nauvoo "as soon as grass is green and water runs." The springtime evacuation of Nauvoo was planned with the usual Mormon attention to detail, and John C. Frémont's reports on his western explorations and Lansford W. Hastings's *Emigrants' Guide to Oregon and California* were read and reread.

But local hostility festered to the point that the departure date had to be frantically advanced. What had been planned as an orderly withdrawal turned into a rout, or close to it, as thousands of Mormon men, women, and children abandoned their homes, farms, businesses, and community. The first wagons pulled out of Nauvoo on February 4, 1846, some reportedly crossing the Mississippi on solid ice in twelve-below-zero weather. The exiles set up a tent city on the west side of the Mississippi at Sugar Creek, Iowa, then continued across Iowa to Kanesville (now Council Bluffs, Iowa).

Having fought their way out of Missouri and Illinois, in the rain-soaked spring of 1846 the Mormon trains slogged across Iowa, with wagons, animals, and people getting mired in the prairie gumbo, heavy as lead. All along the trail from Nauvoo to Winter Quarters, sickness and death stalked the emaciated Saints. Typhoid, whooping cough, scurvy, and more ambiguous ailments such as the "bloody flux" and "black canker" did not always respond to the chief Mormon remedies: anointing with sacred oils, rebuking of the illness by one of the Apostles, and the laying on of hands.

It took the Mormons four wearying months to work their way from Nauvoo, on the Mississippi, to Council Bluffs on the east bank of the Missouri River, and then to Winter Quarters on the west bank. But mingled with the bad times were signs that the Lord had not forsaken them: timely thunderstorms that doused threatening prairie fires and a covey of quail that darkened the sky and rained down upon the famished Saints like manna from heaven. In an amazing display of vitality, new settlements were started at Garden Grove and farther west at Mount Pisgah, with cabins built, gardens planted, bridges erected, and ferries established. During most of 1846 some sixteen thousand Saints, a virtual city on wheels, made this painful crossing.

During their stay at Winter Quarters in eastern Nebraska (1846–47), six hundred Mormons died of illness and accidents—including two of Brigham Young's wives and one of his little sons. The encampment hunkered down while Young and his council made plans for a group to make their way to the Great Salt Lake Valley in the spring and spy out land for the New Zion. In the interim Young and his followers remained at Winter Quarters, where they built 621 log and sod dwellings for about thirty-five hundred people and waited anxiously for spring.

Above: WILFORD WOODRUFF, *1853. Daguerreotype by Marsena Cannon.*

The intensity of the Mormon spirit shows in the face of Wilford Woodruff, one of Brigham Young's staunch supporters.

Opposite, left: A DESERTED NAUVOO, *1846. Daguerreotype by Lucian Foster.*

A majestic Mormon Temple rises above the empty streets of Nauvoo, Illinois, in 1846, the year the Mormons were driven from the town.

Back at Nauvoo, the 150 or so Mormons who had been left behind to sell off their property were violently harassed by non-Mormon gangs who took over the city. In a letter to Elder Franklin Richards, who was on missionary duty in England, Thomas Bullock described the scenes of Gentile brutality. A few months later Young's non-Mormon friend Thomas Kane passed through a desolate and ravaged Nauvoo, the great temple and its baptismal font defiled and in shambles. Once proud Nauvoo, the shining city on the hill, had been sacked as surely as Rome or Carthage. Clearly the New Zion was still to be discovered, somewhere farther west, and the eviction from Nauvoo only stiffened the Mormon determination to find it.

Above: Frederick Hawkins Piercy. RUINS OF NAUVOO TEMPLE, *1853. From Piercy's* Route from Liverpool to Great Salt Lake Valley, *1855.*

Piercy's on-site sketch testifies to the ruined grandeur of the Mormon Temple at Nauvoo, seven years after its forced abandonment.

On April 14, 1847, the Pioneer Company started west from Winter Quarters. The 148 or so Saints—mostly vigorous young men but also including three women, two children, and six or so black servants, several of whom were baptized Mormons—were in search of a New Zion. According to the journal of Thomas Bullock, official historian of the Pioneer Company, the mile-long train (sometimes spread five wagons abreast for quicker corralling in case of emergency) comprised seventy-two wagons, sixty-six oxen, nineteen cows, seventeen dogs, and some chickens. Led by Brigham Young and his Council of Twelve Elders, this Pioneer Company was the advance party and pride of Mormonism, the first wave of Mormon migration across the Great Basin to the Rockies and the first large body of Saints to cross South Pass.

Their route to South Pass was not too difficult since it retraced a course followed by earlier Oregon-California Trail wagons and described by Frémont in his 1843 exploration report. For over eight hundred miles after leaving Winter Quarters, the wagons followed the north bank of the Platte River and rumbled along the bed of a long-vanished sea so gradually uptilted that the ox teams scarcely bowed their massive necks. The Mormons had chosen the north bank in order to avoid the antagonistic Gentile traffic bound for Oregon and California on the south bank; being less traveled, the north bank also promised better grass for the stock.

The Saints had turned their faces away from the hostile East, but would the Great Salt Lake Valley smile on them at the end of the trail? The mountain men Moses "Black" Harris and Jim Bridger would say "No!" when they met Young on the trail only a day or two after his company had left Pacific Springs, the first watering place on the western side of the pass. The skeptical Bridger offered to pay Young one thousand dollars for the first bushel of corn grown there. Even Father Pierre Jean De Smet—the knowledgeable Belgian Jesuit priest who had ridden his mule around the western wilderness almost as many miles as covered by Frémont and Jed Smith put together—had stopped at Council Bluffs that winter and spoken dubiously about the valley to the Mormon leader and his counselors.

Undeterred, Young kept the Saints moving, having organized them into companies of ten, fifty, and one hundred, with lead wagons rotated daily so no one ate dust day after day. He saw to it that each morning at five o'clock the company was roused by trumpet call, and he thereafter issued the orders of march in minute detail, requiring a man with a loaded rifle to walk on the off side of every wagon, every gun to have a piece of leather over the nipple, with caps and powder flasks ready at a moment's warning. Young did not spare himself, and in Pawnee country he and Heber Kimball, perhaps his most trusted counselor, took first watch on guard duty. Special committees were designated for hunting, trail marking, and road improvement. Everyone had an assignment, everyone felt personally essential to the company's higher purpose. Taking everything into account, the Pioneer Company was probably the best-supplied, best-armed, and most trail-experienced group to go west up till then.

Even so, being led by a determined man armed with a dream probably made all the difference.

Despite the tight organization, the usual run of trail misadventures took their toll. One of the brethren accidentally discharged his gun, striking Young's horse in the belly and killing it; another Saint knocked the eye out of a friend's ox while chopping down a tree; rattlesnakes buried their fangs indiscriminately in the legs of men and the noses of animals; and worse, apostasies occurred in significant numbers. Platte River crossings had been the scene of many accidents, with wagons slowly cartwheeling over and over in the rushing waters. Harriet Crow, one of the Mississippi Saints who had joined the company at Fort Laramie in June, was run over by a wagon but survived unhurt—a bit of good fortune taken as another sign and portent.

Trail life for the Saints had its moments of bounty: babies were safely born in the wagons or by the trailside; May and June flooded the prairie with wildflowers, and masses of wild strawberries left scarlet stains on the shoes of men and women trudging patiently beside their animals, matching a deeper red

FORDING THE RIVER NEAR FORT SEDGWICK, COLORADO TERRITORY, *1867. Photograph by Savage and Ottinger.*

A Mormon wagon train of 1867 threads its way through the treacherous quicksands of the South Platte River, where Nebraska and Colorado Territory met. Frustrated emigrants often described the Platte as "a thousand miles long and six inches deep."

from cracked and blistered feet. And in May, too, there was the first buffalo hunt, with twelve bison killed. In his journal William Clayton eulogized the meat as "sweet and tender as veal,"[1] although some might smile skeptically at that judgment, knowing that hunger is better than a French chef.

All across Nebraska that summer the industrious and needy Saints found work to do for others, hiring out to split rails, clear land, shuck corn, and give evening concerts with their band in return for provisions. Near present-day Casper, Wyoming, the Mormon advance party camped on the swollen North Platte close to two companies of Oregon-bound Missourians who needed a way to cross over before the river rose any farther. Rejoicing that man's extremity is God's opportunity, the Saints used their large leather boat, whimsically called the "Revenue Cutter," to transport the travelers' loads to the far side. For this service they received payment in flour, a most useful commodity, especially at a price that worked out to $7.50 less per pound than the going rate at Fort Laramie, where they could sell it for a profit. To transport the 108 wagons themselves, the resourceful Mormons built a huge ferry from cottonwoods planked together and worked all night in the chill water to get the wagons across—for a good fee. Mindful of others coming up rapidly from the rear, Young left a crew in charge of the ferry operation and continued on his way with a heavier pocketbook and a heart no doubt made lighter because his profit had been paid by Missourians, whose state had earlier cost him such pain.

On the north side of the Platte River, near Fort Laramie, the Saints left a mileage sign penciled on a post and plank to mark their passage from Winter Quarters. Such primitive milestones, often established by Brother Orson Pratt's calculations based on celestial observations, were planted along the entire way, establishing for the first time accurate distances between points and sometimes correcting Frémont's earlier estimates. This improvement was due mainly to William Clayton—company clerk, musician, director of the Saints' band, and later author of *The Latter-day Saints' Emigrants' Guide* (1848). After

Opposite: MITCHELL PASS, *1990. Photograph by Randall A. Wagner.*

Mitchell Pass, in present-day Nebraska, still bears traces of the passage of Mormon Saints.

ORSON PRATT, *c. 1880. Photograph by Charles W. Carter.*

Orson Pratt, Mormon Apostle and scientific advisor to Brigham Young, took celestial observations for the Pioneer Company en route to Great Salt Lake Valley.

walking behind a wagon wheel for days, laboriously counting its rotations per mile, Clayton decided there had to be an easier way and invented the odometer, a system of wooden cogs attached to a wagon wheel, to count the revolutions and measure the mileage covered each day. According to his calculations, Fort Laramie was 543¼ miles from Winter Quarters. By the time they reached South Pass, the Pioneer Company had traveled 818¾ miles from Winter Quarters. On the way to South Pass the Saints marveled at the land's natural wonders: Chimney Rock, the slender rock spire that soared up from the plains, pointing to heaven like the finger of God; Independence Rock; and then Devil's Gate, where even the sober Saints had briefly turned excursionists, climbing the Gate's steep walls, rolling rocks off the top, and firing guns to laugh at the echoes. The place was more aptly named than they could have imagined at the time. A few years later at that very spot scores of Saints

would perish in the worst disaster in the history of western migration.

There was ample time on the long trail for the Mormon leader's thoughts to turn to his several wives. Clary, a relatively new bride whom he had married when she was sixteen, traveled with him in the Pioneer Company; his third wife, Mary (mother of his sons Joseph and Brigham, Jr.), waited for him back in Winter Quarters. He had sent her a long, and for him tender, letter by express courier his first week out:

> 9 o'clock pm April 20, 1847
> Pioneer Camp of Israel 95 miles from
> Winter Quarters
> My dear Companion Partner in Tribulation. . . .
> I lade abed and thought a grate deal I should like to say to you. . . . I due think the Lord has blest me with one of the best famelyes that eney man ever had on earth. I due hope the children will be good and mind there mother when I am gon. My son Joseph you *must not go away from home* and Brigham also must stay at home. How due you sapose I would feele when I come home and find one of my children destroyed by the Indens? I pray this may not be the case. . . . On Saturday last we saw buffalow for the first time. They went on a chase after them, the got 4 old ones and 5 calfs which has made us plenty of meat. . . . We shall have to cross the Platt River here on acount of feed. The prairie is all burnt over on the north side of the River—the Pawneas have gone ahead of us and burned. . . .
>
> —Brigham Young[2]

A month later Young revealed a different side of his nature, blistering his company with a tongue-lashing penitently noted in their journals by Bullock, Clayton, and Wilford Woodruff. Even brief extracts from Woodruff's account give a sense of the fire-and-brimstone style that Young adopted when he felt it necessary:

I am about to revolt from travelling with this camp any further with the spirit they now possess. I had rather risk myself among the savages with ten men that are men of faith, men of mighty prayer men of God, than to be with this whole Camp when they forget God & turn there hearts to folley & wickedness. . . .

For A week past nearly the whole camp has been card playing, chequres & dominoes have occupied the Attention of the brethren dancing & Nigering & hoeing down. . . . If these things are suffered to go on it will be but a short time befor you will be fighting knocking each other down & taking life & it is high time it was stoped. . . . What did you do when you went to seek out Zion, & find A resting place for the Saints whare the Standard of the Kingdom of God would be reared & her banners unfurled for the nations to gather unto? [Did] you spend A good deal of your time in dancing pitching quate, Jumping wrastleing &c? Yes. Yes. Did you play Cards, dice, checkers & dominoes? O! Yes. What Could you do with yourself? Why you would shrink from the glance of the eyes of God Angels & men even wicked men. Then are you not ashamed of yourselves for practicing these things? Yes you are & you must quit it.[3]

Young then called upon the Twelve, the High Priests, and the Elders to humble themselves and to renew their covenants by raising their right hands as a pledge. Clayton recorded that the sermon had administered a moral and spiritual catharsis, through which "we had emerged into a new element, a new atmosphere, a new society."

After leaving South Pass, Young headed the company southwest to Fort Bridger, where his men traded some of their firearms for buckskin clothes before continuing on the final one hundred miles to the valley of the Great Salt Lake. Only five days out of Bridger, however—about the time they crossed Bear River—Young and several others fell ill with mountain fever (now thought to be Colorado tick fever). Probably picked up at Fort Bridger, the affliction was marked by blinding headaches and by sharp pains in the spine and joints that made travel in a jolting wagon real torture. Chills and fevers swept Young, interspersed with waves of delirium, and he was unable to leave Woodruff's carriage. On July 17 Woodruff noted in his journal: "Br. Young is vary poorly this morning," and on the eighteenth Heber Kimball called an emergency meeting at which he urged sending an advance party to the valley in search of a suitable place to plant the first crops, while the rest stayed with their ailing leader.

Orson Pratt's advance party took the lead in searching out the last section of the trail down into the valley; part of the trail, Reed's Cutoff, had been cut through the rough canyon forests the year before by the westbound Donner Party. In only six days Pratt's party covered the thirty-six miles that the Donners had traversed in sixteen. For several days the advance party cleared the trail of boulders and stumps, slashing their way through willows twenty feet tall and filling the swampy canyon bottom with willow branches to make a makeshift corduroy road for the wagons. Canyon Creek was crossed eleven times in a single day, and wagon covers were shredded by the heavy brush. Clayton, in something of an understatement, confided to his journal, "This is truly a wild looking place!" On July 22, having climbed to the top of the hill, he saw Salt Lake sparkling in the distance and was moved to describe the view as "one of the most beautiful valleys and pleasant places for a home for the Saints which could be found."[4]

Pratt and Erastus Snow were the first of the Pioneer Company to make their way into the valley, on July 21, 1847. Ground was broken and cleared at once, and within forty-eight hours a dam and irrigation ditches had been built and five acres planted in potatoes. On July 24, Brigham Young, still in Woodruff's carriage, was brought to the mouth of Emigration Canyon to gaze for the first time on the New Zion. According to tradition, the ailing leader announced, "This is the right place. Drive on!" Heber Kimball declared the next day, Sunday, July 25, "We have reached the promised land." Eight days after entering the valley the Mormons had consecrated the land, blessed the seeds, broken fifty-three acres of ground, and planted forty-two of those acres with potatoes, corn, buckwheat, oats, and beans. In addition to the dam and irrigation ditches, they had laid out a forty-acre temple plot and begun a survey for the future city of Salt Lake. The company had come 1,032 miles from Winter Quarters in a hundred days and—remarkably—not a man, woman, child, horse, mule, ox, cow, or chicken had perished on the journey (except for Young's horse, which had been shot by accident). Young had indeed led his people to their land, as he had promised. Under the circumstances, it seemed only fitting that during the winter of 1847–48 he was "sustained" as Prophet, Seer, and Revelator of the Latter-day Saints.

By the beginning of August 1847 some 450 people inhabited the new settlement in Great Salt Lake Valley. Later that same month Young, the Council of Twelve, and others left the valley to return to Winter

SALT LAKE TEMPLE SQUARE, *1893. Photograph by Charles W. Carter.*

After forty years of construction, the great Mormon Temple towers over Temple Square in Salt Lake City, as it nears completion at the turn of the century.

Quarters, leaving behind only three hundred Saints to continue the intensive farming and building before the early mountain winter set in. Writing on September 8 from a camp twenty miles east of South Pass to his young wife Clary, whom he had left in Salt Lake Valley, the generally formal Young commented with unusual warmth: "You have been a grate comfort to me this summer. I miss your society." His nineteen-year-old wife replied in a long letter brimming with tenderness, housewifely solicitude, and local news:

My Dear Brigham
. . . I felt very lonesome after you left it seemed to me I was a lone child though in a pleasant land everything I saw reminded me of you and your goodness to one who feels herself quite unworthy of it. . . . I put your clothes away and every thing else you wished me to as soon as you left. I will aire your clothes when they need it your little desk sits on a shelf beside the looking glass it shall not be disturbed. . . . May heaven's choicest blessings ever attend you is the prayer of your friend
Yours affectionately
Clara C. Young[5]

Returning to Winter Quarters, Young and his party unexpectedly crossed trails with a westbound group of some two thousand Saints, known to Mormon historians as the Big Company, led by Parley Pratt, John Taylor, and John Young. By the end of 1848 five thousand residents filled Salt Lake City. Young himself led a company back to the valley that same year, and this time he stayed, never to leave Utah again.

By 1870 a total of eighty thousand Saints had trekked to the Mormon capital over the Mormon Trail, with six thousand having died on the way. Emigrants were given a joyous welcome. Brigham, some of the Apostles, and many citizens would often ride out on horseback and in carriages to greet the new arrivals at Emigration Canyon, bringing with them generous gifts of bread, melons, and cakes. Captain Pitt's Brass Band would play for dancing and singing by all, even the weatherbeaten, trail-weary newcomers. One woman Saint, who had walked barefoot every step of the way, then put on the slippers she had carried the entire trek so she could enter Zion with dignity.

THE MORMON WAR

Back east, President-elect James Buchanan, sniffing the political winds in 1856–57, detected public outrage at Mormon polygamy, at the concentration of civil and religious authority in the hands of Brigham Young, and at the high-handed way Mormons treated Washington's emissaries to Utah. Choosing to view this behavior as tantamount to rebellion, Buchanan dispatched twenty-five hundred troops to stamp it out. It was a politically motivated decision that he would regret.

Several thousand Saints were at Big Cottonwood Canyon, Utah, on July 24, 1857, celebrating the tenth anniversary of their entry into Zion, when Porter Rockwell galloped in with news of the advancing army. In response, Young quickly mobilized the Nauvoo Legion, or militia, and assigned harassing missions to Lot Smith and his guerrillas, who promptly burned down Fort

Frederick Hawkins Piercy.
SALT LAKE CITY IN 1853.
From Piercy's Route from Liverpool to Great Salt Lake Valley, *1855.*

Piercy's view of Salt Lake City only six years after Brigham Young and his people had entered the valley.

Supply and Fort Bridger, stampeded thousands of army cattle, and set fire to the prairie grass and seventy-two army supply wagons. (This last depredation caused enormous financial losses to Russell, Majors and Waddell, the later organizers of the Pony Express). In Tabernacle, Young announced a scorched-earth policy, thundering: "Not one building, nor one foot of lumber, nor a fence, nor a tree, nor a particle of grass or hay, that will burn, [will] be left in reach of our enemies."[6] Young did not have to carry out this threat immediately because, caught by bad weather, Colonel Albert Sidney Johnston wintered his troops one hundred miles short of Salt Lake City. The next spring, when Johnston planned to enter the city, Young withdrew thirty thousand Mormons to live for two months along the Provo River bottoms in lean-tos, tents, and dugouts, while in a deserted Salt Lake City, Nauvoo legionnaires were posted in houses stuffed with straw, poised to send Zion up in flames at a word from their Prophet.

But the political winds had shifted again. Buchanan backed off and extended a pardon to the Mormons in return for good behavior. Consequently, in June 1858, when Colonel Johnston marched his troops into Salt Lake City (guided by Peg-leg Smith and Jim Bridger), he kept on marching—right on out

the other side. As they filed quietly through town, one officer, Philip Saint George Cooke, doffed his cap in a respectful salute to the Mormon Battalion he had commanded ten years before on their epic march to San Diego.

Although not a shot had been fired, the expedition was criticized back east as a clumsy political maneuver by Buchanan. For Young and his followers, however, it proved a godsend. The Mormon community prospered from selling provisions to the army that had come to suppress them, and when the troops finally pulled out to go home in 1860, a four-million-dollar auction of army supplies and equipment enabled many Mormons to profit considerably, laying the foundation for several family fortunes. Once again, Mormon ingenuity had turned adversity into opportunity.

MASSACRE AT MOUNTAIN MEADOWS

All that anniversary summer of 1857, Brigham Young's Saints lived under the threat of extermination by the U.S. Army. As Colonel Johnston's troops advanced on Salt Lake City, reviving ugly memories of earlier militia killings of Saints in Illinois and Missouri, tensions had mounted in the Mormon redoubt. Memories of slaughter rose up from the ashes of the

ORRIN PORTER ROCKWELL, c. 1870s.

Though peace-loving people by precept, when persecuted the Mormons could fight fire with fire. The Sons of Dan, an enforcement group within the church, were sometimes called on to retaliate against hostile Gentiles. Orrin Porter Rockwell, frontiersman and Danite, once shot and wounded Lilburn Boggs, ex-governor of Missouri.

past, inflaming Mormon hearts and minds and summoning dark thoughts of atonement for such atrocities.

At the same time, local Indians were becoming restive, covetously eyeing the livestock and arms of emigrant trains passing through Salt Lake City before turning south to pick up the California Trail. Two trains—the Missouri Wildcats and the Fancher Train, numbering some 160 men, women, and children (reports vary as to the actual figures)—grew particularly abrasive to natives and Mormon settlers alike. Provocations proliferated: the Indians claimed that the emigrants had poisoned a well; one Missouri Wildcat brandished a gun that he claimed had killed Joseph Smith; and the Mormons, desperately conserving food in case of war, refused to sell supplies to the two trains; surly fistfights erupted. The Indians, whom Young said he would rather feed than fight, finally attacked the emigrants but were driven off. When asked for guidance by the Mormon settlers, Young counseled them to let the Missouri Wildcats and the Fancher train "go in peace" and sent his friend John Lee to calm the Indians. Although more Indian attacks followed, the Mormons refused to help the emigrants, leaving the two trains to huddle fearfully in an encampment at Mountain Meadows, thirty-five miles from Cedar City, holding the Indians at bay. The furious emigrants threatened to return from California someday and assassinate Brigham Young—an act that could have led to a devastating holy war.

At this point John Lee was induced to enter into a treacherous conspiracy between the Indians and some of the other Mormon settlers. Lured by an assurance of safe passage, the unarmed emigrants ventured out of their fortified camp in a single file. Women and children walked in front, a detachment of the Iron County Militia brought up the rear. At Lee's prearranged signal, "Halt!" Mormon settlers and Indians fell on the emigrant column. The carnage lasted only a few minutes, followed by the hollow silence of death, deepened by shame and horror. The official monument marking the Mountain Meadows tragedy records that of one hundred forty emigrants attacked, one hundred twenty-three died and seventeen children survived. The exact figures remain unknown.

When Lee later lied to Brigham Young, reporting that the slaughter had been perpetrated solely by the Indians, Young burst into tears. It took twenty years and two trials to bring Lee to justice, by which time most of the other witnesses and participants had disappeared. He was finally convicted by a Mormon jury, taken back to the scene of the massacre, and executed by a Mormon firing squad.

Today, a century and a half later, what remains important about the massacre at Mountain Meadows is not so much the identity of either the victims or the villains but rather the recognition that it was a tragic instance of religious zeal and discipline run amok. The horrifying episode of September 11, 1857, haunts the conscience of the Mormon community to this day.

THE HANDCART COMPANIES

Mormon Trail traffic increased greatly after 1849, when the church expanded its missionary activities and established the Perpetual Emigrating Fund (PEF). This transportation organization assisted poorer converts

C.C.A. Christensen. HANDCART
PIONEERS, *1903. Oil on canvas,
11 x 15 in. (27.9 x 38.1 cm). Museum of
Church History and Art, Salt Lake City.*

*Christensen painted a cheery picture of
the Mormon handcart pioneers on their
way to Zion. But in reality the thousand-
mile trek on foot—often barefoot—
hauling a three-hundred-pound cart was
so grueling an ordeal that one in ten
emigrants perished along the way.*

who wished to emigrate to the New Zion by providing low-cost ocean passage from Liverpool to New
Orleans, Boston, or New York. Transport from these
coastal cities varied, but out of Boston and New York
the newcomers usually continued by rail to Iowa City,
Iowa, or Florence, Nebraska, and then on by wagon,
or the cheaper handcart, to Great Salt Lake Valley.
The PEF sent some twenty-six thousand English and
European Mormons to New Zion between 1849 and
1887, a critical infusion into the Mormon melting pot.
The Mormon Trail of those years stretched all the way
from Liverpool to Salt Lake City, making it by far the
longest of any trail west.

Of all the emigrants who traveled west on any
trail the Mormon handcart companies were unques-
tionably the most desperate, the most committed,
and the most impressive. Predominantly church converts from Scandinavia and England, they were often
destitute victims of the Industrial Revolution who saw
a golden opportunity in the church's offer to pay their
passage to America at nine pounds sterling a head,
provided they signed a contract to pay it back through
labor once they reached Great Salt Lake Valley. Still,
many no doubt felt the same pangs recorded by Jane
Rio Griffiths—a forty-one-year-old widow of some
means and experience, who sailed out of Liverpool
on January 4, 1851. "I this day took leave of every
acquaintance I could collect together; in all human
probability never to see them again on earth. I am
now (with my children) about to leave for-ever my
Native Land, in order to gather with the Church of
Christ, in the Valley of the Great Salt Lake, in North
America." Eighteen years and many tribulations later,

an embittered Jane Griffiths described her life in Utah
as "a bubble that has burst in my grasp."[7]

The long pipeline from Liverpool to Salt Lake
was highly organized. In England church representatives chartered ship after ship and stationed themselves at the docks to tally and load the emigrants.
Passengers were divided into groups of one hundred,
with a captain designated for each company. The
routine at sea was also rigorously controlled: the new
Saints awakened to a bugle at 6:00 A.M., and bells
clanged at various times, calling them to morning and
evening prayer and to the tasks shared by all. Unmar-
ried men and women were segregated; the men often
sleeping on deck while cabins were occupied by women
and children. Meals were prepared by the passengers
in relays, each shift leaving the galley spotless for the
next. The discipline and cleanliness of Mormon ships
during the crossing greatly reduced the incidence of
disease and death compared with that among other
travelers, and Mormon ships became models for other
emigrant vessels. Crossings were often enlivened by
marriages and births, but sometimes darkened by death
and burials at sea. Jane Griffiths, on February 22,
noted sadly in her journal that her little son, Josiah,
had "breathed his last" and that his body was "committed to the deep, nearly a thousand miles from land,
there to remain till the word goes forth for the sea to
give up its dead, then shall I have my child again. . . .
Elder Booth conducted the service in Long. 44'/14
west, Lat. 25'/13 north."[8]

At Liverpool in the spring of 1856 Apostle Franklin D. Richards bustled around the docks overseeing
the departure of one ship after another, all loaded with

church converts. Passengers destined to become the first three handcart companies to cross into Zion had already shipped out, and now he was dispatching the fourth and fifth companies, but sending them off late—a lapse that was to provoke the gravest consequences at the other end of the six-thousand-mile journey. In New York, Apostle John Taylor awaited the newcomers, eager to hurry them by train to Iowa City, where they would be outfitted with supplies and the humble handcarts that they had so far heard little about. The handcart being simply a glorified wheelbarrow, there was actually little to say about it: a wooden box about four feet by four feet, with eight-inch sides, that rode an axle between two large wheels. Two shafts projecting forward from the box enabled a person walking between them to pull the cart along behind. The early handcarts were all of seasoned wood (those of the fourth and fifth handcart companies, unfortunately, were green), and some were fitted with bows and cotton covers, like miniature covered wagons.

Children rode inside on the bundled clothes, tents, and blankets, and an occasional cart had a tethered milch cow ambling in the rear. When a cart was fully loaded, the man between the shafts could find that he was hauling about four hundred pounds—over all kinds of terrain and in every sort of weather—for nearly fourteen hundred miles. Traveling under good conditions on dry, level ground, free of stumps and rocks, a cart could make ten to twenty miles a day, but the mileage fell off quickly with deep sand or spring muck underfoot, or with frequent river crossings. Still, most handcart companies made it through to Salt Lake relatively smoothly. Women often helped pull the carts to spell their flagging husbands, and one seventy-three-year-old woman in Handcart Company Number Three walked all the way.

The first three companies left Iowa City in June 1856 and arrived at Salt Lake in late September—a speedy journey of just under four months. But such an easy crossing was not to be the fate of the fourth and fifth handcart companies, captained by James Willie and Edward Martin, respectively. Willie's fourth company was late getting to Iowa City, where it was outfitted, and late again reaching Florence, where it was held up for cart repairs. The same held true for Martin's fifth company. The fourth company finally pulled out of Florence on August 18 with high hopes and good spirits, and the fifth company left a week later. The two companies were followed by two ox-drawn wagon trains captained by W. B. Hodgett and John A. Hunt. Willie's company was made up of 500 men, women, and children, organized into units of one hundred, while Martin's had 576, similarly organized. The companies' equipment included one handcart for approximately every five people, and one round tent for every twenty people. Bulk supplies, such as the ninety-eight-pound sacks of flour, were carried in the ox-drawn wagons and sparingly issued to handcarts as needed. Each person was restricted to seventeen pounds of clothing and bedding; individual food rations were limited to a half-pound of beef (on occasion), one pound of flour per day, and some molasses, sugar, bacon, and other items. The PEF members of the company, for the most part paupers, had to make do with these minimal provisions, but other members with greater means supplemented them with private supplies.

T.B.H. Stenhouse. THE HANDCART EMIGRANTS IN A STORM, *n.d. Denver Public Library, Western History Department.*

Stenhouse, a Mormon apostate, presented a realistically grim image of handcart emigrants crossing the plains in winter.

Trouble on the trail was not long in coming for the fourth and fifth companies. The extreme dryness of the plains made the cart wheels of green wood shrink and separate, and the dust ground away the axle shoulders; in desperation, the travelers used greased boot leather, soap, and finally bacon as makeshift (and ineffectual) lubricants. More serious problems awaited the companies near Grand Island, Nebraska, where a buffalo herd stampeded their cattle. A three-day search recovered only part of the ox teams, forcing a reduction in the beef ration and the hitching of a single yoke of oxen to each wagon. Since this was not enough to pull wagons loaded with three thousand pounds of flour, wagon trains were augmented by yoking up the beef cattle and milch cows. Loads were also redistributed and each handcart was now required to carry an additional ninety-eight-pound sack of flour. These measures, dictated by necessity, were a triple impediment to the company's efficiency of movement.

About September 1, Handcart Company Number Four pulled into Fort Laramie, where Captain Willie foresightedly bought several barrels of hard bread. He also took inventory and discovered that the group's flour and food would run out while they were still 350 miles from Salt Lake Valley. Willie, however, had been promised earlier by Apostle Richards (the same Richards who had seen the company off in Liverpool, overtaken them at Florence, Nebraska, and then passed them along the Platte) that fresh supplies would be sent out from Salt Lake to meet Willie's company at South Pass. Under the circumstances, Willie decided to go ahead. All belts tightened, the flour ration was first cut to three-fourths of a pound per day, then to ten ounces, and the little carts dragged forward, trying to move faster.

As the fourth company traveled up the Sweetwater they were also gradually climbing toward the summit of South Pass, over seven thousand feet high, where the cold grew so severe that their allotted seventeen pounds of clothing and bedding provided inadequate warmth. Fatigue, hunger, and cold began to take their toll among the sick and elderly, as John Chislett, captain of a hundred in Handcart Company Number Four,

wrote in his narrative: "Our old and infirm people began to droop, and they no sooner lost spirit and courage than death's stamp could be traced upon their features. Life went out as smoothly as a lamp ceases to burn when the oil is gone. . . . We soon thought unusual to leave a campground without burying one or more persons. . . . Many a father pulled his cart, with his little children on it, until the day preceding his death."[9]

Sixteen miles from a campsite farther west, where wood and water were available, the fourth company was astonished to see two young Saints out of Salt Lake, Stephen Taylor and Joseph A. Young (a son of Brigham's), ride up bringing glad tidings: supplies from the valley would reach them in a day or two. Hope flared up again, but a blizzard soon extinguished it by dumping a foot of snow overnight, killing five men and women. Supplies "in a day or two" was fine, but people were ravenous with hunger now. Broken-down cattle were butchered, eaten, and regretted after waves of dysentery added to the roster of the dead, dying, or those who wished they could die. Willie and a companion rode west to meet the incoming supply wagon and try to speed it up, while Young and Taylor continued east to find Martin's company, far back down the trail, and the Hodgett and Hunt wagon companies, which were even farther behind. Three days later, on October 21, the rescue party of several horse-drawn wagons from the valley rode into view, setting off a pandemonium of joy and relief. The night echoed with the laughter of heavy hearts suddenly made light, with songs of Zion, and with prayers of thanksgiving. But the trials were not yet over. Although the rescuers did all they could, building fires, cooking

Clark Kelly Price. THE MARTIN HANDCART CO., *1980. Oil on canvas, 36 x 48 in. (91.4 x 121.9 cm). Museum of Church History and Art, Salt Lake City.*

In 1856 two Mormon handcart companies, trapped by blizzards near South Pass, wrapped their dead in blankets and buried them in unmarked shallow graves on the frozen prairie.

meals, and distributing clothes and blankets, nine more people died that night.

Meanwhile, the fifth company lagged a hundred miles behind. Because of their failing strength, members of the company had lightened their loads by jettisoning almost half their clothing, including most of the heavy buffalo robes that Martin had procured for them at Fort Laramie. The Saints were now learning that they were at risk every single day that they traveled on the trail, and that each extra day escalated the risk as worsening cold, hunger, and exhaustion left them ever more vulnerable. Confronting the prospect of fording the Platte at Last Crossing, just west of present-day Casper, Wyoming, Captain Martin had few options: like it or not, the Platte had to be forded, no matter how frigid it was, no matter how frail the travelers. Patience Loader, a young woman of the fifth company who had buried her father on the trail a few weeks previously, told of the fording ordeal:

The water was very deep and cold and we was drifted out of the regular crossing and we came near being drounded the water came up to our arm pits poor Mother was standing on the bank screaming as we got near the bank I heard Mother say for God Sake some of you men help My poor girls. . . . Several of the breathren came down the bank of the river and pulled our cart up for us and we got up the best we could . . . when we was in the middle of the river I saw a poor brother carreying his child on his back he fell down in the water I never Knew if he was drowned or not I fealt

sorry that we could not help him but we had all we could do to save ourselvs from drownding.[10]

Josiah Rogerson recorded in his account of that crossing how a score or more of young women tied up their skirts and waded across the waist-deep river. The shock from the icy water was so intense that they suffered "dementia" (Rogerson's word) from which some did not recover until the next spring. Aaron Jackson, an older man who had been totally immersed in the river, died the same night in a crowded tent. His wife discovered his death during the night but remained quietly at his side until morning, for fear of disturbing the others.

It was early October when Young, in Salt Lake Valley, first learned that a thousand handcart Saints and nearly four hundred wagon emigrants were still on the trail, a very long way from Zion. He immediately called for a rescue effort, supported by all Saints, at the semiannual conference of the Mormon church. As usual, his demands were specific and detailed, calling on the Saints to give forty good men as teamsters, twenty-four thousand pounds of flour, and sixty good spans of mules or horses, with harness, whipple trees, neck yokes, stretchers, lead chains, and so on. Without delay Young mounted an advance rescue party that included George D. Grant, William H. Kimball, Brigham's son Joseph, and Cyrus Wheelock.

These were some of the missionaries just back from England, who had originally converted many members of the endangered handcart companies and who, along with Franklin Richards, had encouraged the emigrants to press forward when they passed them on the trail. Now, after two years away from their families and after only two days at home in Salt Lake, they backtracked hundreds of snowy miles to save the incoming Saints. Pushing hard, Kimball and five others were already east of South Pass when a totally spent James Willie and Joseph Elder of Handcart Company Number Four rode their wasted mules into camp and told their story. Kimball's party hurried on to Willie's camp, where half the rescue party remained to assist that company; the three others continued east to find Martin and his company, wherever they might be. As soon as possible, Kimball started west with Willie's company, the weakest riding in the wagons but others still on foot.

Chislett told of trying to encourage the worn-out, hollow-eyed survivors to go on living: "We talked to them of our improved condition, appealed to their love of life . . . but all to no purpose. We then addressed ourselves to their religious feelings, their wish to see Zion; to know the Prophet Brigham. . . . But all our efforts were unavailing; they had lost all love of life, all sense of surrounding things, and had sunk down into a state of indescribable apathy."[11]

Martin's company turned out to be with Hodgett's wagon company, about a day west of Last Crossing. Since fording the Platte at that point, the two companies had lost fifty-six people. Fifteen miles farther back down the trail, the three rescuers found the Hunt wagons and continued their wintry roundup by shepherding the Martin, Hodgett, and Hunt companies to Devil's Gate, a stone's throw west of Independence Rock. Here at least animal feed was available, but protection was lacking against temperatures that dropped to eleven degrees below zero. On November 3 Joseph A. Young headed for Salt Lake City to report on the calamitous chain of events and ask for reinforcements; his father had already anticipated the gravity of the emergency and dispatched 250 wagons to travel east even before Joseph had left Devil's Gate. Rescue wagons and survivors ultimately met and made their painful way to sanctuary at Salt Lake. The Willie company, assisted by Kimball, came in on November 9, and Kimball turned back immediately to help herd the remaining companies safely in. Martin's company and the others made it in by November 30, but not before many more emigrants died and others suffered primitive trailside amputations of frozen extremities.

The strains imposed by extreme cold, hunger, and the accumulating deaths took a heavy toll on mental stability as well. One night a girl sleeping with her family in a tent awoke screaming with pain to discover one of her famished brothers gnawing on her fingers. A Scottish woman in Martin's company, close to the end of the trail—and clearly at the end of her own tether as well—pushed her handcart over the edge of Emigration Canyon to watch with satisfaction as it splintered asunder. Yet there were bright spots in all this dark and frozen nightmare: in Echo Canyon, just before the group entered the valley, a child was born to a young woman who, miraculously, had come through the handcart ordeal safely from start to finish. Once back in Salt Lake, the survivors received a heartfelt welcome inspired by Young, who urged his people to take the emigrants into their homes and wash, nurse, and wait upon them. Again combining his pragmatism

Just west of Independence Rock, at
Devil's Gate on the Sweetwater River,
Mormon handcart companies suffered
one of the worst disasters in western trail
history, when sixteen people died in a
single night as temperatures plummeted
to eleven below zero.

and faith, Young pronounced in Tabernacle: "You know that I would give more for a dish of pudding and milk, or a baked potato and salt, were I in the situation of those persons who have just come in, than I would for all your prayers, though you were to stay here all the afternoon and pray. Prayer is good, but when baked potatoes and pudding and milk are needed, prayer will not supply their place on this occasion."[12]

In all, the fourth and fifth handcart companies suffered over two hundred deaths—the count is uncertain—out of the 1,076 who started out in Liverpool. Young was widely criticized for such grim results as well as for the cost in time and money of the rescue effort. Answering his detractors with a furious tirade in Tabernacle, he castigated Franklin Richards, who, in Liverpool, had urged the Saints to ship out and go west despite their late start. Young concluded with a blistering rebuttal to his critics: "If any man, or woman, complains of me or of my Counselors, in regard to the lateness of some of this season's immigration, let the curse of God be on them and blast their substance with mildew and destruction, until their names are forgotten from the earth!"[13]

The traumatic experiences of the fourth and fifth handcart companies, however, did not sound the death knell for this mode of gathering to Zion. Five more handcart companies crossed the plains between 1857 and 1860, although the number of such travelers fell off dramatically: the first five companies in 1856 (including the tragic fourth and fifth companies) carried 1,891 people—nearly double the 1,071 who crossed during the succeeding, and final, four years. Overall, about one handcart traveler in ten died in the traces, and more died shortly after arrival in the valley.

After the handcart era ended in 1860, church wagon trains would depart from Salt Lake for the Missouri River, dispose of their Mormon-grown agricultural cargoes, gather up a cargo of new Saints in the east, and head back to the valley. In the process, the Mormon Trail developed into a well-traveled road, and many thousands of emigrants reached Zion this way until the railroad effectively drove a golden spike in the trail's coffin.

Grim as the fourth and fifth handcart companies' experiences were—both the trek and the rescue effort initiated by Brigham Young—this heroic episode of Mormon history exemplifies many of the enduring qualities of nascent Mormonism itself: thorough organization, iron discipline, unswerving devotion to a cause, and limitless self-sacrifice. It suggests that the true Mormon Trail was not on the prairie but in the spirit.

6 | THE PONY EXPRESS

"NEITHER RAIN NOR SNOW NOR HEAT OF DAY nor gloom of night shall stay these couriers from the swift fulfillment of their appointed rounds." The Pony Express performance seems to personify this inscription above the portico of the main post office building in New York City, yet surprisingly the Pony Express was never an official part of the U.S. Postal Service. It was a private mail system, a hell-for-leather bucket brigade on horseback—instead of water, the young Pony Express riders hauled saddlebags stuffed with mail. Riding night and day around the clock, the unbroken chain of Pony Express couriers delivered its mail nearly two thousand miles, between Saint Joseph, Missouri, and San Francisco, California, in only ten days. Never before in human history had written communication been moved so swiftly, over such distances, and with such regularity.

The Pony Express operation had all the ingredients of daring and danger—even death—needed to fire the public imagination. Riding through violent storms, crossing mountain ranges in winter through thirty-foot snowdrifts, fording flooded rivers in spring, and traversing searing western deserts in summer were all in a day's work for the couriers.

The Pony Express was a private business conducted by the Central Overland California and Pike's Peak Express Company (COC&PP). The COC&PP, in turn, was created and owned by Russell, Majors and Waddell (RMW), one of the most powerful of the many freighting firms in the country, with headquarters

PLUME ROCKS, WYOMING, *1985. Photograph by James L. Amos.*

at Fort Leavenworth, Kansas Territory. Its principal business was conveying, largely by ox-drawn wagon, millions of pounds of War Department supplies to military posts throughout the frontier. In its heyday the firm employed six thousand men and owned seventy-five thousand oxen in addition to thousands of wagons and coaches, as well as warehouses, stores, corrals, real estate, a sawmill and lumberyard, a meat-packing plant, a bank, and an insurance company— all part of Russell, Majors and Waddell's sprawling commercial empire.

Each of the three partners brought special talents to the firm. William Hepburn Russell, an aristocratic, immaculately tailored financial wizard with a quick

temper, felt most at home in banks and boardrooms. William Bradford Waddell, a one-time lead miner and successful grain merchant, administered office affairs. Alexander Majors, an ex-farmer, was the hands-on partner who coordinated the massive logistical problems of the operation. Despite varying temperaments and backgrounds, the three made a highly effective team.

Following its formation in 1854, RMW had expanded in every direction, embarking on a series of brilliant mergers and acquisitions engineered by Russell. Unfortunately, as their holdings mushroomed, a mountain of ultimately disastrous debt grew with them. A $493,000 loss on a government freighting deal

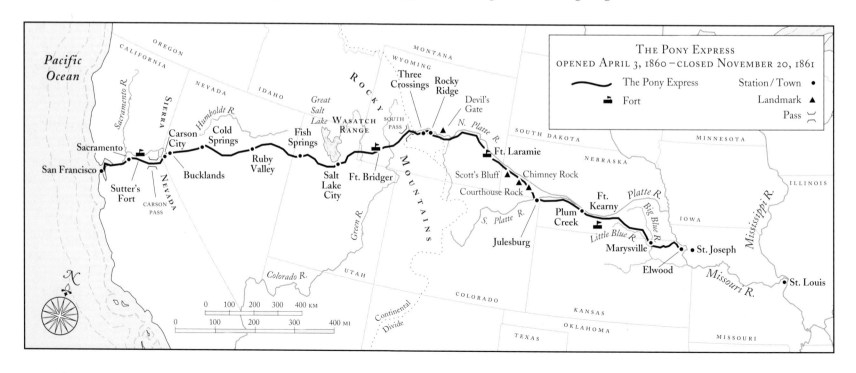

Left: WILLIAM H. RUSSELL, *1860.*

William Hepburn Russell was often called the Napoleon of the Plains because of his predilection for business plans on a grand scale.

Below: WILLIAM B. WADDELL, *1860.*

William Bradford Waddell, a former miner and grain merchant, administered office affairs for the Russell, Majors and Waddell partnership.

Left: Alexander Majors, a founder of the Pony Express, required every rider to sign a pledge of temperance in language, use of alcohol, and general behavior. He also provided a Bible and a pair of Colt revolvers for self-defense.

during the army's Mormon Expedition of 1857, when Mormon guerrillas burned three RMW wagon trains and sixty tons of supplies and drove off twelve hundred animals, further undermined the firm's financial standing. Nevertheless, by 1860 RMW still occupied a strong position, influential enough to vigorously lobby the Post Office Department for the lucrative mail contract from Missouri to Placerville, California, via stage on the Central Overland Route.

This bid was a direct challenge to RMW's arch-rival, John Butterfield, whose Overland Mail Company already held the contract (due to expire in 1863) from Saint Louis to San Francisco by the Southern, or Ox-bow, Route. Butterfield's route was eight hundred miles longer than the Central Overland Route and took twenty-five days to cover, but it was open all year round. Using the shorter Central Route, a dream of Russell's since 1858, mail could cross the continent in half of Butterfield's time, but its carriers had to hurdle the formidable Wasatch and Sierra Nevada ranges before reaching the Pacific terminus. Grizzled heads who had seen Sierra blizzards block the mountain passes for weeks at a time doubted whether the Central Route would be usable twelve months a year. Still another east-west mail route then in use, but an even slower alternative than the Ox-bow Route, was by ship around the southern tip of South America. This treacherous voyage, however, took four to seven months, provided the vessel didn't founder en route—which happened with alarming frequency. The only other option for mail was by steamer to Panama, then a slog across the fever-ridden, jungle-choked isthmus, and by another steamer up to San Francisco. These conditions improved only marginally after the completion of the Panama Railroad in 1855, while freight costs increased across the isthmus and health conditions remained appalling.

All this posed an increasingly urgent problem for the Post Office. Ever since the Pikes Peak gold rush there had been mounting pressure from the West Coast for improved mail service. Now, with the Civil War brewing, both northern and southern interests in Congress wanted to win California to their own side of the impending conflict. The problem had suddenly gone beyond awarding a simple mail contract to determining a matter affecting national unity. It was widely felt that a new and unbroken line of communication to the West Coast, running through northerly Union territory (opposing the Ox-bow Route through southerly Confederate territory) would greatly strengthen California's ties to the Union side. The strategy worked, and thanks in part to Russell's dramatic and daring solution—the Pony Express—California did remain loyal to the Union.

From the Pony's first run on April 3, 1860, until its last on November 20, 1861—a span of barely nineteen months—the riders covered some 616,000 miles, enough to circle the earth twenty-four times.

FOUR-LEGGED FORERUNNERS

Innovative as Russell's idea was, the Pony Express did have precursors that had also used animals as mail carriers. The first of these to run eastward from Sacramento to Salt Lake City—a seven-hundred-mile stint—was Major George Chorpenning, Jr.'s "Jackass Line"—so called not as a reflection on its proprietor but because it used a mule train to transport mail over the Sierra Nevada and across the deserts of Nevada and Utah. Chorpenning and his partner, Absalom Woodward, made their system work for a time, but over the years they suffered one disaster after another. In the autumn of 1851 Woodward's mail train was attacked by Indians; all his men were killed and the mail scattered. Woodward himself, though severely wounded, escaped with two mules and traveled three hundred miles—to within thirty miles of Salt Lake City—before he died. The next year five Chorpenning men with ten mules and horses, who again headed east out of California, were caught in blizzards. They spent fifty-three days on the trail and watched every one of their animals freeze to death. The party lived on mule meat for days, went without food altogether for four days, and made their way through the snow on foot for two hundred miles to finally arrive in Salt Lake City—with the mail still intact on their backs.

Later unsuccessful experiments using animals to carry the mail over the Sierra Nevada included dog teams and even horses wearing snowshoes, but perhaps the most bizarre was the Camel Corps, organized in 1855 with enthusiastic support from Jefferson Davis, then secretary of war. Davis was convinced that the dromedary, accustomed to traveling for days without water in sand and heat, was not only a creature born to carry the mail across the American desert, but one that could also pack a howitzer on its hump for use as mounted artillery in battles against the Indians. Pursuing his inspiration, Davis had a small navy vessel, the S.S. *Supply*, fitted out to resemble Noah's Ark and dispatched a young navy lieutenant and an army major to the London Zoo to acquaint themselves with the ways of camels. There were additional research stops along the way in Paris, Florence, and at numerous Mediterranean ports of call in Arab countries. In the course of their eight-month junket the two officers acquired thirty-three camels, including both Bactrian (two-humped) and Arabian (one-humped) breeds, accompanied by five Bedouin attendants. Some of the beasts were pregnant when purchased; others conceived during the monotonous voyage to America. When all were finally unloaded at Indianola, Texas, training began promptly and just as promptly revealed unforeseen shortcomings. Horses and mules stampeded at the sight and smell of the strange creatures. And unlike the soft Sahara sands, the rocky deserts of the Southwest soon made the camels footsore; they dropped to their knees and refused to budge. Even when outfitted with leather boots, they still did not perform up to expectations, and after trudging listlessly around Texas, Nevada, and southern California for a few months, the Camel Corps was discreetly retired from service.

THE BIRTH OF THE PONY EXPRESS

It appears that about 1859 Senator William H. Gwin of California discussed with William Hepburn Russell the Pony Express concept of using a relay system of men on horseback. To encourage the project Gwin promised his best efforts

To recruit riders for their new transcontinental Pony Express mail route—ten days to cover the 1,838 miles between Saint Joseph, Missouri, and San Francisco—Russell, Majors and Waddell may have placed a similar advertisement in western newspapers.

in persuading Congress to reimburse RMW for any losses that might be incurred through the operation of the Pony Express. Gwin then made legislative attempts to launch the service, but unfortunately they never came to fruition. Establishing it on a private basis was a bold—or more accurately, desperate—move by Russell, whose firm was already edging toward insolvency. Never intended to be a profitable and permanent mail service, the Pony Express was essentially a temporary grandstanding gesture by Russell to focus attention on his Central Overland Route as the best year-round way to carry mail by stage to California. If the Pony Express succeeded, RMW would capture Butterfield's fat mail contract; if not, RMW would go under. Faced with these alternatives, Russell's partners allowed themselves to be persuaded, much against their better judgment, to go along with his scheme, and the Pony Express was off and running.

WANTED
YOUNG SKINNY WIRY FELLOWS not over eighteen. Must be expert riders willing to risk death daily. Orphans preferred. WAGES $25 per week. Apply, *Central Overland Express, Alta Bldg., Montgomery St.*

Advertisements were placed in newspapers of major cities along the Pony Express route urging "young skinny wiry fellows" who were "willing to risk death daily" to apply as riders at a salary of one hundred dollars a month plus food and shelter. Many were called, but few were chosen; out of the first 160 applicants only 80 made the cut and assured themselves of a coveted place in frontier history (over its short life the Pony Express probably had a total of 180 riders). Within a scant three months of the partners' agreement, RMW performed a logistical miracle by setting up, staffing, and equipping some 190 relay stations from Saint Joseph to San Francisco, in a beeline that stretched almost two thousand miles across plains, deserts, and mountains. The Pony Express became the first non-stop line of communication to span the continent.

RMW's stage line, the Central Overland California and Pike's Peak Express Company, already had stations in place as far west as Salt Lake City, which could serve double duty for the Pony Express, but west of Salt Lake it was pretty much empty wilderness until the trail ran down the western slope of the Sierras. New stations consisting of shelters, corrals, and storage facilities had to be built along three-fourths of the route; some four hundred station keepers and stock tenders were quickly hired. Nearly five hundred horses—mostly mustangs, thoroughbreds, and Morgans, chosen for speed and endurance—as well as saddles, bridles, *mochilas* (saddlebags), and feed were purchased in double-quick time and distributed along the trail. William Finney, RMW agent in Sacramento, personally led a mule supply train over the trail to Salt Lake City, dropping off men and supplies at previously selected station sites.

The Pony Express and Overland Stage station at Rock Creek, Nebraska Territory. Station agent David McCanles, the gentleman holding the bottle, is said to have been gunned down later by Wild Bill Hickok.

Ruins of the Pony Express station at Fish Springs, Utah. Such isolated and primitive living conditions probably helped account for the high turnover rate; few riders lasted more than six months.

The route fixed by RMW began on the western border of Missouri and ran directly east-west through six other present-day states: Kansas, Nebraska, Wyoming, Utah, Nevada, and California, barely nicking the northeast corner of Colorado at Julesburg. Across the Great Plains it essentially followed the Oregon-California and Mormon Trails along the Platte River, almost parallel to the route later chosen by the Union Pacific and Central Pacific Railroads. Between Salt Lake City and Sacramento the route stuck close to Chorpenning's former "Jackass Line." This overall line led the Pony through a dozen or more established communities, including Sacramento, California; Carson City and Fort Bridger in Utah Territory; Forts Laramie and Kearny in Nebraska Territory; and Marysville in Kansas Territory. Although long stretches were unpopulated, except for the isolated Pony Express stations, there were times and places along the way where emigrant wagon outfits, pack trains heading for the golden gravel of the Sierra Nevada and Rockies, and Mormon handcart companies toiling toward the City of the Saints created temporary traffic jams or detours for the racing couriers.

Over the life of the operation the number of stations varied from 160 to 190 or so as the route was modified from experience. Stations were of two kinds: relay stations (also called swing stations) and home stations. Generally the relay stations were located about ten to fifteen miles apart; approximately seventy-five to one hundred miles separated home stations. A rider normally made a run of four or five legs between two home stations. Each rider was assigned to his own home station as a base where he received the mail from an incoming rider. The fresh rider, changing horses at succeeding relay stations, galloped on to the next home station, where he turned over the *mochila* to his successor. The original *mochila* that left Saint Joe had to change hands, i.e., horses, about 190 times before it was delivered in San Francisco ten days later.

A rider usually stayed at the second home station to await the next return mail, although the procedure was somewhat flexible. This system meant that each rider had a regular run, both east- and westbound, seldom going beyond it except in cases of dire necessity—of which there were surprisingly few, considering the

many thousands of rides made. Russell's concept also assumed, and the assumption proved correct, that a horse and rider could average better than eight miles an hour, an incredibly high average to sustain, given the night riding, rugged terrain, and bad weather that ranged from blizzards to blistering heat. Multiplied out in round figures, about two hundred miles could be covered by four men in a day, and the entire run of some two thousand miles completed in ten days by forty men.

Such a finely tuned schedule dictated the decision to slash weight to the absolute minimum by providing riders with spare and uncluttered equipment. The special wafer-thin saddle, designed and made by Israel Landis, master saddler of Saint Joseph, was slimmed down to weigh about a third as many pounds as the

standard western saddle. The *mochila,* with its four *cantinas,* or pockets, had a hole and a slit on top so it could be slung quickly over the saddle horn and cantle. Together saddle and *mochila* weighed about thirteen pounds empty and perhaps ten to fifteen pounds more when filled with mail. Dispatches, letters, and newspapers were printed on special tissuelike paper in order to save weight, and letters were wrapped in oiled silk bundles to protect them when fording streams. Some riders carried a small horn, sounding a blast as they approached a station to alert the keeper to ready the next pony for instant departure. The rifle originally issued for self-defense was abandoned early on as needless weight, but each rider carried a brace of navy Colt .45-caliber revolvers. Every logistical detail was planned to reduce fatigue—of horse first and rider second—and to enhance the fleetness of the animal on which rested the rider's ultimate security of life and limb.

THE FIRST RIDE

Johnny Fry must have relived many times in his mind the scenario that unfolded in Saint Joseph, Missouri, on the third of April 1860, surely the most unforgettable day of his young life. Since early afternoon the curious crowd had begun to gather in front of the Pike's Peak Stables. At first they circled at a distance, admiring Sylph, the little bay mare who stood patiently in the

JOHNNY FRY, *1860.*

Fry was first to ride the Pony Express out of Saint Joseph, and the last to ride in. Two years later he was killed while serving as a Union scout in the Civil War.

spring sunshine waiting for Fry to appear. Then souvenir hunters began to pluck strands of hair from her tail while the pony shook her head, nervously wheeling and shifting her weight before riding into history.

April 3 was a day of excitement not only in Saint Joe but throughout the country. The first rider ever to vault into a Pony Express saddle had been scheduled to leave Saint Joe at 5:00 P.M. on the opening leg of the first nonstop transcontinental mail delivery in history. But as luck would have it, the special train

bringing mail from New York and points east had been detained, delaying the departure until 7:15 P.M. Across the continent, in San Francisco, Fry's western counterpart, James Randall (who was not an official Pony Express rider), had already stepped into his stirrup more than two hours earlier, at 4:00 P.M. San Francisco time. Nevertheless, to Fry belongs the glory of being the first authentic Pony rider onto the trail because William (Sam) Hamilton, the official western Pony courier, did not leave Sacramento until April 4.

CHIMNEY ROCK, NEBRASKA, *n.d.*

Chimney Rock was one of the first of many astonishing natural landmarks along the Pony Express route.

As afternoon faded into evening, with little activity other than some music and flowery speeches in front of Patee House, where RMW had its local offices, some of the crowd lingered; others probably drifted away to home and supper. Those who stayed to witness the departure saw Johnny Fry saddle up and trot to the U.S. Express office (a freight and parcel company), followed by a parade of well-wishers.

Postmaster William A. Davis bustled out importantly, greeted Fry, and swung into place on Fry's saddle the *mochila* filled with some fifty pieces of mail or more, including a congratulatory message from President Buchanan to Governor Downey of California. Somewhere a cannon boomed, the crowd hurrahed, and the nervous pony pranced and snorted. F. M. Posegate, publisher of the *Daily West,* standing on one side of the animal, heard Major Jeff Thompson on the far side, perspiring and flushed with excitement, say a few brief words of encouragement to the rider before he gave the pony a slap on the hip and shouted, "Go!!!" Away went Fry, clattering down Jules Street to the Elwood Ferry, where he boarded the *Ebenezer* and crossed the Missouri River to Kansas Territory. The great Pony Express relay race was underway.

Fry first stopped for a change of horses at Cottonwood Spring Station, then came Cold Spring, Kennekuk, Kickapoo, Log Chain, and Seneca, where he passed the *mochila* to Don Rising, his first relay, who rode on to Marysville, Kansas, in just over eight hours. The mail had then traveled 112 miles in thirteen hours. At Marysville, Jack Keetley took over the *mochila* and dashed to Hollenberg's Station. Three riders later, following the well-worn '49ers' trail hugging the north bank of the Little Blue River and then going along the south bank of the North Platte, the mail had reached Fort Kearny, Nebraska, 230 miles west of the starting point at Saint Joe and a bit behind schedule. Relay upon relay, rider after rider rushed the precious *mochila* westward across a progressively more austere and mountainous landscape. Chimney Rock and South Pass fell behind on the trail, then Fort Bridger and, on April 9, Salt Lake City. Three more days were spent crossing one of the most rugged deserts in America before the Pony Express reached Carson City, in what would within the year become Nevada Territory.

At Carson City the telegraph line from California had its easternmost terminal, so telegrams were taken from the *mochila* at that station and wired ahead to Sacramento. The rest of the mail continued on, winding through Carson Pass and down the western slope of the Sierra Nevada to reach Sacramento, the Pony Express western land terminus, on April 13, at 5:25 P.M. Elapsed time from Saint Joe, nearly two thousand miles to the east: a shade under ten days—right on schedule.

Sacramento went wild! The *Sacramento Daily Union* exulted on page one of its April 13 edition that "Loryea's crockery establishment had a hobby horse mounted before the awning posts, decorated with flags and inscribed 'Pony Express. Russell, Majors & Co., take the skates!' Dale and Cox, nearly opposite . . . rigged out their largest doll (a perfect bouncer) on a wooden pony, stuffed letters and papers in his hand,

mounted a soldier cap on his head, and set him off with the motto, 'Pony Express, forever!'"

Storefronts and streets were draped with banners and bunting. Women filled windows, balconies, even rooftops, straining to catch a first glimpse of horse and rider. A high-spirited detachment of the Sacramento Hussars galloped out to Sutter's Fort to meet the exhausted incoming courier, William (Sam) Hamilton, who had carried from Sportsman's Hall. Reported the *Union*, "First a cloud of rolling dust in the direction of the Fort, then a horseman bearing a small flag, riding furiously down J street, and then a straggly, charging band of horsemen, flying after him, heralding the coming of the Express."

The celebration grew more boisterous by the minute. Bells rang out from church towers and firehouses, and cannon fired by Young America Fire Companies Nos. Two and Six boomed out nine-gun salutes. There were shouts and a pall of gunpowder hanging over crowds beside themselves with excitement. Out of the pandemonium suddenly rode Hamilton on his roan horse, trotting up to the door of the Alta Telegraph Company with his battered *mochila*. After a change of horses (here accounts vary), he continued to the levee, where he boarded the steamer *Antelope* for the trip down the Sacramento River to an even more eagerly awaiting San Francisco.

The *Antelope* docked at San Francisco, according to the *Daily Alta California*, at 12:38 A.M. on April 14, 1860. Unable to contain themselves, the city press had already organized a celebratory and planning meeting at the Reporters' Union a day or two before Hamilton's arrival in San Francisco. The reporters toasted

warmly and at length the annihilation of space and
time, a giant step toward the distant goal of printing
the same news on both coasts the very same day. As
the *Alta* good-humoredly noted, "A number of baskets
of champagne were opened, and wit and sentiment
were soon freely circulating." Important committees
burgeoned like mushrooms: a Nominating Committee, a General Committee, and a Committee of Citizens at Large were designated, a Grand Marshal
anointed, fire companies alerted, and elaborate plans
laid to meet the Pony Express rider when he arrived in

the city, even though that would take place near mid-
night. The *Antelope* did indeed arrive in San Francisco
on schedule; Hamilton (whose name the paper forgot
to mention in the excitement), described as mounted
on "a bay horse" (which had been "a roan" in Sacramento), disembarked to the cacophony of rockets,
bells, the eighteen-piece California Band, and a roar
of welcome from two thousand throats. Unfortunately,
the fire companies had failed to get powder in time
to set off the cannons, but they showed their goodwill by racing their engines full speed around the

Montgomery Street block. Fireworks and huge bonfires were set off at numerous points in the city—so many that a fire alarm was sounded for fear the city might burn to the ground. Hamilton and the bay horse proceeded to the *Alta* telegraph office, surrounded by a torchlight procession and accompanied by strains of martial music and "See the Conquering Hero Comes." It was well after one in the morning before the enthusiastic crowds finally dispersed.

By curious coincidence, the cities at each end of the Pony Express route, Saint Joseph and San Francisco, bore the names of saints. Also curious is that the first leg of the route from each city was not by land but by water: from Saint Joe by ferry across the Missouri to Elwood, Kansas Territory, and from San Francisco upstream to Sacramento.

The first Pony Express rider out of San Francisco, eastbound for Saint Joe, on April 3, followed the same trail as the first westbound rider. The take-off from San Francisco by James Randall had all the earmarks of a publicity stunt: the pony's headstall was bedecked with two small American flags, and the *Daily Alta California* tartly observed the next day that Randall, to the applause of a modest throng, had mounted the little khaki-colored pony from the wrong side. Surprisingly, the animal did not object and together they rode down to embark on the 4:00 P.M. boat for Sacramento.

In Sacramento, William Hamilton, the next—really the first official—eastbound rider waited impatiently. There was no crowd of well-wishers to speed him on as it was now about two in the morning of April 4, and Sacramento was asleep. Hamilton swung into the saddle and settled onto the *mochila* beneath

him. Giving his horse a reassuring pat on the neck, he began his solitary ride up the Sacramento Valley. Riding blind in inky darkness, with no sound but the breathing of his horse and the clatter of hoofs on the trail, Hamilton rode toward the Sierra Nevada foothills. He knew it had been snowing heavily for days in the mountains ahead, with roads blocked and stages stalled at Strawberry Valley. Anxious to make time while he was still on the flat, he pressed ahead. The first swing stations passed: Five Mile House, Fifteen Mile House, and Mormon Tavern. Even though the going had turned uphill, Hamilton pulled into Placerville a half-hour ahead of schedule. Then on to Sportsman's Hall, where Warren Upson, his relief man, was waiting to carry the mail over the Sierra Nevada. Upson, son of a Sacramento newspaper editor,

VIEW OF THE LEVEE, SACRAMENTO CITY, CALIFORNIA, *1850s. From original letter sheet published by Forrest and Borden, Sacramento.*

At Sacramento the first eastbound Pony Express rider disembarked from a river steamer, and the next rider took the mochila for the first overland leg east.

On the final leg of the Pony Express's two-thousand-mile run, the river steamboat Antelope *carried the first westbound horse and rider from Sacramento to San Francisco, on April 13, 1860.*

was not only a top-notch horseman but also thoroughly acquainted with this stretch of the Sierras in all seasons. Only such a man could fight through deep snow and cold without slipping off the trail and down a canyon into oblivion. Upson started out about 7:00 A.M. on April 4 and struggled for thirty miles under impossible conditions, sometimes forced to dismount and lead his floundering horse through the drifts. Late that night he reached Carson City after having ridden eighty-five miles. The crux passage of the entire Pony Express trail had been successfully crossed.

The rest of the trail to Saint Joe proved relatively uneventful once South Pass and the worst of the mountains and snows had been left behind. Fording the Platte farther east, however (near Julesburg in present-day Colorado), a horse and rider were swept downstream into quicksand before the eyes of onlookers come to cheer the Pony Express along. In a twinkling the rider, name unknown, disentangled himself from the animal, grabbed the *mochila* and thrashed his way safely to shore. There he leaped on a borrowed horse and sped on his way, leaving his mount to be rescued (which it was) by the people lining the bank.

Somewhere along the trail, it is not known exactly where or when, a historic moment took place: the first encounter of the east and west mails when a westbound Pony Express rider and an eastbound rider (identities unknown) passed each other. It was an encounter that foreshadowed the meeting of the eastern and western railroads eight years later at Promontory Summit, some two hundred miles farther west. Without venturing here into the swamp of a time-rate-distance problem, one reconstruction of the incident suggests that the encounter occurred about 9:00 P.M. on April 8, 1860, somewhere along the Sweetwater River on the eastern slope of the Continental Divide, between South Pass and Independence Rock—more precisely, in a twenty-five-mile zone between Rocky Ridge (to the west) and Three Crossings (to the east). At 9:00 it would have been pitch dark; did the two riders even see each other? Possibly. Did they stop to exchange congratulations in the middle of the trail? Not likely.

On April 13, 1860, Johnny Fry, who had been the first Pony Express rider out of Saint Joe, now rode back into town after a hard sixty-mile run from the west. As horse and rider trotted out of the cottonwood trees on the west bank of the river, thousands of people on the east bank, or Missouri side, roared their welcome. He quickly boarded the little Elwood ferry and crossed over to Saint Joe, where he delivered his *mochila* with eighty-five letters to the U.S. Express office at 4:30 P.M., whereupon a delirious celebration began. Fry was home again, and the first round-trip mail delivery by Pony Express between the Atlantic and the Pacific oceans had been completed. Having gone out on April 3 with letters from New York in his *mochila*, Fry returned bringing San Francisco mail from two thousand miles away—and only ten days had elapsed.

"YOUNG SKINNY WIRY FELLOWS"

The young Pony Express riders—many of them boys in their teens—clearly had a sense of mission, a remarkable esprit de corps, and the conviction that they were making history. They also took great pride in their horsemanship. But despite these sustaining factors the constant pounding in the saddle and the lonely life at the relay and home stations took a toll on health and spirits. Long days and nights waiting for the incoming mail must have weighed heavily on the young men, and card games, tending to their tack, and reading old magazines—if they could read—must have done little to lighten the boredom. Turnover of riders was a problem, and few seem to have stayed in the service more than six months.

No observer has painted a more honest—and discouraging—picture of a typical relay station than the English soldier and explorer Richard Burton, who rode the Overland Stage west in the summer and fall of 1860 to visit Brigham Young. He commented that the Sand Springs Station in present-day Nevada was "a vile hole" encumbered "with drifted ridges of the finest sand, sometimes 200 feet high, and shifting before every gale." Its water, Burton continued, "was

In 1860 the Pony Express advertised for "young skinny wiry fellows," preferably orphans, as riders for its new mail service. Four of the eighty who signed up—Billy Richardson, Johnny Fry, and the Cliff Brothers, all out of Saint Joseph, Missouri—are presumed to be pictured here.

Above: Fernand Lungren (1857–1932).
WHY ONE RIDER WAS LATE,
from Century, *October 1898.*

*Few frontier enterprises have been so
sensationally romanticized as the Pony
Express, as this grim illustration from
Century magazine shows. Although a
number of Pony Express station keepers
were killed by Indians, there is only one
such confirmed death of a rider.*

Right: MOUNTED MESSENGERS
ATTACKED BY INDIANS ON
THE PLAINS, *from* Harper's
Weekly, *January 13, 1866.*

For the titillation of readers, Harper's
Weekly *kept alive the legend of Indian
attacks on Pony Express riders.*

thick and stale with sulphury salts: it blistered even the hands. The station-house was no unfit object in such a scene, roofless and chairless, filthy and squalid, with a smoky fire in one corner, and a table in the centre of an impure floor, the walls open to every wind, and the interior full of dust. . . . Of the *employés,* all loitered and sauntered about *desoeuvrés* as cretins, except one, who lay on the ground crippled and apparently dying by the fall of a horse upon his breast-bone." Burton had already noted that the diet at the stations was sometimes "reduced to wolf-mutton, or a little boiled wheat and rye, and the drink to brackish water."[1]

During the entire existence of the enterprise, only one—possibly two—rider is recorded as having died in the line of duty; it was the station keepers who bore the brunt of the Indian attacks. The worst violence occurred in present-day Nevada in the spring of 1860, shortly after the Pony began, when a Paiute uprising brought operations to a halt for a month. The final toll: seven relay stations raided, fifteen employees killed, and a seventy-five-thousand-dollar loss to the company. There were other forays. In October 1860, on

galloping up to Egan's Station in driving sleet and snow, Burton's party was shocked to find that the station "had been reduced to a chimney-stack and a few charred posts. The Gosh Yutahs had set fire to it two or three days before our arrival, in revenge for the death of seventeen of their men by Lieutenant Weed's party. We could distinguish the pits from which the wolves had torn up the corpses, and one fellow's arm projected from the snow."[2]

Despite such sobering experiences, a Pony rider's routine was not without its lighter side and even an occasional taste of fame and glory. Since each rider repeated his run of some seventy-five miles between home stations, he became well known to locals and often created a flurry of excitement among young women along the way. Johnny Fry frequently sounded

his horn as he rode into town, alerting a girl in Cold Springs, Kansas Territory, who would hold out a handful of freshly baked cookies so he could scoop them up as he dashed by. On one of his rides he is said to have had his shirttail torn off by a female admirer, who sewed it into her patchwork quilt.

Those dashing young riders lucky enough to be based at a well-situated home station were usually in demand for parties and dances held at surrounding farms. Thomas Owen King recalled that after a two-hundred-mile ride to Salt Lake City he did not feel tired and took his best girl for a walk that same evening. Jack Keetley, apparently on a bet, became the hero of a record-breaking ride of 340 miles nonstop from Big Sandy to Elwood and back to Seneca in under thirty-one hours. He averaged the amazing speed of eleven miles an hour and arrived at his destination sitting sound asleep in his saddle.

Eighteen-year-old Richard Erastus (Ras) Egan, whose father had entered Great Salt Lake Valley in 1847 with Brigham Young's Pioneer Company and had later laid out the three-hundred-mile trail followed by the Pony Express in Utah Territory, one winter night carried the mail five miles on foot after his pony plunged

off a bridge in the dark and broke its neck.

Billy Fisher and his younger brother John also rode for the Pony. Billy's route started from Ruby Valley, heading east to Egan Canyon, in present-day Nevada. On July 4, 1860, he is reported

to have ridden from Ruby Valley to Salt Lake City with news of an Indian uprising in Utah Territory. In the process he covered three hundred miles in thirty-four hours and wore out six horses and two mules. Billy had adventures both summer and winter: in January 1861, carrying the presidential returns, he strayed eight miles off the trail and was lost for twenty hours in a blinding blizzard.

At age nineteen Pony Bob Haslam fit to a T the "skinny wiry fellows" description in the original Pony Express ad. Haslam was one of the few couriers who stayed in the service from beginning to end, and he probably had more hair-raising adventures than anyone else. His exploits have been copiously written about—sometimes in terms that stray a bit far from the verifiable facts. Pony Bob was one of the riders who rushed the first news of Lincoln's election across the country and, later, in March 1861, did the same for Lincoln's inaugural address to Congress. The feat was

Far left: RICHARD ERASTUS EGAN, *1860.*

Egan, whose father and brother also rode for the Pony Express, later became a Bishop of the Church of Jesus Christ of Latter-day Saints.

Left: WILLIAM FREDERICK FISHER, *1860.*

Fisher and his brother John both rode for the Pony Express.

Opposite: Ruby Valley Station was the Pony Express stop halfway between Salt Lake City and the Carson Valley, Nevada.

accomplished between telegraph stations at each end of the line in just seven days and seventeen hours, the fastest time ever recorded by the Pony Express. During that March ride, it was reported, an Indian arrow ripped through Haslam's jaw and a bullet shattered his arm while he was escaping an ambush.

Haslam's assigned route lay principally in the Ute country of present-day Nevada, where the Indians were most hostile. On one of his epic runs during the Paiute uprising Haslam headed east from Friday's Station, planning to change to a fresh mount at Reed's Station. Once there, however, he found that all the horses had been appropriated for a campaign against the Indians. On the same tired horse, the boy continued fifteen miles farther to Bucklands, only to discover that the next rider refused to go. He rode thirty-five miles more on a fresh horse to the Sink of the Carson, changed horses again, and loped across the alkali desert to Cold Springs. Another change, another thirty miles to Smith Creek, and a catnap.

Then he began backtracking to his starting point. This time at Cold Springs he found the Indians had gotten there first, killing the station keeper and driving off all the stock. Without rest or food Haslam rode on through the dangerous night to Sand Springs. There his report of the situation at Cold Springs persuaded the station keeper to join forces with him as far as the Sink of Carson (thereby saving the man's life, for his station was raided shortly after their departure). The Sink proved to be under siege, so Pony Bob rode through to Bucklands where, again, there was no available rider to take over the mail. After an hour's rest he was back in the saddle, retracing his old west-

bound trail to the foothills of the Sierra Nevada and back to Friday's Station. The ride remains an extraordinary feat of courage, discipline, and horsemanship: 380 miles in thirty-six hours, for an average of over ten miles per hour. Pony Bob received a meager bonus of one hundred dollars for his pains.

William Frederick Cody, known throughout the world as Buffalo Bill, occupies a special niche in the pantheon of Pony Express riders—a place largely of Cody's own creation and one that recent historians have questioned. By his own account, Buffalo Bill went to work at the age of eleven as a cattle driver for RMW's freighting firm. After some hit-or-miss schooling, he rejoined the firm as a Pony rider at age fourteen. Writing many years after the event, Cody claimed to have made a 320-mile ride in twenty-one hours and forty minutes after he found his relief rider had been killed in a drunken brawl. The story probably belongs with many another apocryphal frontier tale, even though Alexander Majors, a founder of RMW, confirmed in his own memoirs that Cody did ride with the Pony Express for a time. The fact remains that Buffalo Bill Cody was probably the youngest of all the riders and that, as he modestly wrote, "excitement was plentiful" during his brief stint with the Pony Express.

Cody's richly deserved fame did not rest on his Pony experiences, however, but on his cumulative reputation as an Indian fighter, scout, army officer, buffalo hunter, horseman, and supreme showman. From the fabric of his life he created his own larger-than-life myth and more. By force of character and spirit, and through his colorful Wild West shows and

Rosa Bonheur (1822–1899). COL. WILLIAM F. CODY, *1889. Oil on canvas, 18½ x 15¼ in. (47 x 38.6 cm). Buffalo Bill Historical Center, Cody, Wyoming.*

When world-renowned Buffalo Bill Cody took his Wild West Show to Paris in 1889, his buffalo-hunting, scouting, Indian-fighting, Pony Express days were long past, but Bonheur's nostalgic painting sums it all up in the most celebrated of his portraits.

Rosa Bonheur 1889

ghostwritten dime novels, he vividly communicated to crowned heads and crowds alike some of the powerful frontier forces that had formed him and the nation. To this day his image remains the popular symbol of all the knights in fringed buckskin who helped win the West.

THE BITTER END

After the initial triumph of their Pony Express, William Hepburn Russell and his partners momentarily had reason to be optimistic. Their venture had proven beyond doubt that the Central Overland Route to California was viable year-round; the Post Office contract seemed within their grasp. But powerful forces—political and military as well as economic—were working against them, and in the end they were to drink the bitter tea of defeat.

The Pony Express had inaugurated its service with a letter charge of five dollars per half-ounce, although over time this dropped to one dollar per half-ounce, and the weekly schedule was shortly stepped up to semiweekly. Reports vary from source to source regarding the total amount of mail carried, but the estimate of thirty-five thousand pieces handled during the brief nineteen-month life of the Pony Express (with eastbound mail outnumbering westbound by two to one) is probably close enough. These figures work out to about fifty-seven letters for each of the transcontinental runs made, considerably less than might have been expected. In monetary terms the picture is even bleaker: the estimated cost to the Pony Express per letter was sixteen dollars, while the average revenue

per letter was only three dollars. The bottom line—a loss of nearly five hundred thousand dollars—confirmed the worst fears expressed earlier by Russell's two partners. Their empire was heading for a crash.

The firm's credit standing plummeted, and operating funds became so scarce that wags said COC&PP stood for "Clean Out of Cash and Poor Pay." Russell made a desperate move to maintain RMW's financial credibility by illegally using government Indian bonds as collateral for his bank loans. This only made matters worse. Russell was arrested and tried in January 1861, but the charges against him were dismissed on a legal technicality. After that, events closed in swiftly on Russell and his partners. Confederate troops cut Butterfield's rival southern Ox-bow Route, stopping the flow of mail to California. Congress, finally galvanized into action by this disruption, decreed that the Ox-bow Route be moved north to the Central Overland Route and granted a million-dollar subsidy to the Overland Mail Company, Butterfield's old outfit. It was a gesture fraught with irony since the Overland Mail Company was now controlled by Wells Fargo and Company, the major creditor that had forced Butterfield out of business the previous year for nonpayment of debts. In one last coup of financial legerdemain, Russell released the western half of COC&PP's route to the Overland Mail Company and worked out a deal to split both the million-dollar subsidy and the costs of operating its stage and Pony Express services. But this coup came too late. In April 1861 Russell was shouldered out as president of COC&PP, and Ben Holladay (the "Stage Coach King"), who had helped finance the Pony Express initially, took control and installed his own hireling, Bela Hughes, as president. Within a year the bankrupt COC&PP and its assets, including the Pony Express, were sold at a rigged auction for the trifling sum of $100,000—to Holladay. Russell had met his master at financial maneuvering.

By the summer of 1861 the run serviced by the Pony Express should have been getting progressively shorter: the eastern telegraph lines had extended nearly one hundred miles west of Fort Kearny, Nebraska Territory, while the western telegraph crew moved east of Carson City, in the new Nevada Territory, at the amazing speed of twenty-five miles a day. The fact is, however, that while the Pony Express carried telegraph messages across the shrinking gap between the eastern and western telegraph termini as they rapidly approached each other, it also continued to carry mail all the way from Saint Joe (later from Atchison, Kansas) to Sacramento up until November 18, 1861.

Nevertheless, the days of the Pony Express were numbered, and on October 26, 1861, two days after the eastern and western telegraph lines were linked at Salt Lake City, it came to the end of its official life. A terse notice in the *Sacramento Union* served as its epitaph: "Pony Express will be discontinued from date. Wells, Fargo & Co., Agents Sacramento, Oct. 25, 1861." By the time the last rider delivered the final mail to San Francisco on November 20, 1861, the press had lost interest and failed to note the historic event.

The original page-one editorial of the *Daily Alta California* for April 13, 1860, best speaks for the entire nation in its thoughtful appraisal of the Pony Express, a summing up as valid at the end of the remarkable service as it had been at the beginning:

Yesterday [*sic*] was the commencement of another important epoch in the history of California—the arrival of the first pony express overland, with news from New York, to the 3rd April—less than

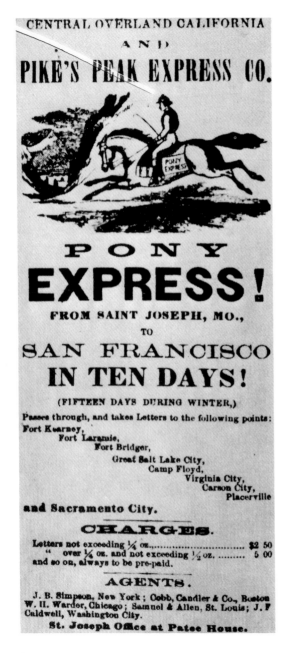

CENTRAL OVERLAND CALIFORNIA
AND
PIKE'S PEAK EXPRESS CO.

P O N Y
EXPRESS!
FROM SAINT JOSEPH, MO.,
TO
SAN FRANCISCO
IN TEN DAYS!
(FIFTEEN DAYS DURING WINTER,)

Passes through, and takes Letters to the following points:
Fort Kearney,
Fort Laramie,
Fort Bridger,
Great Salt Lake City,
Camp Floyd,
Virginia City,
Carson City,
Placerville

and Sacramento City.

CHARGES.

Letters not exceeding ¼ oz. $2 50
" over ¼ oz. and not exceeding ½ oz. 5 00
and so on, always to be pre-paid.

AGENTS.

J. B. Simpson, New York; Cobb, Candler & Co., Boston
W. H. Warder, Chicago; Samuel & Allen, St. Louis; J. F
Caldwell, Washington City.
St. Joseph Office at Patee House.

ten days old. One by one the chains of darkness and the desert are broken, and we are brought nearer and nearer to our brethren on the other side of the continent. We are still a growing people; nations have reached a summit of prosperity, and then declined, but we are still going ahead. American life is a continuous revolution of business, activity, and national progress; and revolutions never go backward. One of our most glorious advances of late is the Pony Express; its achievements will be famous through the world. Wherever men think, and books are read, there the Pony Express will be heard of, and the news welcomed. Honor, then, to the men who have planned it, and with so little bragging, and yet with so much efficient management, have made it a perfect success from the beginning. The day of the ox team, which required four or five months time to make the journey from the Missouri to the Sacramento, has passed away, and lightning and ponies have succeeded them, to be superceded in their turn, by lightning and steam. Let us then have the Overland Telegraph and the Pacific Railroad as soon as possible; but until we get them, let us foster and support those men who have been so enterprising as to establish the Pony Express, with its reduction of the time across the continent to nine days.

Although the demise of the Pony Express is often blamed on the completion of the Transcontinental Telegraph, the fact is that the two were not mortal enemies since each carried a different sort of traffic.

This early advertisement soliciting mail for the young Pony Express shows a classic but erroneous image of the horse in motion; a running horse never has all four feet off the ground in the "rocking-horse" position seen here.

The Pony Express had been created as the means to an end: winning the cross-continental mail contract for RMW's Central Overland Route. Though failing to achieve that aim, primarily because of the Civil War and Post Office politics, it did cut in half the transit time for mail between East and West, and played a significant role in keeping California on the Union side in the North-South conflict.

After the last Pony Express horse and rider trotted wearily into Sacramento in 1861, the tattoo of hoofbeats fell silent, to be replaced by the clicking of the telegraph key—and not far behind, a mere eight years away, the snort of the iron horse.

Many former Pony Express riders lived to a ripe old age, while others came to untimely ends. Bill Carr, for example, was hanged for murder in Carson City, Nevada, and Joseph A. Slade, former Pony Express division agent at Julesburg, Colorado, with time grew so unruly and dangerous that he was ultimately lynched by the Vigilantes Committee at Virginia City. He was buried in the Mormon cemetery at Salt Lake City in a zinc-lined coffin filled, it is said, with the whiskey so dear to him in life. Some riders who had left the Pony to join the army were no doubt injured or killed in the War Between the States. Johnny Fry—his cookie-catching, shirttail-snatching days barely two years behind him—fell in 1863 as a Union scout in a brush with William Clarke Quantrill's Confederate raiders. Jack Keetley became a successful mining man in Salt Lake City and died there in 1912. Pony Bob Haslam, after several years' association with Buffalo Bill's Wild West show, became a steward at the Congress Hotel in Chicago, where he passed away at age seventy-two in 1912. Billy Fisher was ordained a Mormon Bishop in 1876, and Ras Egan was later set apart as a Mormon Bishop and Patriarch; in 1895 he was elected to the first Utah legislature. The last survivor of the elite corps—a contested claim—seems to have been Billy Campbell, who died at age ninety-three in Stockton, California, in 1934. Buffalo Bill Cody made and lost several fortunes but left a still-living legacy in the town of Cody, Wyoming. When he died in Denver on January 10, 1917, at age seventy-one, the nation's telegraph wires were cleared of the day's World War I news to flash the word that the most widely known of all American plainsmen—and the most vivid reminder of the glory days of the Pony Express—had at last gone under.

Handstamped franks on envelopes for eastbound and westbound Pony Express mail in 1860–61. Wells Fargo and Company were then western agents for the service and saw to it that their imprimatur was prominently displayed, almost overshadowing that of the Pony Express and its owner, the Central Overland California and Pike's Peak Express Company.

7

THE FIRST TRANSCONTINENTAL TELEGRAPH

A SINGLE THREAD OF WIRE STRETCHED TAUT against three thousand miles of sky between New York and San Francisco. At long last, on October 24, 1861, the continent was endowed with a central nervous system: the first Transcontinental Telegraph. This was a brand new kind of trail, hailed by the Mormon *Deseret News* as an "electric highway." Now, for the first time, people a continent apart could converse together by the miracle of electricity converted to sound.

But the Transcontinental Telegraph was more than a new link between the Atlantic and Pacific. It created a new technological barrier between the Native American and the expanding white cultures—a barrier made even more formidable eight years later by the first Transcontinental Railroad. America's pretelegraph and prerailroad trails had relied on wagon trains powered by ox, mule, and horse. No more. Electricity and steam, iron wire, and iron tracks had come to stay.

Before the telegraph it had taken three months and twenty days for news of President William Henry Harrison's death in 1841 to reach Los Angeles (then a tiny village), but word of Abraham Lincoln's assassination in 1865 was flashed across the continent in mere minutes. As of October 24, 1861, the Golden State could no longer feel it was a forgotten backwater, out of touch with the power centers of Boston, New York, and the nation's capital. True, by 1860 telegraph wires had already crisscrossed the country east of the Mississippi, but once west of Fort Kearny in Nebraska Territory travelers would get all the way to Carson City, Nevada

LIGHTNING, EAST OF CLAUDE, TEXAS, *May 25, 1977.*
Photograph by Charles A. Doswell III.

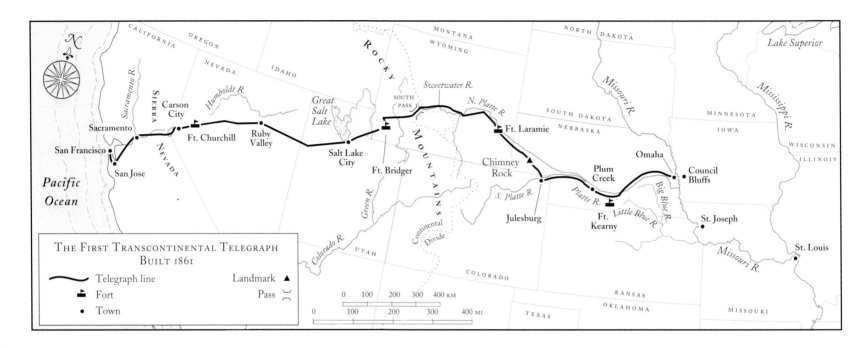

THE FIRST TRANSCONTINENTAL TELEGRAPH
BUILT 1861

Telegraph line   Landmark ▲
Fort   Pass ⌣
Town

Territory, near the California border, before finding another "singing wire."

It was only a fragile strand of iron, but of all the ties that bound the West Coast to the Union at that time, the Transcontinental Telegraph was the strongest. Lewis and Clark, the overland trails, and the Pony Express had all, in their time, stirred intimations of coast-to-coast unity. Now there was a new reason for people to view themselves not simply as Californians or Oregonians but as Americans. As it was widely observed at the time, the Transcontinental Telegraph annihilated time and distance, and such a tremendously accelerated transmission of information was bound to alter the basic rhythm of life for the entire continental United States.

.—— .... .— — .... .— — .... ——. . . ..
.— . . . .— ——. . .... —

"WHAT HATH GOD WROUGHT!"

Samuel Morse was an established artist long before he turned inventor in 1832, but over the next dozen years he perfected the communication system that would bring him far greater and more lasting fame than his painting. Morse, however, neither discovered electromagnetism nor invented the telegraph. He was one among many who had devised telegraph systems, including Alexander Bain of Scotland, Sir Charles Wheatstone in England, and Royal E. House and David Hughes in America. Yet Morse can be singled out as the first to design and develop a simple, practi-

Opposite: SAMUEL F. B. MORSE AT AGE SEVENTY-FIVE, *1866. Photograph by Mathew Brady.*

Morse, artist and inventor, developed a practical electromagnetic telegraph system that changed the world, as confirmed by the decorations from many nations in this photograph taken a few years before Morse's death in 1872.

cal apparatus that used electromagnetic current to send and receive intelligence over a wire.

When Morse returned home from Europe in 1832, as he walked down the *Sully*'s gangplank, the forty-one-year-old painter carried in his baggage the unfinished sketch of his masterpiece, *The Exhibition Gallery of the Louvre* (Terra Museum of American Art, Chicago), and, burning a hole in his pocket, the rough sketches of his telegraph—then still in the conceptual stage. Electricity was a relatively new field of inquiry; little was known about it, even by eminent scientists. Despite all his ingenuity and imagination, Morse was to struggle with one technical failure after another in his long quest for a telegraph system that really worked. This required designing a transmitting unit (consisting of battery, armature, and key) that sent the signal down the wire; a relay device (to push the signal farther along); and a receiving unit to record the message. Initially Morse was unable to transmit his signal over even a forty-foot wire, but when, on the advice of his colleague Professor Leonard D. Gale, he multiplied his power source from a one-cell battery to twenty cells and increased his feeble armature magnet from a few turns of wire around the core to one hundred turns, the signal passed readily through the tangles of wire festooned around Morse's workroom. Such improvements ultimately enabled his signal to pass through a remarkable ten miles of wire. Morse, ever careful to protect his own interests, filed for a pat-

ent in his sole name in 1837.

In late 1842 Morse's lobbying efforts were at white heat as he tried to win funds from Congress to build a telegraph line from Washington to Baltimore. To be near the officials whose support he sought, Morse had cannily procured work space in the Supreme Court chambers of the Capitol building, where he set up a model capable of transmitting messages. Despite any number of successful demonstrations to congressmen and others who observed the procedure with skeptical fascination, the general reaction was to dismiss the system as a novelty with no future. It was about this time that Hiram Sibley, at the request of a Washington lady of his acquaintance, put in a word for Morse with the chairman of the committee dealing with Morse's project. Little by little, but with painful slowness, events seemed to be moving in Morse's favor.

On March 3, 1843, Congress deliberated an appropriation bill authorizing thirty thousand dollars for Morse to build the first government telegraph line from Washington to Baltimore. A dispirited Morse hovered anxiously in the Senate throughout the day. Nothing had been decided by the time he returned home that night, and he was further discouraged to

find that after paying his travel expenses he would have exactly thirty-seven and one-half cents left. But next morning Annie Ellsworth, daughter of the commissioner of patents, brought him the news that his bill had finally passed. The jubilant Morse promised Annie as her reward that she could choose the first message to go over the wire.

With the government appropriation secured, Morse, his colleague Alfred Vail, and a new associate, Ezra Cornell (later founder of Cornell University), began construction of the experimental line. Their plan called for burying the telegraph cable in a trench, a feat to be facilitated, they hoped, by a special plow that Cornell had invented for the purpose. Trouble soon developed, however, in the form of faulty cable insulation, and work came to a halt. To allay congressional fears and a possible cutoff of funds, Cornell announced that the plow had broken and, together with Vail, saved the day by suggesting an alternative: stringing the wire overhead between poles, a system that became the norm for many decades. The Washington-Baltimore line, the U.S. government's first experimental telegraph line, was successfully completed, and on May 24, 1844, the first message came down the wire, not in Morse's words but in a biblical phrase (Numbers 23:23) chosen a year earlier by Annie Ellsworth: "What hath God wrought!"

THE RISE OF WESTERN UNION

Only a year and a half later, on November 24, 1845, America's first commercial telegraph line, built by one of Morse's rivals, Henry O'Rielly, connected Harris-

burg and Lancaster, Pennsylvania. William B. Wilson, who helped string that line, later described it as "a primitive affair. Small unbarked chestnut poles were planted about 100 yards apart [18 per mile]. . . . Through the top of each pole was inserted a turned black walnut cross-arm, the ends of which were covered with gummed cloth. The conductor was a No. 14 copper wire attached to the poles by giving it a double twist around the gummed cloth ends of the cross-arm."[1]

An early improvement replaced the gummed cloth with cotton cloth dipped in molten beeswax, and both devices were later made obsolete by glass insulators. For convenience, the Harrisburg-Lancaster telegraph was strung along the tracks of the Harrisburg, Portsmouth, Mount Joy, and Lancaster Railroad, thus setting a pattern for the first Transcontinental Telegraph line of 1861, which basically followed the Pony Express route, and for the second line, in 1869, which ran along the Transcontinental Railroad right-of-way and was constructed simultaneously with it.

The Harrisburg-Lancaster line was a success, but it had drawbacks. The system needed clear, cold weather in order to function, and wire breakdowns were frequent. The public, too, could be a problem since people were quite in the dark about how the system worked. "The general opinion," according to W. S. Bryan, who saw the first telegraph line to cross

Below: Insulators, made in New York for the telegraph, sometimes caused construction delays because they had to be shipped the long way around Cape Horn and then overland from San Francisco to Carson City and beyond as the line stretched eastward.

Opposite: TELEGRAPH CORPS AT WEBER CANYON, *1869. Photograph by A. J. Russell.*

Planting poles and stringing wire in Weber Canyon, Utah, a telegraph crew works its way west with the railroad in 1869, augmenting the original Transcontinental Telegraph of 1861.

the Mississippi, "was that the messages were written on very thin paper, which was rolled up tight and shot through the wires by pneumatic arrangement, the wires being made hollow for the purpose."[2] Fearful of language sent by "thunder and lightning," some folks were suspicious of the wire and its humming sound, and gave it a wide berth. One woman along the line fenced in a pole on her property so her cow couldn't rub against it and sour the milk. And at Fort Madison, Iowa, as the wire moved west a few years later, old Isaac Johnson, hoping to intercept free news, attached a wire of his own to the telegraph line. To the lower end of his wire he carefully fastened a potato, which he then floated in a tub of water. The potato bobbed and tossed, but to his chagrin it remained silent as the grave. Johnson could not beat the system, but he was neither the first—nor the last—to try.

The age of innocence for the telegraph industry did not last long. In barely a decade it matured from the superstitions of the cow lady and the ventures of eager entrepreneurs like O'Rielly to a culture of increasing financial and technical sophistication dominated by full-blown tycoons. Although platoons of other scientists, businessmen, and political figures played significant roles in the ultimate development of Morse's telegraph system into a national network, several emerge in retrospect as the Big Four of American telegraphy: Samuel Morse, Hiram Sibley, Jeptha Wade, and Edward Creighton.

Samuel F. B. Morse, born in 1791, carried into the nineteenth century the stamp of the Age of Enlightenment. Endowed with talents in both art and science, he became a professor of art at New York University, a trustee of Vassar College, and a founder and first president of the National Academy of Design. Together with J. W. Draper he made one of the first daguerreotypes in America.

Hiram Sibley first saw the light of day in North Adams, Massachusetts, in 1807. His formal education was limited to the village school, which he left early to take up shoemaking. There followed a succession of employments: a cotton factory, a machine shop, and a wool-carding business. In 1838 he moved to Rochester, New York, where he was elected sheriff—an early sign of the political deftness he would demonstrate when he lobbied successfully for the congressional appropriation for Morse in 1843 and again for the Telegraph Act of 1860. With Ezra Cornell he staged a master coup by founding the Western Union company in 1856. He remained its head for nine years, proving time and again not only his farsighted ability to read the future but also his determination to help shape it. At the time of his death in Rochester, in 1888, Sibley was the largest owner of improved land in the United States.

Jeptha H. Wade entered the world of telegraphy as a telegraph operator—a glamorous new occupation at the time—after an early stint as a carpenter and several years as an itinerant portrait painter and daguerreotype artist. His shrewdness quickly propelled him into the booming business of constructing telegraph lines throughout Ohio—experience that greatly increased Wade's usefulness to Sibley and his efforts to build Western Union.

Edward Creighton, who came of Irish stock and was raised on farms in Ohio, epitomized the self-made man whose image marches time and again across the pages of nineteenth-century American history. His boyhood was cut short when he left school after the fifth grade to go to work. By age fourteen he began to earn his way as a cart-boy on the pike-roads with a companion, Phil Sheridan (later the famous Civil War general). For a time Creighton hauled supplies from Ohio to Maryland, supplementing his meager income by prizefighting. He got his first experience with the telegraph when he won a contract in 1847 freighting telegraph poles from Springfield to Cincinnati, Ohio, and went on to build telegraph lines, including several for Henry O'Rielly, the newspaper-editor-turned-telegraph-contractor. Creighton ultimately rose to the post of general superintendent of the Pacific Telegraph Company, which built the eastern section of the Transcontinental Telegraph.

In the 1840s, when the telegraph industry was in its feverish infancy, more than fifty small local companies had set themselves up east of the Mississippi to build telegraph lines linking any two towns that would have them. Telegraph developers were a special breed, typified by smooth-talking, fast-moving Charles M. Stebbins, an early promoter in the Kansas-Arkansas area. With all the seductive flair of a Music Man, Stebbins would breeze into a town and persuade the citizens that they badly needed a telegraph (whether they did or not), and that they should pay him to build one. It was a classic example of innovative entrepreneurship, a pattern to

Hiram Sibley, together with Ezra Cornell, organized the Western Union company in 1856, a masterstroke that established Sibley as the world leader of the telegraph industry and Western Union as the nation's first monopoly.

Edward Creighton, one of the Big Four of the transcontinental telegraph, risked his life riding across the Nevada desert and the Sierra Nevada in winter to identify the best route for the line from Omaha to Sacramento.

be endlessly repeated in evolving America: create a need and then satisfy it for a profit.

The problems encountered in actually building the Big Line, the Transcontinental Telegraph, seemed almost anticlimactic compared with the bedlam in the telegraph environment that preceded it. Frenzied construction throughout the eastern United States, coupled with ferocious competition and bitter legal clashes over patent infringements, had led to financial chaos. Companies clawed at each other to keep alive, and few potential investors were willing to risk buying telegraph stock. So great was the confusion that Samuel Morse, uncertain as to the best application of his own invention, offered the patent to the government for one hundred thousand dollars. Fortunately for him, the Post Office, with its habitual myopia, decided the system would not succeed commercially and rejected Morse's offer.

As the tangled telegraph web spread over the East, clearer heads discerned that consolidation was the only route to efficient operation—and to profit. In the vanguard were Cornell and Sibley, who recognized that many of the existing companies were on the verge of bankruptcy and could therefore be bought for a few cents on the dollar. It was clearly a buyer's market and, with Wade's help, Cornell and Sibley gobbled up some twelve rival companies in five years.

The explosive growth of the telegraph industry after 1850 was phenomenal, and the Western Union system became the major factor in that growth. Western Union began life in 1851 as the New York and Mississippi Valley Printing Telegraph Company. At that time it controlled only 550 miles of wire. Five years and a number of acquisitions later, Sibley and Cornell formed Western Union by merging Mississippi Valley with the other regional telegraph companies they had bought. After swallowing their nearest rival, the American Telegraph Company, in February 1866, Western Union controlled 75,686 miles of wire. In fifteen years it had become one of America's largest corporations, with annual revenues of $6.6 million—an enormous figure for the time. Only three years later, upon completion of its second transcontinental line, along the Union Pacific right-of-way, the Western Union system had become the largest and most efficient telegraph network in the world. By then it owned 121,595 miles of wire, or ten times more than its remaining rivals. The years of grinding work finally made wealthy men of Sibley, Cornell, Wade, Creighton, and of course Morse, as well as those associates and investors who had had the nerve to run awesome risks and the stamina to stay the course.

WIRING THE CONTINENT

Although Sibley was the one who finally implemented the first Transcontinental Telegraph, the concept of a single telegraph line across the entire continent did not originate with him, or even with Morse. Like the telegraph itself, the transcontinental wire was an idea that had been in the air for some time. Even the ebullient Henry O'Rielly, with Senator Stephen A.

Douglas of Illinois as his advocate in Congress, had offered a bill to fund such a venture in 1848 and again in 1851, but the time was not yet right and the bills failed. For the ensuing decades Congress, already sorely divided by sectionalism, shunted Transcontinental Telegraph proposals aside for fear that the tail might wag the dog—i.e., that building such a line along either a northern or a southern route might determine the ultimate location of the vital Transcontinental Railroad, the prize that North and South each coveted. By 1860, however, both the politics and the telegraph had changed dramatically. Having formed his powerful Western Union in 1856, Sibley had lobbied successfully for passage of the Telegraph Act in 1860. (That act, interestingly enough, had been introduced by William H. Gwin, the senator from California who had earlier introduced legislation to create the Pony Express.) The Civil War was not far off. It was time to take action.

The Telegraph Act of 1860 authorized the government, with certain restrictions, to award a construction contract to the low bidder for a telegraph line from Missouri to California. The low bidder proved to be Sibley, who was in fact the sole bidder since, by a curious coincidence, all his competitors—Theodore Adams, Benjamin Ficklin, and John H. Harmon—withdrew at the last minute. Sibley left nothing to chance in realizing his vision of a transcontinental wire. His board of directors had previously rejected as too risky his proposal that Western Union erect the transcontinental line. In return, Sibley blustered that if they refused, he would do it himself. The board then agreed, in order to insulate Western Union

from risk if things turned out badly, to form a separate company for the line's construction: the Pacific Telegraph Company.

On January 11, 1861, the Pacific Telegraph Company was chartered in Nebraska, with Wade as president and, to no one's surprise, with the three nonbidders under the Telegraph Act of 1860—Adams, Ficklin, and Harmon—as directors. The company's objective was to build the line from Omaha only as far west as Salt Lake City; it was hoped that the western section would be completed by one of the California telegraph companies. This stratagem further diluted Western Union's risk.

Seventeen years had passed since Morse's stringing of the first government telegraph line between Washington and Baltimore. Now, in the space of only a few months, a transcontinental wire would connect New York to San Francisco, rendering the Isthmus of Panama crossing ever more obsolete and prefiguring the next trail to come: the Transcontinental Railroad.

In November 1860 Sibley sent Creighton on a cross-country survey from Omaha to Sacramento to determine the best route. At the same time, Wade was dispatched to San Francisco by sea, crossing Panama on muleback, to organize support for the transcontinental project among the California telegraph companies. November was dangerously late for Creighton to cross the western plains and mountain ranges. Traveling partly by stage, but most of the time by horse or mule, he rode west eleven hundred miles in winter, a solitary, antlike figure, black against the snow, following the Pony Express route west from Fort Kearny.

Creighton reached Salt Lake City in mid-December,

FREDERICK A. BEE *built a telegraph wire across the Sierra Nevada in 1859. Running from Sacramento, California, to Carson City, Nevada, the fragile line, nicknamed "Bee's Grapevine" because it was strung between trees, carried messages between the Nevada gold fields and the West Coast.*

and there he met with the commercially alert Brigham Young, who confirmed his financial and logistical support of the project. Continuing west, Creighton fought through the valley of the Humboldt and, as one account has it, "Stumbled into Carson City after 12 days, snow blind and half dead." Three times during the ride, snow and alkali driven by gale winds had flayed the skin from his face until it looked like raw beef. After only a short rest Creighton crossed the Sierra Nevada—an ordeal that had earlier killed nearly half of the eighty-seven members of the Donner Party—to keep his Sacramento rendezvous with Jeptha Wade.

While Creighton was slogging westward, Wade had already reached San Francisco and opened delicate negotiations with the four leading California telegraph companies, urging them to join forces in building the western sections of the line. This was a ticklish task since each company, jealous of its own prerogatives, aspired to assume the dominant role. Wade's overtures, as he put it, "had raised a breeze" in a situation already rife with discord, acrimony, and suspicion. Just how carefully Wade danced on eggs in these discussions is revealed in a discouraged letter he sent back to Sibley, on January 4, 1861:

> The present state of the case seems to be this. I am still trying the plan mentioned in my last and am getting it somewhat talked up for the Capitalists which I will call A. I have in tow some of the best and wealthiest men here and as good as can be found anywhere. Next is Messrs. Bee which I will call B. Also Mc C and S. which I will call C. & Mr. Carpentier and associates of the State

Tel. Co. which I will call D. . . . Each of the 4 have a special regard for self and want . . . to play sharp. "A" would evidently like to close with us to build half way and then use their "Lemon Squeezer" to bring in the other B. B and C both like my plan and say they are willing to go into it on fair terms. D don't object to the plan, but (feeling suspicion to the other Tel. Co's which is correct in some respects) wants to treat with us on their own hook, squeeze or choke . . . B and C, and leave A out, having as they pictured all the money they need. . . . "D" is the hardest of the lot to get along with.[3]

For nearly two months Wade maneuvered between the recalcitrant western companies, cajoling and bullying by turns. Finally he threatened that Western Union would go it alone and build its own western section if the Californians refused to cooperate. In the end it was agreed to form the Overland Telegraph Company as a counterpart to the Pacific Telegraph Company in the east; both Overland and Pacific were to be under the control of Western Union. The Overland Telegraph Company was chartered April 10, 1861, and by May its construction crews were assembled at Sacramento and rumbling east toward Salt Lake City.

The 1861 Transcontinental Telegraph was to be a continuous two-thousand-mile wire suspended between Omaha at the eastern end and Fort Churchill, Nevada Territory (on the California border), at the western end. At these two points it connected with wires already erected and extending to both coasts. In the middle lay Salt Lake City, where the line's east-

ern and western sections would meet. In the west, construction began at Fort Churchill; in the east the jumping-off point was Fort Kearny, since the line had already been completed to that point from Omaha by the confident Sibley, the year before he won the government contract.

At the head of the column out of Sacramento rode James Gamble, a telegraph veteran who had built a number of California lines, including the first wires strung by the California State Telegraph Company in

Despite mountains, blizzards, and delayed deliveries of supplies and equipment, veteran telegraph-line builder James Gamble of California successfully took the western arm of the Transcontinental Telegraph into Salt Lake City in October 1861.

*Sacramento during the Flood.
K Street East from Fourth Street,
January 1862. Photography by
Charles Weed.*

*The year after the completion of the
Transcontinental Telegraph, the great
flood of 1862 gave a Venetian look to
Sacramento at the western end of the
line, floating poles away and creating
havoc with the wire.*

1853. Alongside Gamble rode I. M. Hubbard, also an experienced line builder. To the rear stretched a long file of 50 men, 228 oxen, 18 mules and horses, and 25 jangling wagons of wire, insulators, and other equipment. Toward the end of June the train reached Carson City, where Hubbard took charge of the crew working east out of Fort Churchill while Gamble continued on to supervise the entire route to Salt Lake.

From the outset Gamble's progress was delayed by supply shortages. The telegraph wire and insulators from New York had to make the time-consuming sea voyage around Cape Horn to San Francisco, then a long haul overland to Carson City and points east. Poles presented a special problem, for pole contractors often failed to make timely deliveries to construction sites. In early autumn, stuck west of Salt Lake City without the poles he needed, Gamble was forced to leave the line and lead a crew many miles into the mountains to cut their own poles. During the night an early blizzard buried his sleeping men in gravelike hummocks of snow. At first light and Gamble's sharp command, the hummocks exploded to life. The crew cut twenty wagonloads of poles in two days, enough to finish the line into Salt Lake City. Terrain, logistics, and weather were Gamble's chief worries; his crews had left Fort Churchill in July, digging, stringing wire, and sweating all the way, but as they approached Salt Lake in October they were digging, stringing, and shivering in their boots.

Eleven hundred miles to the east, on June 17, 1861, Creighton and his Pacific Telegraph crews struck out from Omaha for Fort Kearny, the first leg of their route, following the Platte River. Ultimately Creigh-ton's caravan would pass through Fort Kearny, then Julesburg (a hardscrabble clutch of six log huts in the northeast corner of present-day Colorado that would soon become notorious as a "hell-on-wheels" town), past Fort Laramie in Wyoming Territory, over South Pass (which only fifteen years earlier Narcissa Whitman and Eliza Hart Spalding had been the first white women to cross), and down to Jim Bridger's old fort near the Green River, before reaching his goal at Salt Lake City.

Creighton commanded a train of over one hundred wagons, five hundred oxen and mules, and four hundred well-armed men on the march to Fort Kearny and its handful of neighboring adobe huts. The telegraph station was a low, mud-brick structure with grass clumps sprouting from its sod roof like porcupine quills. It was here, in this outpost of civilization—one of only half a dozen between Omaha and Sacramento—that Creighton's men planted their first western telegraph pole on July 4, 1861. Two days earlier and two hundred miles farther west Creighton, who had gone on ahead, had with his own hands dug the first pole at Julesburg.

While the Gamble and Creighton crews toiled toward Salt Lake from opposite ends of the line, two additional crews worked out of Salt Lake City to meet them. James Street and his men headed west to Fort Churchill, while W. H. Stebbins's crew struck east toward Fort Kearny. Crossing the treeless plains between Fort Kearny and Salt Lake City posed a special problem, since poles had to be shipped from as far as 250 miles away.

Along the construction line each crew was divided

MOUTH OF ECHO CANYON, *1866. Photograph by Charles W. Carter.*

Bare telegraph poles near Salt Lake City wait for the stringing of wires that will bring them to life.

into special sections. The surveyors led the way, placing their stakes and markers; next lumbered the wagons, rolling poles onto the ground at the rate of about one every seventy yards. These were followed by the rugged pole diggers, who, using nothing but simple spades and bare hands, buried every pole five feet deep in the hard earth. Last in line trailed the wire stringers, who climbed to the top of the pole and attached the fragile wire to the equally vulnerable insulators.

Translating the accomplishments of Gamble and

THE OVERLAND PONY EXPRESS, *n.d. Print by Savage after a painting by George M. Ottinger.*

A Pony Express rider waves to his rivals, the telegraph linemen, as he dashes down the trail. The telegraph line across the continent was completed in October 1861, and the Pony Express expired in a matter of days.

Creighton and their crews into numbers conveys the magnitude of the effort as nothing else can: they planted an astonishing total of 27,500 telegraph poles across plains, desert, mountains, and rivers, and strung two thousand miles of single-strand iron wire. The crews averaged from three to eight miles a day depending on terrain, although they once strung a record sixteen miles in a single day, hurrying to reach water.

An advance telegraph station was set up daily at the head of Gamble's line so communication could be kept open with Sacramento. The distance between Gamble's and Creighton's advance stations kept shrinking as the eastern and western columns, like tall wooden soldiers in single file, marched steadily toward each other. By special arrangement with Western Union, Pony Express riders interrupted their cross-country rides at the advance stations to deliver telegraph dispatches from the East or to pick up those from the West. Ironically, the Pony Express was delivering messages to the very system that within the year would accelerate its own demise.

GUARDING THE LINE

As if the natural hazards of lightning bolts, howling winds, and the Sierra blizzards whose twenty-foot

Opposite: A LINEMAN OF 1855, *n.d. Engraving from* Shaffner's Telegraph Manual, *n.d.*

An early telegraph lineman cavalierly checks his wire. In the 1850s brittle, but cheaper, iron wire was sometimes used instead of copper, and breaks were frequent.

snowfalls buried lines and poles were not enough, other forces regularly downed wires and interrupted traffic. Curiously, more problems arose on the line after it was finally up than during its initial construction.

Out on the prairie, two-ton bison wandering over the treeless plains suddenly discovered the unaccustomed bliss of upright poles, made to order for scratching. Leaning and rubbing their shaggy hides in ecstasy,

the great beasts would send a tangled forest of poles and wires crashing to the ground. Eventually the railroads and their hunters, William F. Cody included, would eliminate that hazard forever.

Two-legged predators also caused problems. The line had barely been completed when the governor of Missouri, in order to disrupt Northern military communications, ordered the wires in Missouri torn down. This forced a rapid rerouting to avoid Saint Louis, and as of January 1862 the circuit went from Omaha to Chicago and then on east. In the western section of the line, desperate emigrants on the trail would chop down poles for firewood and appropriate wire to repair their wagons.

The Indians were another matter. Late in life Sibley recalled to an interviewer that the Indians had never caused a bit of trouble to the telegraph; some tribal chiefs at various times had, in fact, sent gifts of live animals and other tokens of respect to him at Rochester, New York. During construction little or no trouble brewed in the western section of the line, where Gamble had prudently engaged a number of Shoshone tribesmen to handle the stock.

In one highly impressive demonstration, so one version of the story goes, wire was strung for a mile between two hills, and Shoshone were stationed on each hill. At the sending end of the wire, the Indians composed a message and gave it to the operator, who transmitted it to the

receiving station a mile away. When the receiving operator gave the message to the Indians at the receiving station, they then galloped back to the sending station and recited the message to the senders. To the Indians' astonishment, the messages were identical. As a result of such educational experiences, there was relatively little Indian trouble during the building phase of the Transcontinental Telegraph.

Farther east, where tribal hunting grounds were at stake, Indian interest in the *we-ente-mo-ke-te-bope* ("wire rope express"), as they called it, would turn from curiosity to hostility. In the Great Plains region,

Henry F. Farny (1847–1916). SONG OF THE TALKING WIRE, *1904. Oil on canvas, 22⅛ x 40 in. (56.1 x 101.6 cm). The Taft Museum, Cincinnati; Bequest of Mr. and Mrs. Charles Phelps Taft.*

initial Indian suspicion of the white man's wire—
reinforced by occasional electric shocks inflicted on
them in horseplay by the builders—made them cau-
tious in coming near it. When some expressed the
belief that the telegraph was an animal and asked how
it was fed, they were told it ate lightning. With the
Plains Indians growing increasingly anxious over
white invasion of their hunting lands, and with the
rapid decimation of the great buffalo herds—which
the Indians recognized as a fatal disturbance of the
balance of nature—things took a 180-degree turn for
the worse during the Cheyenne War of 1864. By that
time the Indians fully grasped the importance of the

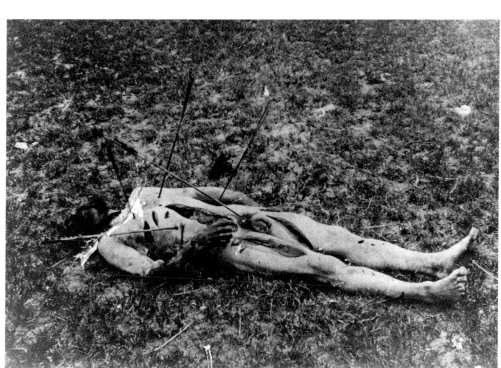

telegraph as a means of military communication and
regularly sabotaged the telegraph line, ripping down
wires, burning poles, and attacking telegraph installations at stage stations.

U.S. Army troops were finally assigned to key
points along the overland trail with the mission—vital
to the Civil War effort—of keeping the Transcontinental Telegraph in operation. Private Hervey Johnson
of Company G, Eleventh Ohio Volunteer Cavalry,
was at first assigned to monotonous duty at Fort Laramie, then in the Idaho Territory, but after being re-
assigned to stations at Deer Creek and Platte Bridge,
Johnson found himself in a more active combat area.
In a letter to his sister he reported that ten men repair-
ing the telegraph near Sweetwater Station had been
attacked by fifty Indians; Edgar M. Gwynn, the telegraph operator, was killed and another soldier badly
wounded. "Gwynn," Johnson continued in a postscript
dated August 24, "was stripped of his clothing, scalped,
his hands cut off, sinews taken out of his legs and
arms, and his heart and liver taken out, nineteen
arrows were in his body."[4]

Johnson's experiences in the service made him
adamantly anti-Indian, convinced that the government's Indian peace program of 1865–66 was pointless.
He wrote indignantly: "I would like for some of our
philanthropists to come out here, I mean some of those
who sympathise with the indian in his benighted condition, some of those who sit there at Washington and
howl and want the authorities to deal leniently with
the *poor* indian."[5] Such negative feelings about the
Indians were not uncommon at the time, especially
among those in the military who had engaged in armed

combat with them. Despite the voices of those who advocated a more moderate policy—and they were many—the congressional chorus of calls for isolation or extermination of the Indian rose to ever more strident levels as the inevitable clash of cultures approached its climax. But that bloody denouement was still more than a decade away.

TWO OCEANS CONNECTED

Progress west by Gamble's Overland section of the telegraph line was relatively slow during July and August 1861. Pole and equipment delays made for faltering headway, and water shortages were severe for crews crossing the Nevada desert in high summer. By July 15 poles had been planted fifty miles east of Fort Churchill, but it took two and a half months, until the end of September, to make Ruby Valley, another two hundred miles east.

Creighton, meanwhile, had strung supply and construction trains out along the line at Fort Kearny and Julesburg, and as time went on he moved farther ahead to Fort Laramie, South Pass, and Fort Bridger. Creighton charged busily up and down the line, directing the hauling of crooked cedar poles from Cottonwood Springs two hundred miles west of Fort Kearny, checking on wire and insulator stocks, and orchestrating the whole performance. For Creighton, life was a crescendo of activity; his brother John, who was in charge of building between Fort Laramie and Fort Bridger, said he had "known him to be 14 days and nights at a time in a coach without rest" except for meals.

Accounts differ as to timing and locations, but apparently by July 22 Creighton's wire had been strung to Chimney Rock, Nebraska; two weeks later poles were up and wired three miles west of Fort Laramie, and on October 17 the eastern wire was complete into Salt Lake City. Creighton, then still at Fort Bridger, tapped into the wire and triumphantly wired his wife in Omaha: "In a few days two oceans will be connected." The western wire being strung by Gamble's men would not reach Salt Lake for another week, but when it did people observed with astonishment that due to the difference in time zones a telegram from New York to San Francisco would now reach San Francisco three hours and fifteen minutes before it left New York.

On October 18 the first test message was sent successfully from Salt Lake to Omaha, provoking widespread celebration but not the all-out jubilation that had met the Pony Express's inaugural run. By 1861 public attention was distracted by the six-month-old War Between the States and by the still unsuccessful but nonetheless dramatic attempts to lay a transatlantic telegraph cable across the sea floor. Nevertheless, ritual greetings were sent by Brigham Young to Jeptha Wade in Ohio, and after Gamble had finally wired up in Salt Lake—thus completing the circuit from San Francisco to Washington—on October 24 Chief Justice Stephen Field of California sent Abraham Lincoln the first through telegram from the West Coast to the East Coast, assuring the beleaguered president of California's loyalty to the Union.

Two days later, on October 26, the *New York Times*, noting the relatively placid public reaction to the line's completion, added a more upbeat salute of its own:

"The work of carrying westward the transcontinental telegraph line has progressed with so little blazonment, that it is with almost an electric thrill one reads the words of greeting yesterday flashed instantaneously over the wires from California. The magnificent idea of joining the Atlantic with the Pacific by the magnetic wire is today a realized fact. New York, Queen of the Atlantic, and San Francisco, Queen of the Pacific, are now united by this noblest symbol of our modern civilization."

The first Transcontinental Telegraph was profitable from the very outset. Admittedly this was partly due to the exorbitant and illegal rates charged in the first euphoria of success. During the first week of operations it cost one dollar a word to send a message, but this was shortly trimmed back to seven dollars for ten words, still far above the rate specified in the Act of 1860, which had stipulated three dollars for ten words. Such arrogant price gouging evoked a chorus of protests from the working press—who were becoming major telegraph clients—and from Congress, which viewed overcharging as a violation of the public trust. The fight dragged on endlessly, rendered more acrimonious by the widely publicized fact that the entire transcontinental line had cost only half a million dollars to erect.

The establishment of the Transcontinental Telegraph—the first American industry based on electricity—now linked the Atlantic and the Pacific by an electric trail of almost limitless promise. It was not an unmixed blessing, however: while revolutionizing America's press and railroad operations, at the same time the telegraph created the nation's first national monopoly. It was miraculous that the entire transcontinental line had been built in only four months, yet it created an even greater miracle than speed. Since the eastern section alone (Omaha to Salt Lake City) had been financed by the sale of a million dollars worth of stock, and since the exorbitant telegraph traffic revenues exceeded all expectations, the first surge of electricity from coast to coast transmuted the galvanized iron wire to pure gold.

John Gast. SPIRIT OF MANIFEST DESTINY, *n.d. Library of Congress, Washington, D.C.*

Westward expansion, embodied here in the "Spirit of Manifest Destiny," leads progress, technology, and civilization westward, illuminating the darkness of an untamed wilderness.

THE FIRST TRANSCONTINENTAL RAILROAD

8

IN 1803–6 LEWIS AND CLARK HAD BLAZED THE first trail to the Pacific in dugout canoes, on horseback, and on foot. A scant sixty years later a highly mechanized iron trail, two thousand miles long, would overtake them.

At its outset, in 1863, the Transcontinental Railroad was not one line but two: the Central Pacific (CP), starting from the west, and the Union Pacific (UP), heading from the east. The two roads met less than six years later in Promontory Summit, Utah, where their joining was celebrated at the famous Golden Spike ceremony.

Although an extensive rail network had been developing in the eastern United States since 1828, all tracks stopped at the Missouri River. For travelers from the Atlantic coast to the Pacific, a steam-powered train all the way to California would be a vast improvement to the dismal alternatives: a spine-cracking stagecoach ride lasting several weeks, a fever-plagued crossing of the Isthmus of Panama, or a four- to seven-month voyage around South America's Cape Horn. In the 1840s and 1850s, after such massive demographic shifts as the Great Migration, the Mormon settlement of Utah, and the stampede of gold seekers to California, a transcontinental railroad seemed inevitable.

But dreaming of a coast-to-coast railroad was one thing, building it, another. Over a twenty-year period many construction plans had been put forward, ranging from the practical to the crackpot. Perhaps the most ambitious of all was New York City merchant

MORNING, DONNER LAKE, CALIFORNIA, *1987.*
Photograph by Frank S. Balthis.

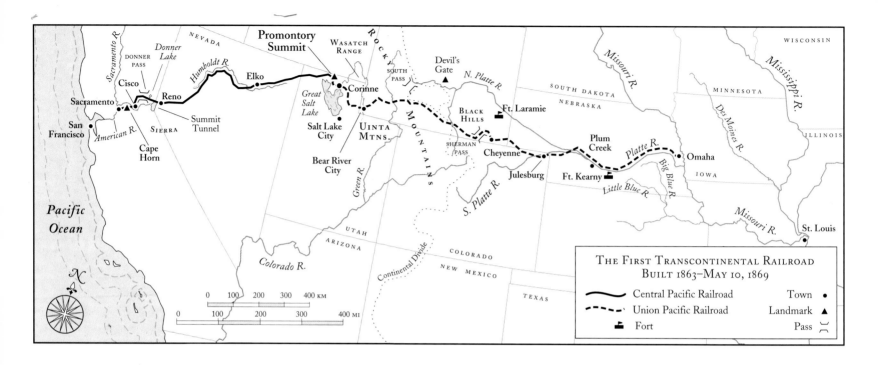

The First Transcontinental Railroad
Built 1863–May 10, 1869

—⁓— Central Pacific Railroad   Town •
- - - Union Pacific Railroad   Landmark ▲
🛇 Fort   Pass ⌣

Asa Whitney's plan of 1848, in which he proposed that in return for his building the railroad to the Pacific at a cost of fifty million dollars, Congress should grant him ninety thousand square miles of land along the right-of-way, an acreage larger than many countries in the world. Southern congressmen, however—including Missouri Senator Thomas Hart Benton, who agitated for a more southerly route than Whitney's—saw to it that the proposal was consigned to the congressional dustbin.

Before a single foot of track could be laid, legislation had to pass through Congress settling such controversial matters as route location, government and private financing, and the organization of the railroad

system itself. Competitive steamship lines and stagecoach companies, like Wells Fargo and Ben Holladay's Overland Stage, threw obstacles in the way, but the railroad's fiercest enemy was the bitter sectionalism in Congress. Regional interests, north, south, east, and west, clamored in the Capitol for years—more loudly as the Civil War approached—repeatedly blocking the passage of enabling legislation. Into this raucous arena, in 1861, finally stepped a brilliant young engineer named Theodore Dehone Judah. Within a year he would tame the congressional lions and rescue the Pacific Railroad Act of 1862.

While still in his twenties Judah had engineered the Sacramento Valley Railroad, the first line in Cali-

Opposite: Theodore Dehone Judah was the brilliant young railroad engineer from California who successfully promoted the construction of the Transcontinental Railroad. He made the first railroad-route survey across the Sierra Nevada before dying of yellow fever at the age of thirty-seven, long before the railroad was completed.

fornia. For years he surveyed the valleys and ridges of the Sierra Nevada searching for a viable railroad pass to the east—often accompanied by his young wife, Anna, who sketched the stunning scenery. It was to Anna that he brashly confided one day, "[A transcontinental railroad] will be built, and I'm going to have something to do with it."[1]

Obsessed by this vision, in 1859 Judah drafted his "Practical Plan for Building the Pacific Railroad" and sent off copies to President James Buchanan and every member of Congress. Shortly afterward, a California railroad convention dispatched him to Washington to present his plan in person to Congress. After wangling an office for his own use in the Capitol building, the young engineer set up a miniature railroad museum, complete with maps, charts, geological specimens, and Anna's artwork. From this cubbyhole Judah buttonholed passing legislators and handed out copies of his plan—without success. The frustrated engineer returned to California to continue his search for a pass over the summit of the Sierra Nevada. When his friend Dr. Daniel W. Strong, a druggist in the hamlet of Dutch Flat, guided him to the Donner Pass area in October 1860, Judah realized that he had finally found his crossing.

Back at Doc Strong's drugstore, Judah promptly drew up the articles of association for the Central Pacific Railroad Company of California. Druggist and engineer immediately began the search for buyers of CP stock, but investors responded coldly to Judah's offer, preferring to earn 24 percent per annum in mining ventures rather than take a complete flyer in a nebulous railroad scheme.

Nevertheless, in January 1861 Judah finally found the mother lode. After a lackluster meeting one evening in Sacramento's Saint Charles Hotel, during which not a single share in the CP was subscribed, a portly hardware dealer named Collis P. Huntington

approached Judah and suggested a private meeting a few days later with his partner, Mark Hopkins. This second gathering led to the organization of the Central Pacific Railroad. After hearty handshakes—but nothing yet in writing—the Big Four (Huntington, Hopkins, and their subsequent associates Leland Stanford and Charles Crocker), with marginal help from others, agreed to buy enough stock to permit CP incorporation and to finance Judah's definitive survey across the Sierra Nevada. Stanford (soon to be elected governor of California) was named president; Huntington, vice president; Hopkins, treasurer; and Theodore Judah, chief engineer. Crocker was designated a director.

When his survey was completed, Judah's 1861 report to the CP board estimated construction costs of thirteen million dollars from Sacramento to the Nevada border. A sobering figure, but not a deterrent to the Big Four. In October 1861 the CP board, confident that their chief engineer knew more about building railroads through high mountains than any other man in the country, dispatched Judah to Washington to lobby for a new railroad bill. This time around he was armed with one hundred thousand dollars in CP stock to sprinkle as he saw fit among hesitant congressmen. A lobbying campaign had begun, sometimes slipping over into outright bribery.

A highly effective lobbyist, Judah soon won appointment as clerk to two House railroad subcommittees, in which capacity he literally wrote the enabling legislation. Congress—recognizing the validity of Judah's plans and prodded by Abraham Lincoln, who foresaw that the railroad would keep California on the Union side and assure access to much-needed gold and silver—finally worked out a compromise bill with the windy title "An Act to Aid in the Construction of a Railroad and Telegraph Line from the Missouri River to the Pacific Ocean, and to Secure to the Government the Use of the Same for Postal, Military, and other Purposes"—more commonly called the Pacific Railroad Act of 1862.

The act was flawed from the outset, but it did create the Union Pacific Railroad and recognize the already existing Central Pacific Railroad as its western counterpart. The act gave the railroad companies sixty-four hundred acres per mile, checkerboarded on alternating sides of the track that each laid, which could be sold to raise additional funds; it also authorized the issuance of government bonds to both lines for track laid: $16,000 per mile over level ground, $32,000 across deserts, and $48,000 in the mountains.

But there was more than one catch. The bonds would be released to the railroads for each forty-mile stretch only after government inspection and approval. Moreover, the railroads had to convert the bonds into cash for construction costs by offering them in the open market, a market sorely depressed by the Civil War. These restrictions alone almost strangled the infant railroad in its crib. In a final flourish of congressional power and prudence, the law also required that the entire railroad be built by July 1874 or be confiscated by the federal government. All in all, it was a well-intentioned but unworkable piece of legislation that had to be revised in 1864, 1865, and 1866. Imperfect as the act was, it nevertheless prompted Judah to wire jubilantly to Sacramento: "We have drawn the elephant. Now let us see if we can harness him up."[2]

As amended, the Pacific Railroad Act of 1862 finally made the railroad a business venture appealing to private investors who saw a chance for profit from the construction phase alone. (Freight and passenger revenue still seemed highly unlikely for a railroad that crossed two thousand uninhabited miles.) With its financial future at last looking rosier, construction of the Transcontinental Railroad soon got underway. On January 8, 1863, dry-goods merchant Charles Crocker said a few inspirational words and California Governor Leland Stanford, the august president of the Central Pacific, turned over the first spadeful of earth at a modest groundbreaking ceremony in Sacramento. Eighteen hundred miles to the east, in Omaha, the Union Pacific was considerably slower off the mark, not celebrating its groundbreaking until December 2, 1863—a ceremony presided over by the Machiavellian vice-president of the line, Dr. Thomas C. Durant, and his ebullient colleague, real estate developer George

Governor Leland Stanford, a founder and the first president of the Central Pacific Railroad. Like his Big Four associates, he became one of the wealthiest men in America.

Francis Train. As it turned out, Durant's financial, organizational, and construction problems were just beginning. He had no technical staff at work, and it would be over a year before the UP would lay a single mile of track. He might well have wondered if the UP December groundbreaking might turn out instead to be a burial ceremony. Modest though it was, the expense of the Central Pacific's celebration exhausted

its treasury, and the Union Pacific's was not much better off. Perhaps this was an omen: both railroads were to be perennially plagued by cash crunches.

THE BIG FOUR

There may never have been four partners in American industry who worked together so harmoniously, for so long, and so successfully as the four men who ran the Central Pacific Railroad: Charles Crocker, Mark Hopkins, Collis P. Huntington, and Leland Stanford. Mutual trust was the hallmark of the relationship, and many of their business decisions were confirmed by a handshake rather than a contract. It was many years before that goodwill deteriorated to the point that Huntington publicly called Stanford "a damned old fool" and Stanford declared that he would trust Huntington as "far as he could throw Trinity Church up the side of Mt. Shasta."

Yet whatever differences they may have had during their association, their character and experience were similar enough to bind them solidly together in the great enterprise they had undertaken. All four were easterners turned '49ers, gone west to seek their fortunes; all became successful merchants there. Each was ambitious, hardheaded, thrifty, and industrious in the extreme—good qualities to have in the rough-and-tumble, cash-on-the-barrelhead environment of Sacramento, still partly a tent city in the 1850s.

Hopkins, senior in years to the others and familiarly known as "Uncle Mark," was dour of manner and spoke with a lisp on the rare occasions when he broke public silence. According to Crocker, Hopkins was not given to administration but preferred to counsel his colleagues and to devote his formidable attention to the details of overseeing the vastly complex Central Pacific financial records.

Leland Stanford, thirty-six years old in 1861, was the youngest of the Big Four. He had studied law in Albany, New York, practiced briefly in Wisconsin, grown restless, and moved on to try his luck in the California mines. There he turned a handsome profit that enabled him to open a wholesale grocery business in Sacramento. Always drawn to politics, he became a leader in the new Republican party, and after a bruising defeat in his campaign for the California governorship in 1857, ran again and won handily in 1861. Stanford, who had peddled vegetables on the streets of Schenectady as a boy, was already a wealthy man when he threw in his lot with Hopkins and the others.

Charles Crocker was the biggest of the Big Four, tipping the scales at 244 pounds (although he confessed to having reached 270 during the most stressful years laying track over the Sierra Nevada). By all accounts he was blunt, stubborn, fearless, and a workaholic who habitually arose at 4:00 A.M. to light fiercely into the day's work. "I had no nursery years," boasted Crocker. When he was only nine years old, Charlie Crocker was already selling fruit and newspapers in his hometown

of Troy, New York, and at age twelve he quit school to help support his family. He approached life as a series of transactions, expecting something in return for everything he gave. Crocker and his brothers Henry and Clark went west for gold in 1850, driving two wagons and four horses over the Oregon-California Trail. Their little wagon train rattled by night across the thirty-mile Nevada desert between the Humboldt Sink and the Carson River, then passed safely over the Sierra Nevada summit to Placerville.

As the driving force behind the Central Pacific Railroad, Collis P. Huntington can rightly be considered its locomotive. He mobilized the first financial support for the infant railroad; he lobbied for it in Washington with resounding success against heavy odds; and he became its in-house logistics expert, who bought locomotives by the dozen, wrought-iron rails by the thousands of tons, and purchased every scrap of material needed to build the railroad, from nuts and bolts to boxcars. At one point he had seven ships afloat loaded with CP cargo. Since most of these supplies had to be shipped from the East Coast either through Panama or around the Cape, timing such massive purchases and deliveries to arrive in the proper sequence at the constantly moving construction site was no mean trick. Most astonish-

Left: Charles Crocker was in charge of the Central Pacific's construction, rushing up and down the line "like a wild bull," as he said, to keep things moving.

Below: Mark Hopkins's associates on the Central Pacific trusted him totally as the "inside man" who oversaw the complex railroad accounts.

ing, he performed all these large-scale miracles during the chaos of civil war. Huntington was forced to compete against the Union Pacific—paradoxically, his rival in a common endeavor—in his desperate search for private funding, and, even worse, with both the UP and the federal armed forces in his nationwide scavenging for railroad hardware. No one was better prepared for these undertakings by temperament and business acumen than Huntington, though he had no previous railroading experience.

Huntington had been raised to be a sharp trader, from his boyhood days in a Connecticut village—aptly named Poverty Hollow—to his year's apprenticeship to a local farmer at age fourteen. There followed five years as a Yankee peddler traveling up and down New England in a horse-drawn wagon. When the news of the California gold strike reached him in 1848, the young entrepreneur promptly sailed for Panama with twelve hundred dollars in his pocket and a stock of whiskey, and other marketable merchandise. In Panama he bought and provisioned a sloop, sold the merchandise at a fat profit, and in the process crossed the Isthmus twenty-four times on foot. He finally arrived in San Francisco five thousand dollars richer. There Huntington went immediately to work. Mooring a dory in the bay, he would row out to be first aboard incoming merchant ships, where he paid for cargo with gold dust from a pouch always ready at his waist. Settling in Sacramento, he stocked six tents and sold supplies to gold miners. He even dug in the gravel himself, but only for half a day, and rued it the rest of his life as a rare mistake in judgment.

Plain-spoken and tenacious, Huntington was a pragmatist to the core. When the Railroad Act Amendment of 1866 had come up for a vote, he later blandly recalled, "I brought over half a million dollars to use [in Congress], every dollar of it if necessary to pass this bill." No one in the country could protect the interests of the Central Pacific Railroad in Washington's corridors of power more effectively than Collis P. Huntington.

Back in Sacramento, it was not "harnessing the elephant" but harnessing the Big Four that proved difficult for Judah, as it became increasingly clear that his associates had focused on profiting from the construction phase of the railroad rather than from freight and passenger traffic revenues. The painfully honest Judah fumed, for example, when Crocker's contracting company siphoned off dollars earned from the railroad construction and used them to build a wagon road from Sacramento to the Dutch Flat mining area. This project gave rise to the persistent (but groundless) rumor of a "Dutch Flat Swindle." A second Big Four action that troubled Judah was Stanford's clever, but unethical, gambit to have unearned federal bonds allocated to the Central Pacific. Aware that the law entitled the CP to forty-eight thousand dollars in bonds for every mile of mountain construction, Stanford (then governor of the state) arranged for a team of geological experts to rule that the western base of the Sierras (where the forty-eight-thousand-dollar rate would begin to apply) was ten miles closer to Sacramento than it actually was. The maneuver worked; the mountain came to Stanford, and overnight the CP was $480,000 richer. Judah, however, deplored this maneuver as compromising his engineering integrity, and he indignantly embarked for New York in quest of backers to buy out the entire Big Four interest in the Central Pacific.

But fate had other plans, and Judah was stricken by fever while crossing the Isthmus of Panama. He lived to reach New York but in such weakened condition that he died there a week later, at the age of thirty-seven. Judah was not remembered kindly by Huntington, Hopkins, Stanford, and Crocker; too often he had rubbed their fur the wrong way. Yet the original and practical vision of the Transcontinental Railroad from Sacramento to the East had been his, and it was Judah who had sold the four reluctant partners on the idea. It was Judah, too, who ran the first trans-Sierra survey, and he had literally written the groundbreaking Railroad Act of 1862. It was Judah who had assembled and trained the crack engineering team of Samuel Montague and Lewis Clement, who posthumously carried out his construction plan. Despite his premature death, Judah left an indelible stamp on the Transcontinental Railroad as the fifth member of the Big Four.

THE UNION PACIFIC ROLLS WEST

Just as the Central Pacific had its Big Four, so it can be said (without diminishing the vital role of many others) that the Union Pacific had its Big Three: Oakes Ames, financier; Thomas C. Durant, promoter; and Major General Grenville M. Dodge, builder.

The Ameses were known as one of the "first families" of Massachusetts, and the Ames Shovel Company of Boston was the largest shovel maker in the world.

Owned and managed by Oakes Ames (a member of the House of Representatives) and his younger brother, Oliver, the firm's three factories were cash cows whose profits eventually funded the company's expansion into railroad construction in Iowa and Missouri. Little wonder that President Abraham Lincoln, in 1865, called on sober, conservative Oakes Ames to take an active interest in the faltering Union Pacific, which as of April 15, 1865, had not yet spiked a single mile of track. Ames became a director of the railroad but was careful never to become an officer of either the UP or its affiliate, the Crédit Mobilier, leaving it to his brother Oliver to become president of the Union Pacific in 1865.

Thomas C. Durant, born in 1820, was a physician who quickly abandoned medical practice, turning instead to the healing of ailing railroads as a career. His early railroad work, beginning in 1850, brought him in contact with several of the engineers: Peter Dey, Samuel B. Reed, and Grenville M. Dodge, who would work with him fifteen to twenty years later on the Union Pacific. Durant, flamboyant in velvet waistcoats and broad-brimmed hats, was a born promoter: intelligent, energetic, guileful, and a manipulator of men. He had conceived the UP railway project in the East, lobbied hard for its charter, and personally taken up most of the first stock subscription.

OAKES AMES, *1865.*

A respected hardware tycoon and financier, Ames was asked by President Abraham Lincoln to keep an eye on the fledgling Union Pacific's finances. Ames's brother, Oliver, became president of the Union Pacific, but for years Oakes was the power behind the throne.

According to Durant's railroad doctrine, a straight line might be the shortest distance between two points, but it was certainly not the most profitable. Accordingly, he arbitrarily rerouted several of Chief Engineer Dodge's line locations crossing the Great Plains, nonchalantly adding curves and mileage. Since the railway earned government bonds by the mile, this increased the construction revenue flowing into UP coffers. A corollary to the doctor's philosophy of distance was his theory of speed: build the line west as quickly as possible in order to lay more miles of track than the rival Central Pacific. Again, the more miles per day, the more revenue. Ames and Durant had a visceral disagreement about how to run a railroad: the former focused on growth through longer-range operations revenues, and the latter on quick income through construction profits.

Durant's unscrupulous and self-serving behavior cast a shadow over the UP's construction-contracting arm, Crédit Mobilier, of which he was president, and over the Union Pacific itself, of which the doctor became vice president and general manager. For better or for worse, Durant will always hold a central position, along with Grenville Dodge and Oakes Ames, in the triptych that dominated the UP. He played a hands-on role—probably too much so—in the line's construction, yet despite his annoying interventions and financial chicanery Durant succeeded in getting the UP built in less than five years, a success partly due to him and partly in spite of him.

Crusty and blunt, Major General Grenville M. Dodge was a soldier's soldier, a patriot who had served with distinction in the Civil War. Dodge was a superb engineer who had made his reputation rebuilding bridges and railroads destroyed in the conflict, but even before the war he had explored and surveyed widely along the Platte River valley while working for Peter Dey and Durant in planning the Mississippi and Missouri Railroad. Perhaps it was this early experience with Durant that made Dodge hesitate two full years before accepting Durant's invitation to join the UP as chief engineer. He finally agreed in 1866, and it was one of Durant's canniest field appointments; Dodge also won election to Congress that same year,

Urbane, clever, and more than a touch unscrupulous, Dr. Thomas C. Durant was the prime mover in organizing and financing the Union Pacific.

and Dodge's friend General Grant became president. Suddenly Dodge was a soldier with political clout that could greatly help the UP advance a project many had seen primarily as a wartime military necessity.

For all his obvious virtues, Dodge's character was not without its paradoxes. A disarming veneer of homespun simplicity overlay a measure of vanity (his own accounts of his exploits invariably end well) and of cunning (he became a skilled lobbyist, boldly working the levers of Washington power). After a few of Durant's arbitrary line changes, General Dodge threatened to resign, then called in the top army brass, including his friends Generals Philip Sheridan and Ulysses S. Grant, who permanently humbled the overreaching Durant.

The expense of building the first Transcontinental Railroad dwarfed by far the initial costs of all the preceding western trails combined. To raise the many millions of dollars needed, the railroads relied chiefly on the sale of their own stocks and bonds, on bonds advanced from the government, and on proceeds from land grant sales. But with stock and bond sales lagging badly in 1864, Durant set up a separate organization named the Crédit Mobilier (CM), with himself as president, ostensibly to raise funds for UP construction and to let out contracts to its builders. The CM device also enabled Durant to spin off construction profits (178% of dividends in a single year) to his cohort George F. Train and an inner circle of CM shareholders. Train boasted later that he had three generations living off his profits from the Crédit Mobilier. Durant's years with the UP and CM were marred by persistent allegations of collusion and fraud, entangling him in lawsuits and once even landing him in jail.

The Crédit Mobilier's most trying days, however, came after the transcontinental line was completed. Rumblings of discontent had risen for years in the press, the public, and eventually in Congress, about fiscal irregularities at the Crédit Mobilier. Rumors also circulated about Ames's "sweetheart sales" of CM stock to some of his fellow congressmen while he served on the House Subcommittee on Railroads.

Such questions inevitably triggered congressional inquiries once national euphoria at the Transcontinental Railroad's completion had subsided. The presidential election of 1872 made the railroad scandal a juicy issue, and two congressional commissions pounced on it with glee. One of them, the Poland Commission, was dubbed "the Inquisition" by its own chairman. At such official inquiries Durant, Dodge, Huntington, Crocker, and others played musical chairs on the witness stand, blandly disclaiming personal knowledge of irregularities or falling prey to severe memory lapses. Congressional inquiries about CP operations were further hampered by the unexplained disappearance of most of its financial records for the construction years.

The Poland Commission finally chose as scapegoat the venerable, but vulnerable, Oakes Ames, who had once pledged his personal fortune to keep the Union Pacific afloat but who now was accused of selling

After a brilliant career in the Civil War, Major General Grenville M. Dodge was named chief engineer of the Union Pacific and discovered the crux passage over the Continental Divide. His close ties to President Ulysses S. Grant and Generals Philip Sheridan and William Sherman were great assets to the Union Pacific.

a few shares of Crédit Mobilier stock at below market prices to selected congressmen in order to curry political favor. Despite having mounted a lame defense, Ames avoided being expelled from Congress, but his official censure by the House on February 27, 1873, proved a public humiliation that probably accelerated his death ten weeks later.

INCHING EAST AND WEST

Two years after the Central Pacific groundbreaking, with construction well underway, in January 1865 the CP had only six hundred men on their construction crews and faced a severe labor shortage, even as demobilization after the Civil War released veterans into the workforce. Desperately needing five thousand men before spring, Crocker finally hit on the idea of Chinese labor. His new construction boss, James Harvey Strobridge, was aghast until Crocker reminded him that people who had built the Great Wall of China could probably build a railroad. Hiring agents were established in China, and within two years the CP had fielded a small army of some twelve thousand Chinese workers—the largest single workforce in the United States at the time.

Often known as "Celestials" because they referred to their native land as the Celestial Kingdom, the Chinese also came to be enviously called "Crocker's Pets," in part because of the special diet they demanded—and got—from the railroad. This included such exotica as dried cuttlefish, seaweed, dried oysters, salted cabbage, bean sprouts, and bamboo shoots. The Chinese also constantly drank tea carried by "tea boys" down

the work line in old powder kegs slung on poles. This preference for tea rather than unboiled water probably spared the Chinese much of the digestive illness suffered by their Irish colleagues ("Terrestrials"), who may have relied too heavily on whiskey to purify ditch water. The logistical problems of feeding alone—moving food from California to end of track in Nevada for twelve thousand men—boggled the mind: the CP then served thirty-six thousand meals every day.

Situated four miles east of Colfax, a thirty-eight-hundred-foot-high granite wall called Cape Horn rose at a dizzying seventy-five-degree angle above the American River. Gouging out a roadbed twenty-two hundred feet above the river was a challenge never before faced by American railroad builders, but Strobridge sent five thousand men and six hundred mule and horse teams on ahead in September to begin slowly hacking out the dangerous line before another Sierra winter shut down the work. Painfully slow progress soon demanded a more daring approach, however, and in October, Chief Engineer Montague suggested that Chinese volunteers might be lowered over the cliff top in woven baskets to drill holes for the explosives. Once the charges were planted and fuses lit, baskets

and occupants would be hastily hauled up—in time to avoid disaster, if all went well. The system did work, though not without human cost: some Chinese workers were injured, and a few plummeted to their deaths into the gray-green river far below. By year's end the basic work was complete, and in May 1866 the first train crawled cautiously around Cape Horn.

Perilous as it was, the work performed by Montague's basketeers was not as dangerous as that done by the one thousand men Strobridge sent that same summer to clear the right-of-way. This task involved felling timber and blowing up stumps, rocks, and other obstacles to cut a one-hundred-foot swath on either

Opposite: HEADING OF EAST PORTAL, TUNNEL NO. 8, *n.d. Photograph by Alfred Hart.*

Using empty powder kegs, a Chinese water boy carries tea to his fellow laborers on the Central Pacific.

Left: MESS CALL FOR A CONSTRUCTION GANG, *n.d.*

Under a canvas roof, with seats improvised from empty kegs and logs, a work crew enjoys an alfresco lunch.

Although the Central Pacific had tracked thirty-one miles to the base of the Sierra Nevada in 1864, back east the year had ended for the UP with fewer than twenty miles of easy grading done and no track laid at all. Worse still, because of insufficient funds, Durant had been obliged at one point to stop all construction and sell off considerable equipment in order to pay company bills. Against this dismal background, the year 1865 also dawned without promise.

The Union Pacific was without a chief engineer. Dey had resigned, and Dodge, still in the army, had not yet succumbed to Durant's persistent cajoling to join the UP's high command. Jack Casement, a Civil War general, and his brother Dan would not be brought on staff as track-laying contractors until 1866. In short, the team that would ultimately drive UP construction

Right: A Chinese track crew poses on its handcar. At the peak of construction, the Central Pacific employed about twelve thousand Chinese laborers, many recruited in China.

side of the roadbed. Since it took a three-hundred-man gang ten full days to clear a single mile, it is not surprising the work cost Crocker as much as five thousand dollars per mile. Ancient redwoods, among the world's tallest trees, fell grudgingly beneath the ax and saw. Ten kegs of powder were often needed to blast loose a stubborn stump, sending redwood projectiles wildly in all directions and mowing down many a luckless worker in the forest's final revenge. In one week the clearing gangs blew up as many explosives as Lee and McClellan had used at Antietam.

was not yet even on the train. Meanwhile, Durant and his consulting engineer and acolyte, Silas Seymour, were frantically directing surveys to determine the UP line west from Omaha, with James A. Evans the engineer responsible for the region east of the Continental Divide and Samuel B. Reed the one in charge of the area west of it. Evans succeeded in locating a new line, which Durant named Evans Pass, but Reed could not find a good line south of the Uintah Mountains to Salt Lake City. His journal for July 8, 1865, reported with dismay, "Snow banks near telegraph station 15 to 20 feet deep." In the end, Reed abandoned the idea of a crossing at South Pass because, although it required an ascent to only 7,470 feet, it turned out to be seventy miles longer.

The whole region from the west end of the Platte Valley through to the Humboldt River valley proved discouragingly short of improvements or communities but long on troublemakers and hostile nomadic Indians. One stroke of luck, however: following an Indian skirmish General Dodge accidentally discovered a passage through the Black Hills, which he mentally filed for later use by the Union Pacific. He named it Sherman Pass to honor his friend and former superior, William Tecumseh Sherman (soon to be commanding general of all troops west of the Mississippi and a good friend to have at court). At 8,560 feet, Sherman Summit would rank as the highest point on the whole UP line.

Nagging construction problems cropped up constantly. What little grading and other work had been done was managed mostly with shovels, wheelbarrows, and dump carts. Lumber for ties was scarce. Most

common was a pulpy cottonwood that required the application of zinc chloride under pressure (a process called Burnettizing) to help preserve the twenty-five hundred ties used for every mile. Thousands of these treated ties deteriorated so badly that they had to be replaced even before the railroad was completed, adding significantly to the cost.

UP financial prospects looked even more bleak. After the Civil War ended, Durant's attempt to float a public sale of Union Pacific stock, in April 1865, had fallen flat. Not a single share was sold, and the UP had to borrow funds at the crushing rate of 19 percent per annum to meet its mounting obligations. No U.S. government bonds had yet been earned, let alone received. Then, that summer, at President Lincoln's urging, a group of New England financiers headed by Oakes Ames made a major investment in the sagging Crédit Mobilier. With new money in the bank, the CM and its UP affiliate could shift construction from idle into high gear. On July 8 the first UP locomotive—called the *General Sherman*—reached Omaha, and on July 10 the first Union Pacific rail was laid near the ferry landing in that city.

By November the length of completed track encouraged Durant to organize a promotional excursion for UP investors and supporters. A select coterie rode on flatcars, with General Sherman perched on a nail keg, drinking in the view and doubtless other stimulants as well against the autumn chill. By the end of 1865 forty miles of UP track had been completed, extensive rolling stock had been acquired, and sidings, machine shops, water stations, and other important installations had been built. The UP had finally quali-

fied to receive $640,000 in U.S. government bonds and could now issue the same amount of its own first mortgage bonds as well.

After the basketeers' cliff-hanging at Cape Horn, the CP crews sweated eastward to Cisco, overcoming major challenges en route by building the long, high, and elegantly curving Secrettown Gap trestle, the Long Ravine Bridge (878 feet long and 120 feet high), and the first and second of the CP's eventual fifteen tunnels: the 498-foot Grizzly Hill Tunnel and the 300-foot Emigrant Gap Tunnel.

CP investors and the government alike rightly felt shaken after reviewing the alarmingly meager progress

made by the Central Pacific between groundbreaking in Sacramento on January 8, 1863, and December 31, 1866. Yet even though the CP had laid only ninety-four miles of track in these four years, it had already accomplished one of the wonders of the railroad world by climbing thirty-eight hundred feet in only thirty-nine miles.

The cost of the CP railroad up to the end of 1866 was variously reported as being from seventeen to nineteen million dollars, a staggering sum for those

days. But by now the Big Four were accustomed to thinking big, as Huntington coolly recalled: "I have gone to sleep at night in New York when I had a million and a half dollars to be paid by 3 o'clock on the following day, without knowing where the money was coming from, and slept soundly."[3] He would sleep less soundly in 1867, when the Central Pacific again teetered on the brink of bankruptcy. That year, record-breaking Sierra Nevada blizzards buried much of the CP line and kept crews from closing a seven-mile gap in track (near Donner Lake, where members of the ill-fated group had perished twenty years earlier). Since only continuous track was eligible for compensation, that gap delayed the release of millions of dollars in government and CP bonds due for other track.

THE TORTOISE AND THE HARE

Competition between the CP and the UP to lay the most track (and thus earn the most subsidies) escalated, and by 1866 there was little doubt who would win. The CP, burrowing through the Sierras at a pace of only inches a day, plodded along like Aesop's tortoise, while the UP, though it had broken ground a whole year later than its rival, was laying track at a speedy three miles a day across plains as flat as a barn floor, leaping ahead like the proverbial hare.

Having scampered past the One Hundredth Meridian milepost on October 5, 1866, a year before

Left: While crossing the Sierra Nevada, the most rugged terrain in the entire line, the Central Pacific created engineering miracles like this curved trestle at Secrettown Gap, California.

eastern terminus of the UP was bound to sharply boost Omaha land values, and he had already secretly bought up so many of the best lots in Omaha that insiders called it "Train Town."

The five-day affair began on October 22 with a grand ball staged for over two hundred people. The guest list included the governor of Nebraska; several U.S. senators and members of Congress; the high society of Omaha, military officers (including now Major General Philip Saint George Cooke, of earlier Mormon Battalion fame); various high officials of the Union Pacific; the secretary of the French legation, the Marquis de Chambrun; a smattering of European nobility; and other dignitaries. The next day an imposing cavalcade steamed out of Omaha, including in its entourage the Lincoln car (which had been especially built for President Lincoln but now was personally owned by Durant), the resplendent directors' car, and seven passenger cars, which boasted a refreshment salon, mess car,

the December 1867 deadline set by Congress, the hare decided to celebrate the achievement with a grand excursion for dignitaries from Omaha to the One Hundredth and beyond. Although the finish line still lay some four hundred miles away, at Promontory Summit, this seemed a favorable moment to focus public attention on the UP's astonishing performance and to attract both investor and congressional support. The celebration was Durant's brainchild, and he named his crony George Francis Train as coordinator. Train, a real estate speculator, applied himself to the assignment with relish, for drawing attention to the and mail car—all profusely decked out with flags and banners.

The first night out a lavish supper was served under a camp tent while a specially arranged Indian war dance was performed by Pawnee braves around a dying campfire. The following afternoon the Pawnee and thirty mounted "Sioux warriors" (also Pawnee) staged a mock battle complete with rearing and plunging horses and combatants grappling with each other in sham death struggles.

Next morning everyone bathed in the Platte River. After a hearty breakfast, orders for the day's activities were posted—musical events, buffalo and antelope hunts, and other diversions. A mobile printing press

Two years after the completion of the Transcontinental Railroad, in 1871, this is how the infant eastern terminus, Omaha, still looked from Seventeenth and Farnham Streets.

published issues of the *Railway Pioneer*, and a telegraph line was opened to permit contact with the outside world. At 11:00 A.M. the party headed for the end of track, some ten miles west, where Jack Casement's men put on a track-laying demonstration before the return to camp and a rich dinner of game bagged by what Silas Seymour called "the shootists." After dinner a dazzling fireworks display filled the night sky with "rockets, falling stars, golden serpents," and "other ingenious contrivances." Then came a grand concert, capped by a humorous phrenological reading of George Francis Train's head. The next night, after a thirty-mile-an-hour trip eastward, at the lower end of the Platte Valley the excursionists witnessed a huge fire, twenty miles long (set at Durant's orders two days before), sweeping the prairie as a fiery climax to the excursion.

Back at end of track, Casement and his Irishmen picked up their pace, and the hare was off and running again, while the tortoise plodded on toward Cisco, still fifteen grinding miles short of the Sierra summit. Three years later, however, at Golden Spike time, it was the tortoise that pulled up first to the finish line at Promontory Summit, well ahead of the hare.

BLOOD ON THE TRACKS AND HELL ON WHEELS

From 1865 on, the Union Pacific suffered recurring Indian troubles, but the total number of railroad workers who lost their lives to the Indians between 1865 and 1869 was probably well under one hundred. Usually mounted by small bands of warriors, the spo-

radic attacks did not seriously block the line's westward progress. Casement's track-laying crews were periodic targets, but these men were mostly Civil War veterans who prudently stacked rifles near their picks and shovels, and who relished a good scrap. More at risk were the advance grading crews and isolated survey parties scattered across the countryside, beyond the protective fringe of stretched-out troops commanded by Generals Sheridan and Sherman.

Sherman's uncompromising thinking on the Indian problem found blunt expression in 1867: "The more we can kill this year, the less will have to be killed in the next war, for the more I see of these Indians the more convinced I am that they all have to be killed or maintained as a species of paupers."[4] Admittedly, the army's feelings ran particularly high at the time as a result of the Fetterman massacre in December the year before. In that engagement Captain William J. Fetterman and a party of eighty dispatched to rescue some ambushed woodcutters were themselves ambushed by fifteen hundred Sioux sixty miles north of the UP line. Fetterman and his entire party were slaughtered and brutally mutilated, and the army, as well as the public, would cite those deaths as justification for retaliatory action against the Indians until the massacre was overshadowed a decade later by an even more violent disaster: Custer's bloody defeat at the Little Big Horn.

From time to time, Indians derailed UP trains, and one such foray reportedly took place near Plum Creek, Nebraska, when a small party of Cheyenne tore down some telegraph wire to lash a stack of ties to the rails. A handcar carrying six repairmen soon came

JAMES H. STROBRIDGE ON THE ROOF OF A SNOW GALLERY AT CRESTED PEAK, *n.d. Photograph by Alfred Hart.*

James Harvey Strobridge—Crocker's ham-fisted superintendent of Central Pacific construction, who could wade into a fight with an ax handle if necessary— stands watchfully on the roof of a snow shed in the Sierra Nevada.

speeding down the track and crashed into the ties. Five were slaughtered on the spot, but William Thompson escaped—even though he had been shot, scalped, and left for dead. Inflamed by their success, the Cheyenne piled more debris on the tracks and

waited in the dark for another train. Before long a five-car freight hurtled into the barricade, flew off the track, and burst into flame. The Cheyenne reportedly watched while the fireman, Gregory Henshaw, roasted to death in his cab. Brookes Bowers, the engineer, was killed and his body flung onto the pyre.

News of such murders was suppressed by Grenville Dodge as much as possible since it might have adversely affected railroad revenues and the price of UP stock. In fact, the inflammatory term "massacre," so much abused by the press of the time, rarely applied to a formal military engagement where white soldiers faced Indian warriors in large numbers. The total number of whites and Indians killed in "massacres" during the 1860s cannot now be determined, but it was doubtless surprisingly small.

The Central Pacific seeded its share of towns seething with vice along the track, with its Renos, Elkos, and Argentas, but Crocker and Strobridge kept the lid on pretty tight. Such towns roared only briefly and in muted tones compared with the hell-on-wheels towns that followed the Union Pacific. As it rattled westward across the plains in 1866–69, the UP was constantly plagued at end of track by swarms of card sharks, saloon keepers, *"nymphes du grade,"* rumheads, and thieves who followed the train like voracious flies feasting on an open wound. Ramshackle brothels, saloons, gambling parlors, and dancehalls would be thrown up in tents and shacks in a matter of hours, flourish a few days, and then wither, only to open again at the next town.

Cheyenne, Kearney, and North Platte were among the first hell-on-wheels towns, and Corinne,

Utah (only twenty-eight miles from Promontory Summit), was the last. In between, many others enjoyed a brief life as movable feasts where the pleasure-starved railroad gangs turned out to be the main course. Murders occurred daily, and graveyards rapidly became overcrowded.

In July 1867 Dodge and Casement decided to investigate conditions in Julesburg, a town on the Colorado-Nebraska border that billed itself proudly as "The Wickedest City in America." Engineer Samuel B. Reed had written of it that "vice and crime stalk unblushingly in the mid-day sun."[5] Since the sinning was taking place on Union Pacific land, Dodge bluntly ordered the sporting fraternity to either buy the land, pay rent, or get out. They flatly refused, so Dodge ordered Casement (to his great delight) to take two hundred UP toughs and clean the place out. Casement's men fired blindly into a threatening mob. When the smoke had cleared, over thirty people lay dead. This bloody "cleaning" spree, it seems, brought peace and relative quiet to Julesburg. In June the town boasted a population of forty men and one woman; the number swelled to four thousand in July; by autumn little was left except the cemetery and a litter of tin cans.

Opposite: Henry F. Farny (1847–1916). MORNING OF A NEW DAY, *1907. Oil on canvas, 22 x 32 in. (55.9 x 81.3 cm). National Cowboy Hall of Fame and Western Heritage Center, Oklahoma City.*

More than most western artists, Farny sensed the psychological drama behind the collision of Indian and white cultures.

Right: DANCE HOUSE, KEYSTONE HALL AT LARAMIE, *c. 1867–68. Photograph by A. C. Hull.*

Though ladies were scarce, toes tapped and heels rocked to fiddle and piano at dance halls along the Union Pacific track.

Right: BEAR RIVER CITY, *n.d. Photograph by A. J. Russell.*

As the head of Union Pacific track moved west, small temporary towns, mostly shacks of board and canvas, sprang up overnight—like Bear River City, Wyoming. Saloons and eating houses catered to railroad gangs with whiskey, gambling, "accommodating" women, and nightly free-for-alls, earning the towns a richly deserved reputation as "hell on wheels."

Perhaps the ugliest drama was played out in November 1868 at Bear River City, Wyoming. Violence and vice of every kind had gotten so out of hand that its citizens organized a body of vigilantes, heavily armed and itching to establish "law and order." The spark that detonated this highly volatile situation was the arrival of the Freeman brothers, Leigh and Richmond, with their newspaper, the *Frontier Index.* Their mobile press traveled on the train and was published every few days from a new town along the track. The Freemans were fiery Southern nationalists whose sheet trumpeted their racist, anti-Republican, anti-army views. At Bear River City they made the mistake of vilifying the late President Lincoln and printing scurrilous attacks on presidential candidate Ulysses S. Grant as a "whiskey bloated, squaw ravishing adulterer

[and] nigger worshipping mogul." Such slander went too far, especially in Bear River City, where most of the UP crews were Union Army veterans. A gang of two hundred UP workers, with mauls and ax handles in their callused fists, marched on the *Frontier Index* office. They swiftly demolished the premises, then noticed an ominous silence building up behind them. Turning to leave, they found themselves eye-to-eye with a line of grim-faced vigilantes who opened fire without a word, killing fifty-three and wounding dozens more. It was Wyoming's bloodiest white-on-white encounter.

Some of the hell-on-wheels towns sobered up after the end of track had passed, maturing into respectable and permanent communities, but the wildness of the old towns lingers still with a certain romantic nostalgia in the American imagination. Colonel C. R. Savage, official UP photographer who had witnessed much depravity firsthand, wrote in sorrow and anger in his diary for May 9, 1869, "Verily, men earn their money like horses and spend it like asses."

Harnessing the Elephant: Final Miles

Financial shortages resulting from gaps in the track between Cisco in the Sierra Nevada and Truckee near the Nevada border continued to plague the CP in 1867. But these were matters for Uncle Mark Hopkins in Sacramento and Collis P. Huntington in New York to worry about. Out on the line, Crocker and his cohorts had other problems to grapple with. One day that summer Chinese work crews, some three thousand strong, quietly lay down picks, shovels, and drills, squatted by the roadside, and went on strike. Their requests for wages of forty dollars a month (up from thirty dollars) and an eight-hour day enraged Crocker and Strobridge. Crocker shot off a wire to Huntington suggesting that he hire ten thousand Negroes as replacements, and then he abruptly cut off the special Chinese diet of abalone and cuttlefish. Faced with these countermeasures, the Chinese shortly negotiated a settlement and returned to working their usual twelve-hour days, but at thirty-five dollars a month. The CP knew when and how to compromise—and so did the Chinese.

The second unexpected threat that summer of 1867 came from a small band of Paiutes who fired potshots at a Chinese grading crew. Crocker quickly called the Paiutes into conference, threatened them with harsh reprisals if there was any more sniping, and had them sign a "treaty" embellished with an impressive Central Pacific seal. The Indians were offered free travel on the railroad as well, and that was virtually the end of the CP's Indian troubles. Relations between the CP and the Indians along its route remained so calm that when, in 1868, General Grant finally offered military protection to the CP (as he had provided the UP for years), Strobridge haughtily refused it, scoffing "Damn the military!" But life would not be quite so simple for the Union Pacific, whose westbound tracks were now violating Sioux, Cheyenne, and Arapaho territory.

The granite ridge through which the CP's Summit Tunnel bored was so compact, and the work so agonizingly slow, that Montague and his tunnel specialist, Lewis Clement, decided in desperation to

SNOW COVERING BELOW CISCO, *1864–69. Photograph by Alfred Hart.*

To protect the train from avalanches in the Sierra Nevada, at huge expense the Central Pacific built miles of snow sheds over the tracks, a hazard and expense the Union Pacific was spared crossing the prairie. All told, the Central Pacific used sixty-five million board feet of lumber and nine hundred tons of bolts and spikes to build their sheds.

THE FIRST TRANSCONTINENTAL RAILROAD | 221

sink a vertical shaft from the surface seventy-eight feet deep, bisecting the tunnel's path. This would speed up construction by dividing the tunnel into two sections, thus permitting four facings to be worked simultaneously. The plan worked so well that at breakthrough the opposing tunnel bores fit together within two inches.

Drilling the vertical shaft into the tunnel proved arduous in the extreme because, at the close of 1866, end of track was still back at Cisco, one thousand feet below and fifteen miles behind. All drilling equipment therefore had to be hauled cross-country from Cisco to the summit by wagon over a nonexistent roadbed. Before he could even start clearing the vertical shaft of debris, Strobridge first had to assemble a power source at 7,042-feet elevation. A twelve-ton locomotive, irreverently called the "Black Goose," was to be installed as hoisting engine at the top of the shaft after being dragged overland to the summit by a burr-tongued drover called Missouri Bill. Driving a specially built wagon with sledlike wheels two feet wide and drawn by twenty oxen, laying down heavy corduroy roads as he went, and using wheel blocks with chains snubbed around trees to check runaways, Bill cursed and coaxed his animals during the six weeks it took to cover the tortuous twenty-five miles to the summit. Finally the equipment was skidded into place and the shaft begun.

The winter of 1866–67 was so severe that Crocker sent a third of his crews to the rear and, in a major decision, dispatched three thousand men over the summit and down the eastern slope of the Sierra Nevada, where the weather was better, to grade, cut, and fill many miles ahead of track. This bold attack was supported by freighting forty miles of track equipment—including three locomotives and forty freight cars—from Cisco over the summit and on down to the Truckee River, all by ox sleds. There were times when five hundred tons of matériel a day was shipped this way, testimony to the iron determination of Crocker and his engineers to defeat an awesome Sierra winter and to keep building on both sides without waiting for the completion of Summit Tunnel.

The time was 1:00 A.M., the date May 3, 1867. The place: inside CP Tunnel Number Ten, the Summit Tunnel, 7,042 feet high in the granite spine of the Sierra Nevada. In the dim light of wavering torches, a pickax clanged against rock and a tiny flower of light suddenly bloomed in the dark. Breakthrough! Instantly, the cavernous tunnel rang with shouts and cheers—in Chinese—as more than two hundred Celestials celebrated, exclaiming at the fellow workers now discernible for the first time on the far side of the newly breached facing.

The struggle to reach this climactic moment had taken—in Summit Tunnel alone—nearly two backbreaking years of around-the-clock blasting, hacking, and clearing. Under

claustrophobic conditions of cold, darkness, and air choked with black powder and rock dust, the Chinese had driven doggedly ahead, often at the dispiriting rate of eight inches a day. To make matters worse, the winter of 1866–67 had been one of the worst ever recorded in the Sierra Nevada, with subzero cold and avalanche-prone snowfalls that sometimes drifted to a depth of forty feet. To survive, the Chinese crews had tunneled a torchlit labyrinth beneath the snow, scurrying like moles from their shacks to work sites and back.

Summit Tunnel's entire bore, more than a quarter-mile in length, ranked as the longest tunnel ever cut through native granite. The slowly lengthening tunnel, like some ravenous dragon, had devoured three hundred kegs of black powder a day and countless human sacrifices from blasting misfires, cave-ins, or simply exhaustion. Snowslides swept away entire camps, killing scores of workers—no one knows exactly how many. Summit Tunnel, the crux of all fifteen tunnels on the CP line, exacted a high cost in money, men, and material. Not until it was conquered could it be known for sure whether the CP would ever cross the Sierras. The breakthrough at Summit Tunnel was more than an engineering triumph. It was a psychological victory of preeminent significance for everyone connected with the Central Pacific. The worst construction problems were now behind; ahead lay the prospect of the easy money to be made by laying track across the Nevada flats.

Studying the hectic scene at Summit Tunnel, as he surely did within days after the breakthrough, Crocker could now look more hopefully to the future, turning his gaze eastward to Utah, where he would soon be working with Brigham Young in the final construction phase of the CP line to the Great Salt Lake or thereabouts. "Thereabouts" because although Crocker knew there were six hundred and more rough miles ahead, he was still unsure as to exactly where his tracks were to meet the oncoming UP line. All he knew for sure was the infuriating news that Casement's men were laying track at breakneck speed—a mile a day or better—and qualifying for new government bonds at the rate of forty-eight thousand dollars per mile.

To get to the summit where Crocker now stood, he and his workers had endured four and a half years of trials almost beyond human endurance, such as the death of the Chinese crew swept into a canyon by an avalanche. Uncovered months later by spring thaws, some were still standing rigidly upright, tools in hands, like the long-buried terra-cotta soldiers of Xian. An ominous moraine of debt trailed in the wake of tracks that had crept forward at a glacial pace. The paltry 105.5 miles from Sacramento to the summit had already cost the CP close to twenty million dollars to build, and until the seven-mile gap still open in the line below Donner Pass was closed, the CP could not collect the government bonds due for many additional miles already completed. It now seemed long ago, that day in Sacramento when Crocker had solemnly pledged at the CP groundbreaking ceremony: "All that I have—all of my strength, intellect and energy—are devoted to the building of this section which I have undertaken. Amen!"

WORK ON THE LAST MILE OF THE PACIFIC RAILROAD— MINGLING EUROPEAN WITH ASIATIC LABORERS, *n.d. Engraving after photograph by A. R. Ward.*

Toward the end of construction in Utah, the Union Pacific's Irish work gangs taunted the Central Pacific's nearby Chinese by setting off blasting fuses without warning. After a few such incidents, the Chinese planted charges that showered rocks on the Irish, and peace was restored.

THE GREAT WAGER

In October 1868, after Crocker learned that the Union Pacific had laid seven and three-quarter miles of track in one day, he and Durant struck a ten-thousand-dollar wager: Crocker said the CP men could lay ten miles of track in a single day; Durant bet they couldn't. Crocker, with his usual cunning, waited till the following spring to choose his own place and time of battle, shrewdly selecting flat terrain less than twenty miles from Promontory Summit, so the UP could not have a second chance to outdo him.

The great contest began before dawn on April 28, 1869. Eight hundred fifty men, of whom four hundred were Chinese, all handpicked by Crocker and Strobridge, were offered four days' pay if they succeeded.

At dawn a whistle blasted and the teams exploded into action. What followed was a minutely orchestrated division of labor, in which each man had his assigned place and function: unloading rails, placing ties, pushing handcars, laying rails, tamping, and spiking, all with machinelike precision. In no time sixteen cars of iron were unloaded and processed. A team of eight Irish ironmen, four on each side of the roadbed, seized a six-hundred-pound rail with tongs, staggered to the appointed spot, and dropped it in front of the previous rail. Straightening, aligning, and leveling followed. Spikers sent an anvil chorus reverberating across the plains, and "fishplate" men (who bolted down the metal plates attaching the rail ends together) and tampers pounded down the roadbed ballast to finish the job. It was a stunning performance: 240 feet of rails were laid in one minute and twenty seconds.

The gangs sweated on throughout the morning to a metronomic cadence of lift and carry, place and drop, spike and hammer, with each trackman lifting eleven thousand pounds of rail an hour. No legion of Roman roadbuilders ever worked with more rhythmic discipline. An hour's lunch break, and the robotic march ahead began again. When the final whistle sounded at dusk, ten miles and fifty-six feet of track had been laid by crews now limp with exhaustion. Cheers and huzzahs filled the air, and to drive his victory home, Crocker ordered his heaviest locomotive to race down the new ten-mile track at the blinding

speed of forty miles per hour (the UP trains had groped across the Wasatch Range at six miles per hour). Smooth as silk.

The eight ironmen had worked without relief from dawn to dusk. By quitting time each man had lifted 264,000 pounds, and together they had strained into place 2,112,000 pounds of iron. The operation remains unsurpassed to this day. History, however, does not record whether Durant ever paid Crocker the ten thousand dollars.

THE GOLDEN SPIKE

With their six-year race and the countless problems of construction behind them at last, the two railroads finally met locomotive-to-locomotive on May 10, 1869, at Promontory Summit. The Golden Spike joining ceremony was almost a comic anticlimax to the grimly heroic achievements of the previous six years. Durant, Dodge, and others were there to represent the UP, but many of the other major players were missing. Oakes Ames, now openly hostile to Durant, was in Boston, and Brigham Young, no doubt still smarting from the cavalier treatment he had received from the UP management, saw to it that church business kept him away. Even Charles Durkee, the non-Mormon governor of Utah, remained in Salt Lake City. Of the Big Four, only Leland Stanford made it to Promontory Summit—but barely. His special train, dubbed the *Palace Car,* was nearly derailed en route when it was sideswiped by a log carelessly skidded down the mountainside by CP workers.

The Union Pacific contingent also had their diffi-culties getting to Promontory Summit in time for the ceremony. Casement's work gangs had not been paid for three months, and a nasty strike was brewing. When Durant's special car reached the hamlet of Pied-mont, a surly mob of tie cutters uncoupled the car and shunted it onto a siding. Their demands for immediate payment of several hundred thousand dollars in back pay prompted a two-day flurry of telegrams in which the financial hot potato was tossed from one UP official to another while Durant and his colleagues were de-tained in their car at pistol point. The famished UP treasury, in crisis as usual, could not forward such a sum on short notice, but local Wyoming banks saved the day, and Durant finally proceeded toward Promon-tory Summit. Just east of Devil's Gate, however, a shoddy UP bridge collapsed, forcing his party to aban-don their own elaborate train and board another one, pulled by an ordinary locomotive, *Number 119,* which luckily had waited on the far side of the gorge. And so, in spite of carefully laid plans, it was only old work-horse *Number 119* that faced the CP's opulent *Jupiter* at Promontory Summit.

When it came to the spikes, there was an embarrass-ment of riches: not one spike of gold but two, another of silver, and still another of sil-ver, gold, and iron. Awkwardly raising a heavy silver-headed maul, Stanford had first swing at the Golden Spike—and missed. But since the hammer

Opposite: MEETING OF THE RAILS AT PROMONTORY POINT, *May 10, 1869. Photograph by A. J. Russell.*

Russell recorded the historic "Joining of the Rails," as Union Pacific Engine Number 119 (right) and the Central Pacific's Jupiter (left) gingerly touched cowcatchers, and a bottle of good French champagne was passed between the two jubilant crews.

Below: THE LAST SPIKE, *1995. Photograph by Olie Riniker.*

When the Central Pacific and the Union Pacific railroads finally met at Promontory Summit, on May 10, 1869, a golden spike was slipped into a predrilled hole in a special laurel-wood tie, in symbolic union of East and West.

and rail had been wired to trip the telegraph key anyway, the message flashed to a waiting country: "It is done!" Other VIPs then tried their hand at spike driving, with meager success, until old reliable Grenville Dodge stepped up and put an end to the nonsense by driving the spike into the predrilled hole. Final flourishes with the maul were made by other officials, but the last person to tap the spike home was Hannah Strobridge. The only woman who followed the Transcontinental Railroad from start to finish, she had spent the best part of the last five years living bravely in a converted Central Pacific railroad car with her adopted children.

While the true costs of building the Transcontinental Railroad will never be known, it has been estimated at seventy to eighty million dollars for the

Hannah Strobridge, second from left, lived for several years in this railroad car at the end of track. Her one-eyed husband, James, was the hard-driving superintendent of construction for the Central Pacific.

Union Pacific and thirty-six million for the Central Pacific, for a grand total in the vicinity of $115 million.

For better and for worse the nation was now irreversibly bound together, as Lincoln had foreseen, not only east to west but also north to south. The dreamers had won after all; Judah's dream of a Transcontinental Railroad and Thomas Hart Benton's old vision of Manifest Destiny had finally come to pass.

C O D A

ANYONE READING WESTERN TRAIL HISTORY
from 1800 to 1870 is bound to be struck by the
pungent smells of buffalo chip campfires, leather,
sweat, fur, and alkali dust that rise from its pages.
And, too often, the stench of death. An estimated
ten thousand graves of men, women, and children,
mostly unmarked, line the Oregon-California Trail
alone. But more than that, the hard conditions of
trail travel—rough terrain, atrocious weather, long
distances, and shortages of fuel, fodder, and good
water—all apparently enhanced a latent boldness
and resourcefulness that set the emigrants apart.
Those who dared to go west were a distinct minor-
ity; most Americans remained safely back home
in the East.

Half a million emigrants heading west to free
land and gold were bound to leave marks even deeper
than the wagon ruts that remain today as sacred
wrinkles on the prairie's face. On the way west the
emigrants met, conquered, and almost exterminated
a race that had come to the land twenty thousand
years earlier. The huge bison herds were brought to
the very edge of extinction; only a shift in fashion
saved the beaver from a similar fate. Mines and tunnels were ripped into the earth; ribbons of steel and
wire were stretched across plains, rivers, and mountains. In the process, a continent was joined by an
armature of communications and transportation that
eclipsed any previously known on earth. These material feats of unification seemed like shining corollaries

Albert Bierstadt (1830–1902). OVERLAND TRAIL, *1871. Oil on
canvas, 7 x 11 in. (17.8 x 27.9 cm). The Anschutz Collection, Denver.*

Left: Big Foot, Sioux Chief, lies frozen in the snow after his defeat in 1890 at Wounded Knee Creek, South Dakota, where, as the Indians say, "the dream died."

Below: HYDRAULIC GOLD MINING IN CALIFORNIA, *1850.*

A harbinger of ugly things in store for the earth.

Opposite: KILLING OF BUFFALO, *n.d. Photograph by L. A. Huffman.*

In 1800 some seventy million of these largest of North American beasts roamed free. By 1888 their number had dwindled to a total of 261. When Buffalo Bill Cody served as hunter for the Union Pacific, he reportedly shot 4,280 bison in a single year.

to the political union that emerged from the blood and smoke of Shiloh. And yet for all this extraordinary progress a heavy price was to be exacted. With progress came attitudes and habits that a century and a half ago might be forgiven as matters of survival but that in today's world may usefully be put to question. Such questioning, however, need not dilute the relevance of Frederick Jackson Turner's famous thesis that the American national character, for better and for worse, was largely shaped by the frontier experience. Was Turner right or wrong? We are a young nation; perhaps it is still too early to know.

NOTES

1. THE LEWIS AND CLARK EXPEDITION

1. Jefferson, in Donald Jackson, ed., *Letters of the Lewis and Clark Expedition with Related Documents, 1783–1854*, 2d ed., 2 vols. (Urbana: University of Illinois Press, 1978), vol. 1, p. 61.
2. Lewis to Clark, June 19, 1803, William Clark Papers, box 3, folder 1, Missouri Historical Society, Saint Louis.
3. Clark to Lewis, July 17, 1803, William Clark Papers, box 3, folder 3.
4. Clark, in Gary E. Moulton, ed., *The Journals of the Lewis and Clark Expedition*, 9 vols. to date (Lincoln and London: University of Nebraska Press, 1983–), vol. 2, p. 495. Copyright 1986 by the University of Nebraska Press; reprinted by permission.
5. Ibid., vol. 3, p. 113.
6. Ibid., p. 255.
7. Ibid., p. 291.
8. Lewis to mother [Mrs. Lucy Marks], March 31, 1805, Meriwether Lewis Papers, Missouri Historical Society.
9. Lewis, in Moulton, ed., *Journals*, vol. 4, pp. 9–10.
10. Ibid., pp. 216–17.
11. Clark, ibid., vol. 5, p. 333.
12. Lewis, ibid., p. 74.
13. Ibid., vol. 4, p. 437.
14. Ibid., vol. 5, p. 118.
15. Ibid., vol. 8, pp. 134–35.

2. MOUNTAIN MEN AND THE FUR TRADE

1. John C. Frémont, *The Exploring Expedition to the Rocky Mountains* (1845; reprint, introduction by Herman J. Viola and Ralph E. Ehrenberg, Washington, D.C., and London: Smithsonian Institution Press, 1988), p. 31.
2. James Clyman, *Journal of a Mountain Man* (San Francisco: California Historical Society, 1928; reprint, ed. Linda M. Hasselstrom, Missoula, Mont.: Mountain Press Publishing Company, Copper Mountain Books, 1984), pp. 9–10.
3. Ibid., pp. 9, 13, and 14.
4. Ibid., p. 57.
5. Ibid., p. 97.
6. Ibid., pp. 258, 260, 264, and 266.
7. Hiram Martin Chittenden, *The American Fur Trade of the Far West*, 2 vols. (New York: Press of the Pioneers, 1935; reprint, introduction and notes by Stallo Vinton, foreword by William R. Swagerty, Lincoln and London: University of Nebraska Press, Bison Books, 1986), vol. 2, p. 701.
8. Ashley and Beckwourth, in Fred R. Gowans, *Rocky Mountain Rendezvous: A History of the Fur Trade Rendezvous, 1825–1840* (Layton, Utah: Gibbs Smith, Peregrine Smith Books, 1985), pp. 15 and 30.

3. THE SANTA FE TRAIL

1. James Ohio Pattie, *The Personal Narrative of James O. Pattie* (1st ed., ed. Timothy Flint, Cincinnati: J. H. Wood, 1831; reprint, introduction by William H. Goetzmann, Lincoln and London: University of Nebraska Press, Bison Books, 1984), p. 40.
2. Carson, in David Lavender, *Bent's Fort*, 6th ed. (New York: Doubleday, 1954; reprint, Lincoln and London: University of Nebraska Press, Bison Books, 1972), p. 106.
3. James S. Brown, *Life of a Pioneer—Being the Autobiography of James S. Brown* (Salt Lake City: George Q. Cannon and Sons, 1900), p. 27.
4. Philip Saint George Cooke, journal, October 1846–January 1847, typescript, MS 2688, Archives Division, Church Historical Department, Church of Jesus Christ of Latter-day Saints, Salt Lake City, pp. 121–22.
5. Susan Shelby Magoffin, *Down the Santa Fe Trail and into Mexico: The Diary of Susan Shelby Magoffin, 1846–1847*, 4th ed. (New Haven, Conn.: Yale University Press, 1926; reprint, ed. Stella M. Drumm, Lincoln and London: University of Nebraska Press, Bison Books, 1982), p. 4. Copyright 1926 and 1962 by Yale University Press; reprinted by permission.
6. Ibid., pp. 10 and 12.
7. Ibid., p. 245.
8. Ibid., p. 38.
9. Ibid., p. 57.
10. Ibid., p. 68.
11. Ibid., p. 178.
12. Ibid., pp. 102–3.
13. Gregg, in Marian Meyer, *Mary Donoho: New First Lady of the Santa Fe Trail* (Santa Fe, N.Mex.: Ancient City Press, 1991), p. 27.
14. Magoffin, *Diary*, p. 193.
15. Ibid., p. 207.
16. Bent, in *Reports of the Committees of the Senate of the U.S.*, 39th Cong., 2d sess., 1866–67, p. 96.

4. THE OREGON-CALIFORNIA TRAIL

1. Bancroft, in George R. Stewart, ed., *The Opening of the California Trail: The Story of the Stevens Party from the Reminiscences of Moses Schallenberger* (Berkeley and Los Angeles: University of California Press, 1953), p. 70.
2. Edward Henry Lenox, *Overland to Oregon in the Tracks of Lewis and Clark: History of the First Emigration to Oregon in 1843*, ed. Robert Whitaker (Oakland, Calif.: Dowdle Press, 1904), p. 13.
3. Jesse A. Applegate, *A Day with the Cow Column* (Chicago: Caxton Club, 1934; reprint, Fairfield, Wash.: Ye Galleon Press, 1990), pp. 27–29 and 35–36.
4. Matt C. Field, "Journal on Trip to Rocky Mountains with Sir William Drummond Stewart," 1843, Ludlow Field Murray Papers, Missouri Historical Society, Saint Louis.
5. "D.G.W. Leavitt to a Gentleman in Memphis, Napoleon, Arkansas, January 24, 1846," *Missouri Reporter*, March 9, 1846; in Dale Morgan, ed., *Overland in 1846: Diaries and Letters of the California-Oregon Trail*, 2 vols., 10th ed. (Georgetown, Calif.:

Talisman Press, 1963; reprint, Lincoln and London: University of Nebraska Press, Bison Books, 1993), vol. 2, p. 478.
6. Field, "Journal."
7. Samuel M. Ayres to P. Frances Ayres, June 15, 1850, MSS C995, vol. 29, no. 790, Western Historical Manuscript Collection, University of Missouri and State Historical Society of Missouri, Columbia.
8. Overton Johnson and William H. Winter, *Route across the Rocky Mountains* (1846; reprint, Princeton, N.J.: Princeton University Press, 1932), p. 11.
9. Elijah Bryan Farnham, "From Ohio to California in 1849: The Gold Rush Journal of Elijah Bryan Farnham," ed. Merrill J. Mattes and Esley J. Kirk, *Indiana Magazine of History* 46 (September 1950): 307.
10. Rebecca Ketcham, "From Ithaca to Clatsop Plains: Miss Ketcham's Journal of Travel," parts 1 and 2, ed. Leo M. Kaiser and Priscilla Knuth, *Oregon Historical Quarterly* 42 (1961): part 2, pp. 340–41.
11. William T. Newby, "William T. Newby's Diary of the Emigration of 1843," ed. Harry N. M. Winton, *Oregon Historical Quarterly* 40 (September 1939): 229.
12. Ketcham, "Journal of Travel," part 1, p. 283.

13. Applegate, *A Day with the Cow Column*, pp. 41–42.
14. Henry Wellenkamp, "Diary of a Trip to California," April 23–August 17, 1850, Western History Department, Denver Public Library.
15. Ibid.
16. John M. Shively, "John M. Shively's Memoir," parts 1 and 2, ed. Howard M. and Edith M. List, *Oregon Historical Quarterly* 81 (spring and summer 1980): part 1, p. 23.
17. Ketcham, "Journal of Travel," part 2, pp. 395 and 401.
18. N. M. Bogart, "Reminiscences of Pioneer Days," Overland Journeys Collection, Washington State Historical Society, Tacoma.
19. Samuel M. Ayres to P. Frances Ayres, September 25, 1850, MSS C995, vol. 29, no. 790, Western Historical Manuscript Collection.
20. Wellenkamp, "Diary."
21. James Frazier Reed, in Morgan, ed., *Overland in 1846*, vol. 1, pp. 263–66.
22. Eliza Hart Spalding, diaries, MSS 1201, Oregon Historical Society, Portland.
23. Myra F. Eells, "Journal of Myra F. Eells, Kept While Passing Through the United States and over the Rocky Mountains in the Spring and Summer of 1838,"

Transactions of the Oregon Pioneer Association, Seventh Annual Reunion (1889): 82 and 86.
24. Spalding, diaries.
25. Catherine Sager Pringle, "Reminiscences," MSS 1194–1, Oregon Historical Society. All subsequent quotes in this chapter are from her account.

---

5. THE MORMON TRAIL

1. William Clayton, *William Clayton's Journal: A Daily Record of the Original Company of "Mormon" Pioneers from Nauvoo, Illinois, to the Valley of the Great Salt Lake* (Salt Lake City: Deseret News and the Clayton Family Association, 1921), p. 124.
2. Brigham Young to Mary A. Young, April 20, 1847, MS 5278, Archives Division, Church Historical Department, Church of Jesus Christ of Latter-day Saints, Salt Lake City.
3. Young, in Wilford Woodruff, *Wilford Woodruff Journal, 1833–1898*, ed. Scott G. Kenney, vol. 3, *January 1, 1846, to December 31, 1850* (Salt Lake City: Signature Books, 1984), pp. 187–88.
4. Clayton, *Journal*, pp. 304 and 309.

5. Clara C. Young to Brigham Young, October 8, 1847, MS 1234, Archives Division, Church of Jesus Christ of Latter-day Saints.
6. Young, in Eugene E. Campbell, *Establishing Zion: The Mormon Church and the American West, 1847–1869* (Salt Lake City: Signature Books, 1988), p. 238.
7. Jane Rio Griffiths Baker, diary, January 1851–March 1853 and September 1869–May 1880, MS 1788, Archives Division, Church of Jesus Christ of Latter-day Saints.
8. Ibid.
9. Chislett, in LeRoy R. Hafen and Ann W. Hafen, *Handcarts to Zion: The Story of a Unique Western Migration, 1856–1860*, 5th ed. (1960; reprint, Glendale, Calif.: Arthur H. Clark, 1988), p. 102.
10. Loader, in Wallace Stegner, *The Gathering of Zion: The Story of the Mormon Trail* (New York, Toronto, and London: McGraw-Hill, 1964), p. 247.
11. Chislett, in Hafen and Hafen, *Handcarts*, p. 127.
12. Ibid., p. 139.
13. Young, in Stegner, *Gathering of Zion*, pp. 257–58.

6. THE PONY EXPRESS

1. Sir Richard R. Burton, *City of the Saints and across the Rocky Mountains to California* (New York: Harper and Brothers, 1862; reprint, with foreword, photographs, and biography by Baker H. Morrow, Boulder: University of Colorado Press, 1990), pp. 491 and 460.
2. Ibid., p. 467.

7. THE FIRST TRANSCONTINENTAL TELEGRAPH

1. William B. Wilson, "The Early Telegraph," *Lancaster County Historical Society Historical Papers and Addresses* 1 (1897): 236.
2. Bryan to Colonel Emmons, January 16, 1940, W. S. Bryan Papers, Missouri Historical Society, Saint Louis.
3. Wade to Sibley, January 4, 1861, MSS 3292, "Letters from San Francisco, 1860–61," Wade Family Papers, Western Reserve Historical Society, Cleveland.
4. Johnson, in William Unrau, *Tending the Talking Wire* (Salt Lake City: University of Utah Press, 1979), p. 264.
5. Ibid., p. 281.

8. THE FIRST TRANSCONTINENTAL RAILROAD

1. Judah, in Oscar Lewis, *The Big Four: The Story of Huntington, Stanford, Hopkins, and Crocker, and of the Building of the Central Pacific* (New York and London: Alfred A. Knopf, 1938), p. 9.
2. Judah, in John Hoyt Williams, *A Great and Shining Road: The Epic Story of the Transcontinental Railroad* (New York: Random House, 1988), p. 49.
3. Huntington, in Wesley S. Griswold, *A Work of Giants* (New York: McGraw-Hill, 1962), p. 150.
4. Sherman, ibid., p. 215.
5. Reed, in Williams, *Great and Shining Road*, p. 155.

ACKNOWLEDGMENTS

Like all western writers, I stand on the shoulders of those who preceded us down the trails, among them Bancroft, Billington, Chittenden, Coues, De Voto, Franzwa, Hafen, Lavender, Mattes, Morgan, Moulton, Parkman, Quaife, Simmons, Stegner, Thwaites, Turner, Viola, and many other chroniclers of the Old West in whose giant footsteps I have dared to follow.

In the course of preparing the present work, I have also drawn on the expertise and good will of trail buffs, traditionalists, revisionists, neo-revisionists, and that illustrious dusty fraternity: the chip-kickers. They have each become a part of me, and I am grateful for their contributions to this book—whose flaws are mine alone.

I am indebted to the many organizations who opened their collections and research facilities, and I especially thank: American Philosophical Society: Dr. Martin Levitt and Martha Harrison; Amon Carter Museum; The Anschutz Collection: Elizabeth Cunningham and Darlene Dueck; Bancroft Library, University of California: Anthony Bliss; Beinecke Rare Book and Manuscript Library, Yale University: George Miles; Buffalo Bill Historical Center: Peter Hassrick (Director), Elizabeth Holmes, and Christina Stopka; California State Library: Kathleen Correia, Kathleen Eustis, and John Gonzales; California State Railroad Museum: Stephen Drew and Ellen Halteman; Church of Jesus Christ of Latter-day Saints History Museum and Archives: Ron Barney, Bill Slaughter, and Brian Sokolowsky; Colorado Historical Society: Patrick Fraker; Creighton University: Marge Wannaker; Crocker Art Museum: Janice Driesbach; Daughters of the Utah Pioneers: Edith Menna; Denver Museum of Natural History: John Welles (Director), David Bourcier, Liz Clancy, and Joyce Harold; Denver Public Library: Eleanor Geheres, Kathey Swan, and Barbara Walton; George Eastman House: Janice Madhu and David Wooters; Filson Club: James Holmberg; Huntington Library: Peter Blodgette; Jefferson National Expansion Memorial: Laura Mills and Kathryn Thomas; Kansas State Historical Society, Center for Historical Research: Christie Stanley; Library of Congress: Ralph Ehrenberg; Missouri Historical Society: Robert Archibald (Director), Martha Clevenger, Duane Sneddecker, and Jill Sherman; Museum of New Mexico: Arthur Olivas and Richard Rudisill; National Archives: Fred Pernel, Dale Connelly, and Rod Ross; National Frontier Trails Center: John Lambertson (Director) and Anna Belle Cartwright; National Museum of American History, Smithsonian Institution: Michelle Delaney, Robert Harding, Doug Mudd, and Elliot Sivowitch; National Museum of the American Indian: Laura Nash; National Museum of Wildlife Art: William Kerr (President) and Dan Provo; National Park Service, National Trails Project Office: Thomas Gilbert; Nebraska State Historical Society: Martha Vestecka-Miller; Nevada Historical Society: Caroline Morel; New Mexico Records Center and Archives: Paul Saavedra and Ronald Montoya; New York Public Library; North Eastern Nevada Museum: Lisa Seymour; Oakland Museum: Marcia Eymann; Oregon-California Trails Association: Jackie Lewin (President), Jeanne Miller (Executive Director), and Kathy Conway; Oregon Historical Society; Pony Express National Memorial and Saint Joseph Museum: Rich Nolf (Director), Sarah Elder, Don Reynolds, and the late Bonnie Watkins; Carl R. Samuelson; Jim Sanders; Santa Fe Trail Association: Bill Pitts (President), Leo Oliva, and Ruth Olsen Peters; Stanford University Library: Linda Long; State Historical Society of Missouri: Sharon Fleming and Fae Sotham; Teton County Historical Center: Rita Verley; Teton County Library: Teri Krumdick; Treasures of the Steamboat Arabia Museum: Hawley family; Union Pacific Historical Museum: Don Snoddy; University Club Library: Jane Reed; University of the Pacific Library: Daryl Morrison; University of Wyoming, American Heritage Center: John Hanks; U.S. Geological Survey Photographic Library; Utah State Historical Society: Susan Whetstone; Nelson Wadsworth; Wells Fargo Bank: Robert Chandler; Wyoming Archives, Museums, and Historical Department: Jane Brainerd, Paula West Chavoya, and Ann Nelson; Wyoming Bureau of Land Management: Lander Resource Area.

My warm appreciation to Robert E. Abrams, publisher of Abbeville Press, for making the book possible, and to those whose expertise gracefully overcame challenges along the way: Owen Dugan, production editor; Miranda

Ottewell, copy editor; Molly Shields, designer; Paula Trotto, picture researcher; Richard Thomas, production manager; and particularly Nancy Grubb, executive editor, whose enthusiasm and counsel throughout this project have made all the difference.

Cynthia Henthorn, research director for *Seven Trails West,* contributed editorial and design suggestions and computerized the entire work to most exacting standards. Over a six-year period her mind, eye, and hand touched every aspect of the book to its lasting benefit.

A presubmission manuscript was ably pruned by Jennifer Borum, Anne C. Fredericks, Deborah Henry, R. Bruce Peters, and Margaret Schwed.

Since western history—for better or for worse—is not an exact science, but often a welter of uncertain facts, conflicting opinions, and spotty records, careful research is essential. For such diligence I thank researchers Susan Aberth, Caroline Beraud-Kaufmann, Bill Dillinger, Mary Donahue, Mary Ellen Jones, David Kuhner, Coralee Paull, and Will South. Many thanks to Carol Henthorn, president of Sir Speedy Printing, for years of professional help. Special thanks are due to special people who helped me along the way: Professor William H. Gerdts of the City University of New York Graduate Center identified the location of key images. My son, R. Bruce Peters, piloted me in his plane through electrical storms over the Tetons and Wind River Range to explore Independence Rock, Devil's Gate, the true and false Parting of the Ways, and the Mormon and Oregon Trails in Wyoming and Idaho. Mrs. Dorothy Barker, a Mormon friend, graciously shared with me the unpublished journal of her grandmother who gathered to Zion.

My friend of half a century, Jack Huyler, first introduced me to the West, and together we crossed South Pass on horseback, camped on the Continental Divide, and nooned at Pacific Springs. With him and his wife, Margaret, my wife, Sarah, and I hiked down part of the Oregon, Mormon, and Pony Express trails and retraced Lewis and Clark's trail at Three Forks, the headwaters of the Missouri. John Hay Jr. and his daughter Mary Chant generously granted us access to the Divide at South Pass through the Hay Ranch and hospitably provided hay and water (from the Sweetwater River) for our horses en route. My longtime friend David Lavender—who among today's western historians is father of us all—first encouraged me to undertake this eight-year project and graciously read the raw manuscript. His continued interest has sustained me from start to finish. Albert Edelman, Gregory Franzwa, Fred Gowans, William E. Hill, Jackie Lewin, David Love, and Merrill Mattes all patiently read through the maquette of *Seven Trails West* and made useful critical comments.

And, finally, my deepest gratitude and respect to those sturdy folk who crossed the continent a century and a half ago, in wagons and on foot, painstakingly keeping their journals and diaries at night around thousands of campfires that glowed in the dark from the Mississippi to the Pacific.

CHRONOLOGY OF THE TRAILS, 1800-1890

1801 Thomas Jefferson is inaugurated as the third president of the United States.

1803 May 22—Napoleon Bonaparte sells the Louisiana Territory to the United States.

1804 May 14—Meriwether Lewis and William Clark lead their Corps of Discovery west.

1805 November 17—the Corps of Discovery reaches the Pacific, near Cape Disappointment, Washington.

1806 September 23—Lewis and Clark return to Saint Louis after their five-thousand-mile round trip.

1807 Manuel Lisa sends his first trappers up the Missouri River, launching the beaver trade.

1808 John Jacob Astor founds the American Fur Company.

1811 Astor founds the settlement of Fort Astoria in Oregon Country.

1812 Fur trader Wilson Price Hunt, returning east from Fort Astoria, discovers South Pass—for future decades the gateway to the Far West.

1821 September—Mexico wins independence from Spain.

William Becknell opens the Santa Fe Trail by entering Mexico with his first trade caravan.

1822 February 13—William H. Ashley advertises for fur trappers in the *Missouri Gazette.*

1825 July 10—Ashley organizes the first fur trappers' Rendezvous, on the Green River in Wyoming.

1827 Fort Leavenworth, Kansas, is established to protect travelers on the Santa Fe and Oregon-California Trails.

1830 Joseph Smith publishes the *Book of Mormon* and founds the forerunner of the Church of Jesus Christ of Latter-day Saints at Fayette, New York.

1833 Bent's Fort, Colorado, is completed on the Mountain Branch of the Santa Fe Trail by Charles and William Bent and Ceran de Saint Vrain.

1834 Fort William, Wyoming (later called Fort Laramie), is built by fur traders William Sublette and Robert Campbell.

Fort Hall, Idaho, is erected.

1836 March 2—Texas claims independence from Mexico.

July 4—Narcissa Whitman and Eliza Spalding become the first white women to cross South Pass.

1837 An economic panic grips the United States.

Samuel Morse files for patent on his electromagnetic telegraph system.

1838 October 27—Governor Lilburn Boggs of Missouri issues an order to have the Mormons driven from the state.

1840 Summer—the last fur traders' Rendezvous is held near Green River, Wyoming.

The Mormons receive permission to settle in Nauvoo, Illinois.

1841 The Bidwell-Bartleson party attempts the first planned overland crossing to California by wagon train.

1843 November 6—Peter H. Burnett's company of emigrants is the first to arrive in Oregon City by wagon.

1844 May 24—the first government telegraph message is sent by Samuel Morse from Washington, D.C., to Baltimore.

The American Morse code is introduced as the standard for use on land telegraph lines.

June 27—Joseph Smith is murdered in jail at Carthage, Illinois.

Brigham Young succeeds Joseph Smith as leader of the Latter-day Saints.

1846 February 4—the Mormons are driven from Nauvoo, Illinois.

May 13—war breaks out between Mexico and the United States.

Britain cedes half of Oregon Country to the United States.

September—the Mormon Battalion marches from Fort Leavenworth to Santa Fe and cuts a new wagon road to California.

During the Bear Flag Revolt against Mexico, John C. Frémont raises the United States flag in California.

1847 January 19—Charles Bent, governor of New Mexico, is murdered during the Taos Uprising.

The survivors of the Donner-Reed Party cross the Sierra Nevada after a winter of supreme hardship.

July 24—Brigham Young, leading the Mormon Pioneer Company, reaches Great Salt Lake Valley.

November 29—missionaries Marcus and Narcissa Whitman are killed by Indians at Waiilatpu Mission, Oregon.

1848 January 24—James Marshall discovers gold at Sutter's Mill, California, triggering the gold rush of 1849.

February 2—the Treaty of Guadalupe Hidalgo ends the Mexican War, giving the United States 1.2 million square miles of territory (all or parts of the future New Mexico, Arizona, Utah, Nevada, Colorado, and California).

1850 The first vehicular transport of U.S. mail across the Great Plains, by Waldo, Hall, and Company's mule-drawn wagon, travels from Independence, Missouri, to Santa Fe.

California is admitted to the Union.

1851 Fort Union is established on the Mountain Branch of the Santa Fe Trail.

1854 A cholera epidemic rages along the Santa Fe Trail.

1856 Mormon handcart companies suffer disasters fording the Platte and at Devil's Gate, Wyoming.

Hiram Sibley and Ezra Cornell organize the Western Union telegraph system.

1857 James Buchanan becomes president of the United States.

The U.S. Army mounts an abortive expedition against the Mormons at Salt Lake.

September 11—the Mountain Meadows massacre takes place in Mormon Utah.

1859 Oregon becomes a state of the Union.

1860 April 3—the first Pony Express mail, westbound, leaves Saint Joseph, Missouri, reaching Sacramento, California, ten days later; the first Pony Express mail, eastbound, leaves San Francisco and reaches Saint Joseph ten days later.

The Telegraph Act is passed, authorizing construction of the first Transcontinental Telegraph.

Abraham Lincoln is elected the first Republican president of the United States.

1861 Kansas becomes the thirty-fourth state of the Union.

April 12—the Confederates open fire on Fort Sumter, and the Civil War begins.

The Big Four—Collis P. Huntington, Mark Hopkins, Charles Crocker, and Leland Stanford, together with Theodore Judah—join forces to start up the Central Pacific Railroad.

Dr. Thomas C. Durant initiates organization of the Union Pacific Railroad.

October 24—the first Transcontinental Telegraph is completed between New York and San Francisco.

November 20—the Pony Express makes its final run to Sacramento.

1862 Congress passes the Homestead Act, granting 160 acres of public land to settlers after five years' residence.

Congress passes the Pacific Railroad Act, later revised.

1863 January 8—the Central Pacific Railroad breaks ground at Sacramento.

December 2—the Union Pacific breaks ground at Omaha.

1864 Lincoln wins reelection as president of the United States.

November 29—Colonel John M. Chivington's cavalry attacks a Cheyenne village at Sand Creek, Colorado Territory, slaughtering some two hundred men, women, and children.

1865 April 9—the Civil War ends after General Robert E. Lee's surrender to General Ulysses S. Grant at Appomattox Courthouse.

April 14—Lincoln is assassinated.

1868 Kit Carson dies of an aneurysm in Boggsville, Colorado.

1869 May 10—the Central Pacific and Union Pacific meet at Promontory Summit, Utah, in the Golden Spike ceremony.

Ulysses S. Grant is elected president of the United States.

1880 The Atchison, Topeka and Santa Fe Railroad reaches Santa Fe.

1890 The Bureau of Census officially declares the frontier closed.

The Mormon church prohibits polygamy.

December 29—the Indian Wars effectively end when U.S. Army troops kill about two hundred Sioux men, women, and children at Wounded Knee, South Dakota.

TRAIL AND HISTORICAL ASSOCIATIONS

BUFFALO BILL HISTORICAL
CENTER
720 Sheridan Avenue
Cody, Wyoming 82414
(307) 587-4771
www.TrueWest.com/BBHC/

CALIFORNIA STATE
RAILROAD MUSEUM
111 "I" Street
Sacramento, California 95814-2265
(916) 445-6645
www.csrmf.org

DENVER MUSEUM OF
NATURAL HISTORY
2001 Colorado Boulevard
Denver, Colorado 80205
(303) 322-7009
(800) 925-2250
www.dmnh.org

JEFFERSON NATIONAL
EXPANSION MEMORIAL
11 North Fourth Street
Saint Louis, Missouri 63102
(314) 655-1700
www.nps.gov/jeff/main.htm

LATTER-DAY SAINTS CHURCH
MUSEUM AND ARCHIVES
50 East North Temple Street
Salt Lake City, Utah 84150
(801) 240-2299
www.lds.org
www.indirect.com/www/crockett/
history.html

LEWIS AND CLARK TRAIL
HERITAGE FOUNDATION
P.O. Box 3434
Great Falls, Montana 59403
www.lewisandclark.org
www.nps.gov/lecl

MISSOURI HISTORICAL
SOCIETY
P.O. Box 11940
Saint Louis, Missouri 63112-0040
(314) 454-3150
www.mohistory.org

MORMON TRAILS
ASSOCIATION
c/o Ronald Andersen
3651 Jasmine Street
West Valley City, Utah 84120-5517
(801) 969-4698
history.utah.org/ partners/mta/
www.nps.gov/mopi/

MUSEUM OF NEW MEXICO
Palace of the Governors
P.O. Box 2087
Santa Fe, New Mexico 87504-2087
(505) 476-5100
www.nmculture.org/
cgi-bin/instview.cgi?_
recordnum=POG

NATIONAL FRONTIER
TRAILS CENTER
318 West Pacific
Independence, Missouri 64050
(816) 325-7575
www.frontiertrailscenter.com

OREGON-CALIFORNIA
TRAILS ASSOCIATION
P.O. Box 1019
Independence, Missouri 64051-0519
(816) 252-2276
www.OCTA-trails.org

PONY EXPRESS MUSEUM
914 Penn Street
Saint Joseph, Missouri 64503
(816) 279-5059
(800) 530-5930
www.ponyexpress.org
www.nps.gov/poex/

SANTA FE TRAIL ASSOCIATION
Route 3
Larned, Kansas 67550
(316) 285-2054
www.santafetrail.org

UNION PACIFIC RAILROAD
HISTORICAL MUSEUM
Mailing Address:
1416 Dodge Street
Omaha, Nebraska 68179
(402) 271-3305
www.uprr.com/uprr/ffh/history/
museum.shtml
Collection housed at:
WESTERN HERITAGE MUSEUM
801 South Tenth Street
Omaha, Nebraska 68108
(402) 444-5071
www.omaha.org/heritage/

SELECTED BIBLIOGRAPHY

GENERAL

Bancroft, Hubert Howe. *Chronicles of the Builders of the Commonwealth, Historical Character Study.* 7 vols. San Francisco: History Company Publishers, 1891–92.

Gerdts, William H. *The Plains States and the West: Art across America.* New York: Abbeville Press, 1990.

Mattes, Merrill J. *Platte River Road Narratives: A Descriptive Bibliography of Travel over the Great Central Overland Route to Oregon, California, Utah, Colorado, Montana, and Other Western States and Territories, 1812–1866.* Urbana: University of Illinois Press, 1988.

Thrapp, Dan L. *Encyclopedia of Frontier Biography.* 4 vols. Glendale, Calif., and Spokane, Wash.: Arthur H. Clark Company, 1988–94.

Wagner, Henry R., and Charles L. Camp. *The Plains and the Rockies: A Critical Bibliography of Exploration, Adventure and Travel in the American West, 1800–1865.* 4th ed., edited by Robert H. Becker. San Francisco: John Howell Books, 1982.

Washburn, Wilcomb E., vol. ed. *History of Indian-White Relations.* Vol. 4 of *Handbook of North American Indians,* edited by William C. Sturtevant. Washington, D.C.: Smithsonian Institution Press, 1988.

Wheat, Carl. *From Lewis and Clark to Frémont.* Vol. 2 of *Mapping the Trans-Mississippi West, 1540–1861.* San Francisco: Institute of Historical Cartography, 1958.

1. THE LEWIS AND CLARK EXPEDITION

Ambrose, Stephen E. *Undaunted Courage: Meriwether Lewis, Thomas Jefferson and the Opening of the American West.* New York: Simon and Schuster, 1996.

Appleman, Roy E. *Lewis and Clark: Historic Places Associated with Their Transcontinental Exploration, 1804–06.* Washington, D.C.: United States Department of the Interior, National Park Service, 1975. Reprint. Saint Louis: Lewis and Clark Trail Heritage Foundation, Jefferson National Expansion Historical Association, 1993.

De Voto, Bernard, ed. *The Journals of Lewis and Clark.* 10th ed. Boston: Houghton Mifflin Company, 1953.

Jackson, Donald, ed. *Letters of the Lewis and Clark Expedition with Related Documents, 1783–1854.* 2 vols. Urbana: University of Illinois Press, 1978.

Lavender, David. *The Way to the Western Sea: Lewis and Clark across the Continent.* New York: Harper and Row Publishers, 1988.

Moulton, Gary E., ed. *The Journals of the Lewis and Clark Expedition.* 9 vols. to date. Lincoln and London: University of Nebraska Press, 1983–.

2. MOUNTAIN MEN AND THE FUR TRADE

Carson, Christopher. *Kit Carson's Autobiography.* Chicago: Lakeside Press, R. R. Donnelley and Sons, Co., 1933. Reprint, edited and with an introduction by Milo Milton Quaife, 9th ed. Lincoln and London: University of Nebraska Press, Bison Books, 1966.

Chittenden, Hiram Martin. *The American Fur Trade of the Far West.* 2 vols. New York: Press of the Pioneers, 1935. Reprint, introduction and notes by Stallo Vinton, foreword by William R. Swagerty. Lincoln and London: University of Nebraska Press, Bison Books, 1986.

Clyman, James. *Journal of a Mountain Man.* San Francisco: California Historical Society, 1928. Reprint, edited by Linda M. Hasselstrom. Missoula, Mont.: Mountain Press Publishing Company, Copper Mountain Books, 1984.

Gowans, Fred R. *The Great Fur Trade Road: Discovery and Exploration, 1739–1843.* Orem, Utah: Mountain Grizzly Publications, 1994.

Hafen, LeRoy R. *Mountain Men and Fur Traders of the Far West: Eighteen Biographical Sketches.* Glendale, Calif.: Arthur H. Clark Company, 1965. Reprint, selected and with an introduction by Harvey L. Carter, 5th ed. Lincoln and London: University of Nebraska Press, Bison Books, 1982.

Morgan, Dale L. *Jedediah Smith and the Opening of the West.* N.p.: Bobbs-Merrill Company, 1953. Reprint, 10th ed. Lincoln and London: University of Nebraska Press, Bison Books, 1964.

3. THE SANTA FE TRAIL

Gregg, Josiah. *Commerce of the Prairies.* Norman and London: University of Oklahoma Press, 1954. 4th ed., edited by Max Moorhead with foreword by Marc Simmons, 1990.

Lavender, David. *Bent's Fort.* New York: Doubleday, 1954. Reprint, 6th ed. Lincoln and London, University of Nebraska Press, Bison Books, 1972.

Magoffin, Susan Shelby. *Down the Santa Fe Trail and into Mexico: The Diary of Susan Shelby Magoffin, 1846–1847.* New Haven, Conn.: Yale University Press, 1926. Reprint, edited by Stella M. Drumm, 4th ed. Lincoln and London: University of Nebraska Press, Bison Books, 1982.

Pattie, James Ohio. *The Personal Narrative of James O. Pattie.* 1st ed., edited by Timothy Flint. Cincinnati: J. H. Wood, 1831. Reprint, introduction by William H. Goetzmann. Lincoln and London: University of Nebraska Press, Bison Books, 1984.

Rittenhouse, Jack D. *The Santa Fe Trail: A Historical Bibliography.* Albuquerque: University of New Mexico Press, 1971. Reprint. Jack Rittenhouse, 1986.

Simmons, Marc. *Following the Santa Fe Trail: A Guide for Modern Travelers.* 2d ed. Santa Fe: Ancient City Press, 1986.

4. THE OREGON-CALIFORNIA TRAIL

Bruff, Joseph Goldsborough. *Gold Rush; The Journals, Drawings and Other Papers of J. Goldsborough Bruff, Captain, Washington City and California Mining Association, April 2, 1849–July 20, 1851.* 2 vols., edited by Willis Read and Ruth Gaines. New York: Columbia University Press, 1944.

Franzwa, Gregory M. *The Oregon Trail Revisited.* 4th ed. Saint Louis: Patrice Press, 1988.

Frémont, John C. *The Expeditions of John Charles Frémont.* Edited by Mary Lee Spence and Donald Jackson. 3 vols. Urbana and Chicago: University of Illinois Press, 1970–84.

Hill, William E. *The Oregon Trail, Yesterday and Today.* 2d ed. Caldwell, Idaho: Caxton Printers, 1989.

Meyers, Sandra L. *Westering Women and the Frontier Experience, 1800–1915.* Albuquerque: University of New Mexico Press, 1982.

Morgan, Dale, ed. *Overland in 1846: Diaries and Letters of the California-Oregon Trail.* 2 vols., 10th ed. Georgetown, Calif.: Talisman Press, 1963. Reprint. Lincoln and London: University of Nebraska Press, Bison Books, 1993.

Parkman, Francis. *The Oregon Trail.* Formerly *The California and Oregon Trail: Being Sketches of Prairie and Rocky Mountain Life.* New York: George P. Putnam, 1849. Reprint, edited by David Levin. New York: Viking Penguin, Penguin Books, 1988.

Stewart, George R., ed. *The Opening of the California Trail: The Story of the Stevens Party from the Reminiscences of Moses Schallenberger.* Berkeley and Los Angeles: University of California Press, 1953.

Stewart, George R. *Ordeal by Hunger: The Classic Story of the Donner Party.* 1936. Reprint. Boston: Houghton Mifflin, 1960. Rev. ed. New York: Simon and Schuster, Pocket Books, 1972.

5. THE MORMON TRAIL

Arrington, Leonard J. *Brigham Young: American Moses.* New York: Alfred A. Knopf, 1985. 2d ed. Urbana and Chicago: University of Illinois Press, Illini Books, 1986.

Campbell, Eugene E. *Establishing Zion: The Mormon Church and the American West, 1847–1869.* Salt Lake City: Signature Books, 1988.

Hafen, LeRoy R., and Ann W. Hafen. *Handcarts to Zion: The Story of a Unique Western Migration, 1856–1860.* 1960. Reprint, 5th ed. Glendale, Calif.: Arthur H. Clark, 1988.

Kimball, Stanley B. *Historic Resource Study: Mormon Pioneer National Historic Trail.* N.p.: United States Department of the Interior, National Park Service, May 1991.

Stegner, Wallace. *The Gathering of Zion: The Story of the Mormon Trail.* New York, Toronto, and London: McGraw-Hill, 1964.

Tobler, Douglas F., and Nelson B. Wadsworth. *The History of the Mormons in Photographs and Text, 1830 to the Present.* New York: Saint Martin's Press, 1987.

6. THE PONY EXPRESS

Chapman, Arthur. *The Pony Express: The Record of a Romantic Adventure in Business.* 1932. Reprint. New York: Cooper Square Publishers, 1971.

Loving, Mabel. *The Pony Express Rides On.* Saint Joseph, Mo.: Robidoux Printing, 1959.

Mattes, Merrill J., and Paul Henderson. *The Pony Express: From St. Joseph to Fort Laramie.* Saint Louis: Patrice Press, 1989.

Settle, Raymond W., and Mary Lund Settle. *Saddles and Spurs: The Pony Express Saga.* Harrisburg, Pa.: Stackpole Company, 1955.

Smith, Waddell F., ed. *The Story of the Pony Express.* San Rafael, Calif.: Pony Express History and Art Gallery, Post Centennial edition, 1964.

Townley, John M. *The Pony Express Guidebook: Across Nevada with the Pony Express and the Overland Stage Line.* Reno, Nev.: Great Basin Studies Center, n.d.

7. THE FIRST TRANSCONTINENTAL TELEGRAPH

Ault, Phil. *Wires West.* New York: Dodd, Mead and Co., 1974.

Coe, Lewis. *The Telegraph: A History of Morse's Invention and Its Predecessors in the United States.* Jefferson, N.C., and London: McFarland and Co., 1993.

Gabler, Edwin. *The American Telegrapher: A Social History, 1860–1900.* New Brunswick, N.J.: Rutgers University Press, 1988.

Thompson, Robert L. *Wiring a Continent.* Princeton, N.J.: Princeton University Press, 1947. Reprint. Salem, N.H.: Arno Press, 1972.

Unrau, William. *Tending the Talking Wire.* Salt Lake City: University of Utah Press, 1979.

8. THE FIRST TRANSCONTINENTAL RAILROAD

Bain, David Haward. *Empire Express: Building the First Transcontinental Railroad.* New York: Viking Penguin, 1999.

Combs, Barry B. *Westward to Promontory: Building the Union Pacific across the Plains and Mountains.* Palo Alto and Oakland, Calif.: American West Publishing and Oakland Museum, 1969.

Griswold, Wesley S. *A Work of Giants.* New York: McGraw-Hill, 1962.

Kraus, George. *High Road to Promontory.* Palo Alto, Calif.: American West Publishing, 1969.

Lewis, Oscar. *The Big Four: The Story of Huntington, Stanford, Hopkins, and Crocker, and of the Building of the Central Pacific.* New York and London: Alfred A. Knopf, 1938.

McCague, James. *Moguls and Iron Men: The Story of the First Transcontinental Railroad.* New York: Harper and Row, 1964.

Williams, John Hoyt. *A Great and Shining Road: The Epic Story of the Transcontinental Railroad.* New York: Random House, 1988.

Index

PHOTOGRAPHY CREDITS